124106 eenfem/V4+ 3 16su/15

Condition: V4+/NF → (Ftx)

Edition: 1st

Prtg:

DJ / NO

Comments: A few v fdfp m tgreg aw (33) Pu

Keywords: BIXB 2/6v4F

025/45

SIR WALTER SCOTT

The Man and Patriot

BOOKS BY

MORAY McLAREN

Return to Scotland
The Highland Jaunt
Escape and Return
The Scots (Pelican)
The Capital of Scotland
The Wisdom of the Scots
The Pursuit
A Wayfarer in Poland
The Unpossessed
If Freedom Fail: Bannockburn, Flodden and the Union
Corsica Boswell: Paoli, Johnson and Freedom
Shell Guide to Scotland

SIR WALTER SCOTT
The Man and Patriot

MORAY McLAREN

HEINEMANN : LONDON

William Heinemann Ltd
LONDON MELBOURNE TORONTO
JOHANNESBURG AUCKLAND

First published 1970
© Copyright 1970 Moray McLaren

434 44055 8

Made and printed in Scotland
by Morrison & Gibb Ltd., London and Edinburgh

Contents

Illustrations

Foreword

———◆———

Since John Gibson Lockhart's famous life of his father-in-law which some still place, as a biography in our language, second only to Boswell's Johnson, there have been many books about and lives of Walter Scott. There was a fall in their number as the nineteenth century went on. The centenary of Scott's death in 1932, however, did produce a fresh batch, which continued sporadically in the following three decades.

At the time these words are written the last book that is worth considering as serious, objective yet the fruit of real research and feeling, came in 1964. It was the late Hesketh Pearson's *Walter Scott, His Life and Personality*. Pearson was a vivid writer and very much a professional biographer. His book is eminently readable and factually correct. If it has a fault it is that Pearson did not quite catch the strength of nor understand Scott's ardent and consuming passion for the survival of his native country of Scotland. He reported it most conscientiously. But conscientiousness is not quite enough to convey the quality of such a thing. As a biographer and a man of feeling he was strongly in sympathy with Scott's many other great and good qualities. His factually correct book glows with human admiration and with human feeling on every page.

Pearson's book, having come at the end of a long series of Scott biographies which began, long ago, with Lockhart's great, but factually flawed masterpiece, what need is there of any more? But the bi-centenary of Scott's birth in 1771 approaches and inevitably there are studies and more biographies being prepared.

Recently in the U.S.A. I heard, for example, of a monumental 'Life' in preparation. It is by one of the most eminent American biographers. He has been in labour over it for a dozen years; and the fruit of these labours will, it is said, fill three volumes. Whether it has feeling for its subject or not, it may or may not represent the last purely objective word.

Then why this book? As a result of various writings of mine on Scott, Abbotsford and Scotland and various appearances in the media of mass communication on the subject—appearances seen here and repeated here and in America—a suggestion was put forward. It was that I should 'do' a book on Sir Walter for his bi-centenary to appear at the same time here and in America. I agreed but wished to take the story of his life for granted as 'generally known'. I proposed a study of his immense influence on the world of his era examining at the same time the many rather odd translations of his works into those tongues with which I am familiar.

Proposed also was the theme of Scott's influence in projecting Scotland to the world at a time when her entity as a nation outside her borders was fading fast, and the theme of what was going on in his own mind when engaged on this ardent and patriotic projection.

I should add that the story and the theme were much fortified and enlivened by nine months' stay in the U.S.A. Granted the privacy of the use of the 'Wertheim Room' in the splendid New York Public Library, it was possible to collect evidence of Scott's at one time truly astonishing and unique influence on the United States of America—an influence that was primarily literary, but in its effect on certain Americans more than literary; it may even have led to action.

Back again in Scotland the story began at the source. Starting with the effect that the news of Scott's death at Abbotsford had on the entire civilized world of the West, it seemed to be proper then to return the tale to the Edinburgh in which he had been born—the Edinburgh of the 'Golden Age' of the late eighteenth century, the Edinburgh which, during and after the Golden Age, so profoundly influenced him. Thereafter his Borderland and abroad. So the story went on.

The story went on while I was living at home in Edinburgh and travelling in the Tweedside, Borders and in Perthshire. Intent upon the story, I realized fully and for the first time—despite the obvious changes of our age—how much remains as it was in Scott's day.

One last word. There is here no ordered and chronological attempt at criticism of his work, verse and prose. Where critical comment does intrude it appears only where it suited the purpose of the task or when it seemed relevant to the story and the theme.

M. McL.

Edinburgh, 1969.

1

The News of Scott's Death

In late September, either before or after the brief
equinoctial gales, the East of Scotland in particular, and
including much of the Border country, wears an aspect of
great natural beauty. It is very different from the English
'season of mists and mellow fruitfulness'. Rather it is a
period of reliable calm before storms that are certain to
come and after summer weather that has been far too often
depressingly fickle.

The sharpness of our spring-time, the irregularity of our
uncertain summers are over. The rigours of winter which
with us can restrain themselves until late November or even
December are away in the future. We are in an indefinite
period of delightful suspense. Calm is the operative word.
Noon after noon, afternoon after afternoon can be pleasingly
warm; yet the early mornings and the evenings before the
light has quite gone have an invigorating tang in them which
stimulates the blood. You can be surprised to note how
many leaves in their varying colours of decay hang from
the trees, suspended by the most fragile stalks. A puff of
wind would blow them away, but the puff procrastinates.

We are in Scotland, in the better sense of the word, an
autumnal country. Autumn is the season in which the more
youthful and lively of us are incited to make plans. It is
also the season in which to leave Scotland—that is, if we
wish to part from her when she is at her most benificent,
and looking her best. It was at the beginning of this season
that Sir Walter Scott, world-famous novelist, poet and
Scottish patriot died in the early afternoon at his Abbotsford
house on 21st September 1832, in his sixty-second year.

He had come back from his Mediterranean and Roman

journey, fêted and lauded wherever he had been. In his unfailingly courteous manner he had done his best to respond to the general excitement which the presence of this the most famous man of imaginative letters in the world of that time had aroused, but he was very tired.

Ill, in recurring pain and, as the journey went on, with his faculties decaying, he was, while still in Italy supported by one urgent, indeed restless, longing. That was to see Scotland and his home before his eyes closed forever. He had intended to visit Goethe on the last stages of his Continental tour at Weimar. But upon hearing that Goethe had died while he was moving towards him, he exclaimed: 'Alas for Goethe, but he at least died at home. Let us to Abbotsford.' He did at last, despite some interruptions, some necessary, some infuriatingly accidental, cross the Border between England and Scotland and see Abbotsford —but only just.

As his death grew inevitably near they moved his last bed or couch to a large room on the northern side (now the dining-room at Abbotsford) and by wide windows.

'It was a beautiful day,' Lockhart wrote, 'so that every window was open—and so perfectly still that the sound of all others most delicious to his ears, the gentle ripple of the Tweed, was distinctly audible.'

Lockhart adds that: 'Almost every newspaper that announced this event in Scotland, and many in England, had signs of mourning usual on the demise of a king'.

He did not continue his research amongst the obituaries from outside Britain, or if he did, he did not mention the results. Many French papers reported Scott's death with the same 'signs of mourning'. And in far-off North America, when the news eventually reached them, all journals then in existence reported it in full. The *Richmond Examiner* in the South actually edged *all* the columns in black—an honour then reserved for the death of a President of the United States *while still in office*.

This last tribute was, in a sense, only to be expected; for Walter Scott's popularity in, and effect upon North America was, and remains in retrospect, an astonishing phenomenon. It is more than astonishing, it is unique. No other imaginative writer in our tongue, whether Scottish, Irish, Welsh, English or native American so convulsed the United States, Northern be it noted as well as Southern, as did Scott in his lifetime

2

and for a number of years afterwards. It is safe to say, modern conditions being what they are, that no other novelist or poet will do so again in the same degree.

Tempting though it is to dwell upon this remarkable subject, evidence about it must be postponed until a later chapter—and it well deserves a chapter to itself—'Scott and America'.

The death of Sir Walter Scott, who had returned home to Abbotsford to take his leave of his own Scotland and of the world, was more than a sad literary occurrence. It was a major piece of news for the entire Western world from Russia (as shall be shewn) to the Americas. But, owing to the conditions of travel in 1832, it disseminated itself slowly, like the rings moving outward from the centre of a huge pool into which a stone has been dropped. The simile is not complete in that the rings of news did not abate the further they got from the centre—they kept their size and force, sometimes increasing. Scotland and near home first.

Rather surprisingly *The Scotsman*, by then the leading Edinburgh and Scottish daily journal, had the news on the next day, the 22nd September, and with the black 'sign of mourning' above it. Abbotsford is nearly forty miles from Edinburgh; and someone must have galloped on horseback pretty hard to bring 'the event' in time for the first edition.

Even so there must have been hurried editorial discussions as to whether to print the news, of necessity briefly, thus being the first with it in Scotland and the world, or to hold it over for a full dress account, accompanied by a leading article. They chose the former; and you may see in the issue of the 22nd evidence of the shifts they were put to.

Something on the centre page must have been 'blacked out' and in its place at the last moment the following paragraph of only twenty-two lines hurriedly inserted:

Death of Sir Walter Scott

This distinguished person breathed his last at twenty-five minutes past one o'clock yesterday. He expired safely and easily, but had suffered a great deal for several weeks before. Scotland may well mourn for the loss of the man who spread the glory of her literature far and wide; but the event will awaken a feeling of grief in every part of the globe to which civilization extends. It is the extinction of a mind of unrivalled gifts—the eclipse of a light whose splendour has filled the world. In an age fruitful in great

3

writers, Sir Walter towered, by the force of his genius, to a height which no other person has reached. His work overlapped the common boundaries of language and clime, in a manner hitherto unexampled. Drawing from the depths of human nature, he wrote to men of all countries, all parties, and his fame, like his genius, is *universal*. Sir Walter was only in his sixty-second year. He dies too soon for the wishes of his countrymen—but in the fulness of his glory, with an imperishable name, honoured and lamented by the admirers of genius to the extremities of the earth.

This compressed notice in its journalese ('distinguished person'), in its repetitions on the theme of universality (italicized in its last use) bears the marks of desperately speedy writing—however genuine were the feelings of the writer. It is surprising that *The Scotsman*'s editors, who must have had ample warnings during Scott's protracted illness, should have allowed themselves to be caught napping in this way. But newspaper 'cemeteries' or prepared obituaries were probably unknown in the Edinburgh of 1832.

In the following days *The Scotsman* did its best to make up for this brief and stammering obituary. In particular they reported at three and a half columns' length a posthumous meeting about Scott held in Edinburgh. This they describe as: 'one of the largest assemblages of gentlemen ever met with in the walls of the Great Assembly Rooms, and certainly the most conspicuous in rank and talent ever assembled in Edinburgh'.

This assembly, glittering with the names of the 'nobility, clergy and gentry' supported by the learned professions, met to decide upon a 'suitable memorial' to Scott in Edinburgh. The result of this meeting was to appear in the following decade when the huge Scott Monument arose in Princes Street. It remains possibly (one can go no further than this conjecture) the largest stone memorial to a poet and a novelist in the world.

Facts for the statistically curious—the Scott Monument, which is a large canopy, stands two hundred feet and six inches above street level and is ascended as far as human feet can climb it, by two hundred and eighty-seven steps. The canopy covers a seated statue of Sir Walter carved from Carrara marble; the statue is more than double life-sized. The block of marble from which it was carved was so heavy that when it arrived in Leith harbour it stove out the bottom of the boat and could only be raised from the harbour bottom with the greatest difficulty.

The monument's architect was a young Borderer, George Meikle Kemp who, in appropriately romantic circumstances was drowned in Tweed before his work was finally built.

The monument's style in spiky Scottish neo-Gothic was, in my childhood, despised for its excessive romanticism by the New Town's artistic inhabitants. Today we all enjoy it with affectionate appreciation. It is a part of Edinburgh; the most celebrated street in the capital of Scotland would be unthinkable without it.

The *Edinburgh Evening Courant* was not first with the news of Scott's death but made ample recompense in a carefully written and really judicious leading article on Scott of nearly two columns' length and of some three thousand words. It alludes to Scott's financial difficulties and deep embarrassment and his overcoming of them. It is a human and well-informed document well representing contemporary Edinburgh opinion.

The *Evening Courant* incidentally had beaten its rival *The Scotsman* a few years earlier when it reported in full Scott's tardy public admission that he had really been the author of his novels. He did this by responding to a toast to the 'Author of Waverley' at a crowded banquet in the Edinburgh Assembly Rooms in 1827. By this date the whole world had long known the truth, but this did not prevent Scott's public acknowledgement of it from being official 'world news'. The *Courant* was first in the field and was widely quoted by the world's press. *The Scotsman* must have bitterly regretted their failure in this scoop. Perhaps it was this that urged them at all costs to be first with the inadequately presented news of his death in their issue of 22nd September 1832.

The *Glasgow Herald* did not publish on Saturday the 22nd September and therefore did not carry the immediate news of Scott's death; but it is doubtful, even if they had had an issue on that day, whether the fastest horseman could have reached them in time for its inclusion. Acknowledging by implication that *The Scotsman* had beaten them to it, they contented themselves on Monday the 24th by quoting verbatim the Edinburgh paper's inadequate report, and added a few comments.

They did, however, report one interesting if slightly macabre event on the Monday. That was that in Glasgow on the evening of the 22nd Sir Daniel Sandford, Professor of Greek at Glasgow University, had, at a literary dinner 'proposed the health of Sir Walter Scott'. The subject of this toast had, by the time it was proposed been seven or eight hours dead, or, in the downright manner of the *Herald* 'had long been lying a corpse'.

If *The Scotsman* is to be blamed for not being prepared for the knowledge that for a considerable time Scott had been at Abbotsford obviously and inescapably dying, the literary circles of Glasgow were even more out of touch, more ignorant. One had supposed that, even before the days of mass-communication news of wide interest in a small country like Scotland travelled quickly by the bush telegraph of gossip or common repute. Evidently not so.

But the city of Glasgow made ample amends for their civic paper's neglect. When the news from Abbotsford reached the city on the 24th all ships, of whatever nationality in the river and the wide estuary of Clyde, flew mourning flags. One has perhaps to be a Scot and to know Edinburgh and Glasgow to understand the significance of this gesture shown in the heart of Glasgow's most cherished and beloved element, her river. 'The Clyde made Glasgow and Glasgow made the Clyde' was throughout the nineteenth century and after a familiar saying in that great civic state that for so long had held herself partially independent from the rest of Scotland. By 1832 Glasgow, having deepened her river and made it navigable to the city's centre, having opened thereby her immense trade with the New World, had just coined this phrase and proudly enunciated it—never more proudly than in the presence of Edinburgh folk whose airs and graces ('East-windy, West-endy') they despised with a mixture of irritation and contempt.

Scott had been born in Edinburgh and had passed much of his life there. His own Borderland in the country where he had built his Abbotsford and had made peculiarly his own lay in the east Borders, a part of Edinburgh's ambience. Never before or since has Glasgow spontaneously paid so remarkable a tribute on her Clyde to an Edinburgh man.

The London *Times* newspaper did not get the news till 25th September—not bad going in those days, for four hundred and twenty miles. Their leading article on his death was easily the best to appear in Great Britain. It modestly eschews detailed literary criticism—though praising

6

his great and 'universal works'. It does, however, speak of his great Scottish patriotism and his candid generosity to all other men of letters. Had there been a President of Literature to be elected for all Europe, undoubtedly, *The Times* says, Scott would have been chosen, not only by his innumerable readers but by all his fellow authors. The truth maybe, but the London *Times* 'did him proud' in proclaiming that truth.

A few days later the news reached the Continent. Once one has crossed the Channel and got abroad one could go on at enormous length tediously quoting the entire press of the civilized world on the death of Scott. Enough to say that were one to indulge in such futile research more than half of this biographical bi-centenary tribute would be taken up by it.

Better to consider the extraordinary effect that Scott had had outside his own Borderland and outside the Edinburgh in which he had lived and worked at intervals for most of his life.

In continental Europe the countries that had been most strongly influenced by Scott's genius were France, Spain and Russia. When, well after the Napoleonic wars, peace had returned to Europe, Scott visited Paris and found to his surprise that the French had made a kind of music-drama out of his *Ivanhoe* and were playing it at the Opera House.

He did not, of course, get one penny or bent *sou* for providing obliquely the plot and words of this musical performance which grew highly popular outside France. It was performed in various languages across Europe from St Petersburg to Madrid. No one living today has heard *Ivanhoe*. The score of it must exist somewhere, but no one knows where.

In his lifetime and after his death his stories were seized upon, without any payment in those pre-copyright days, for the libretti of opera. In this Italy led the field. Donizetti's *Lucia di Lammermoor*, based entirely on his novel *The Bride of Lammermoor* was, and still remains the most famous. It is still included in many international repertoires.

The title of this well-known piece with its entrancing coloratura melodies obviously proclaims its origin. Few people realize, however, that that other Italian opera again filled with coloratura and still sometimes performed, *I Puritani*, is based upon the Scott novel *Old Mortality*. There

7

may have been other plays from his stories set to music, remotely composed and remotely performed. If so, they are now forgotten and have sunk without trace.

Certainly his novels were adapted as 'straight plays' for the stage here and in many languages. The most successful with us has been the drama or melodrama of *Rob Roy* taken from the novel of that name. Frequently performed during Scott's lifetime and in later Victorian and Edwardian times, it was recently given a gala presentation in Edinburgh at which Her Majesty the Queen was present.

Certainly, too, as shall be shown later, Scott influenced novelists and poets particularly in France, Italy and Russia. With all this extravagant (but unpaid) use of his imaginative genius, with all the influence upon other writers, it is little wonder that the 'event' of his death was major news throughout Europe.

Again (resisting the temptation to anticipate the chapter on 'Scott and America') one turns to Russia for one outstanding and extraordinary act of courtesy and respect which *may* indeed have been shown to him on his death, but which unfortunately it is impossible to verify from documents accessible here. It seems that, when the news from Abbotsford weeks later reached Russia, the Tsar Nicholas I ordered Court mourning. If this is really true, it is not only highly remarkable but significant.

Long ago, and abroad, the writer distinctly remembers seeing evidence for this story. That evidence is given in the footnote below.[1]

---

[1] In 1932, the centenary year of Scott's death, I recall reading in France and in the French language in some reputable literary journal of the time, an account of how when the news from Abbotsford eventually reached Russia, the Tsar Nicholas I ordered Court mourning for Walter Scott. I read it, of course, with interest and recall that it seemed authoritative.

In 1932 I was not considering adding to the large literature about Scott and certainly did not foresee that, thirty-nine years later, I would be offering a book as tribute to the bi-centenary of his birth. If I had, I would have written notes about the source or at least made strong efforts to retain it in memory.

As it is I have forgotten the source quoted and even the name of the journal, which is not a well-known one.

Short of going to France and combing every lesser and possibly ephemeral literary sheet of 1832 I cannot now get at it. Nor are Russian sources available of any help in this country nor in America (where I was recently) when I endeavoured to find them at New York and at Harvard's fine collection of Russian sources.

Imperial Court edicts of the Russia of the early nineteenth century were not published for the vulgar gaze, and the sparse news-sheets of 1832 would

But enough of the past at the time of his death. Let a celebrated foreigner's spontaneous tribute be quoted.

One of the most famous and certainly the most frequently translated of modern French novelists, Georges Simenon, was, a few years ago, standing upon the summit of the Castle Rock at Edinburgh and surveying upon a bright summer's day the noble prospect from that place. 'What,' he asked the present writer, 'is that huge spiky building down there?' Upon being informed that it was perhaps the largest stone memorial to an author in the world and that it was the Scott Monument, the Frenchman added thoughtfully: 'The largest . . . yes, it must be the largest. They'll never put up anything of that size to any of us again. Certainly they won't put up anything like that for me in Lille.'

He paused once more and finished his reflections more audibly: 'But they were right to put up a thing that size to Scott—he invented us all.'

For a moment the sense of the French phrase escaped me in this context; but Simenon soon made himself clear. 'Without him none of us could have written as we do. He began it all.'

How right was his *mot juste* of 'invented'! One could fill pages more of this brief introductory chapter giving instances of how Scott's life and death influenced the world in countless different places and in countless different ways. But they are all contained in the word 'invented'.

Walter Scott, in the extraordinary influence he exercised on the world of his time, through his novels and poems—an influence, be it remembered, upon the imagination of the then far more numerous illiterate classes as well as upon those who could read—was himself a kind of invention. His power of imagination and his expression of it was as potent in his time as were the inventions of radio and television upon later ages.

He was known throughout the world, and during his life

---

not contain an account of an edict even on a subject of such general interest. The only way to discover any documentary source would be to go to Russia and, with the permission of the U.S.S.R. authorities, delve in old papers at Leningrad and Moscow. This is not possible, and, even if it were, it would be absurd to pursue such a point at such labour and over such a distance.

I repeat, however, that I remember seeing the account, in French and in France of 1832, and that it seemed authoritative. I offer this for what it is worth.

knew as much of the world as he could by travel, reading and talking with countless foreign visitors to Abbotsford. Even when, during the Napoleonic wars, he found himself restricted he read and talked and listened for news of the outside world—past as well as present.

He was, in so far as he was able to become one, a citizen of the world. But his roots were deep-planted in the soil of his native country and in the stones of his ancient native city. He was born here in Edinburgh, lived much of his life here, and died here in his own Border countryside. If he was in a sense an 'invention' it was in Edinburgh and Scotland that he invented himself—or in the Latin sense of that word found himself, discovered himself. His invention or discovery of himself as a citizen of the world, born to influence the world and to project himself and his country to the limits of civilized knowledge, sprang from the place in which he first saw the light.

2

—◦◦◦—

Edinburgh: the City of His Birth

He was born on 15th August 1771, in the Old Town of
Edinburgh, that historic city perched upon and straggling
down the only unprecipitous side of the capital's volcanic
Castle Rock. Walter Scott could scarcely have made his
appearance in his country at a time and place more appro
priate to his genius, his talents, his inclinations and his
profound patriotism so deeply mingled with the past. Nor
could his country have been more ready for, more in need
of what he could give her as he grew and learned to express
himself to the world for Scotland. He was for his native
country a man of destiny.

Napoleon in a very different sense was a man of destiny;
and those who care for coincidence may note that Scott,
who was later to write Napoleon's life, shared, two years
after him, the same birthday. Napoleon was born in Corsica
on 15th August (Assumption Day) 1769. The day on which
the Catholic Church celebrates the Assumption of the
Blessed Virgin Mary has always been, and still is one of the
highest festivals of the Corsican year. It is associated with
that island's strong individual patriotism, and is the day on
which the Corsicans remember the time when they formed,
however briefly, a free and independent country. Boys born
on Assumption Day in Corsica are expected to do well.
Napoleon did.

He began life as an ardent Corsican patriot joining, in his
youth, the struggle to free his country from France. He was
wont, until he was a grown man, to say that he was born
in the year in which 'France deluged his country with blood
and had ravished her'. Then came the Revolution with its
chance of promotion and exciting new life for young men

such as Buonaparte. He chose the ambitious path which led to Imperial glory and, after leaving Corsica never saw his native country again, save when he sailed past it on the way to and from the Eastern Mediterranean. He is said to have noticed how the scent from the island perfumed the sea for miles around. But this was the only thing he did notice. For the rest, he dismissed her from his mind and only used her as a pawn in his great Imperial game.

How different it was with Walter Scott and with his circumstances in his native country, the country of his birth, the country for which to the end of his days he was to have so strong, so nostalgic a patriotism! By the time he was born the Kingdom of Scotland had for sixty-four years officially ceased to exist; and (though this is often forgotten) so had the Kingdom of England. By the Acts of Union passed all but simultaneously in the Parliaments of England and London in 1707 both the Kingdoms that shared this island were officially abolished. Much against the popular will in Scotland, and in the face of some resentment amongst the English people, the 'Establishments' in power had both agreed to sink their identities in the concept of Britain and to cease to exist individually.

There was much to be said for some kind of union or lasting agreement between the two countries commonly enisled and placed geographically so close—the ending of open warfare, the stopping of guerilla fighting upon the Borders, the sharing of the common interests and privileges of these two Kingdoms which (from the same island) had for so long made their mark upon Europe and the world.

Recognizing this, some Scottish patriots with voices to be heard spoke for a federating union in which the two partners would retain their identities. But this did not suit the 'Establishment' in either Kingdom; most certainly it did not suit the English Government who saw in the union, which would make London the capital of the new Britain, the hope of establishing and recognizing once and for all England's superiority.

So the federating idea lost the day. It was 'union complete' or, as it came to be known, 'the incorporating union' with, for Scotland, all the sinister undertones of the word 'incorporating' allowed full play. Within a century all Europe was calling the whole island England, and regarded Scotland, if they regarded that once independent ancient Kingdom at all, as an appendage of England. It was in this direction that things were remotely moving in the year of Walter Scott's birth—only remotely as shall be shown below, on account of Edinburgh's 'Golden Age' which, intellectually speaking, drew the attention of Europe far more strongly than did London. He was, in the latter part of his life, through his talents and genius in the world of his powerful imagination, to show that Scotland did still exist.

Of course she existed. Two groups of politicians, whether venal and ambitious or not, could not with a few strokes of the pen obliterate two long-established kingdoms and countries, each against their different historical backgrounds. England continued to exist and grow in importance. Scotland, if she did not grow in importance, even if she later declined as a unit in Europe, continued in her own eyes to be herself. It is as herself that she looks upon herself, even today. How much more then must she have felt her individual identity in the eighteenth century and at the time of Scott's birth when men were still alive who could from their childhood recall the independence of their native land!

The passage by coach between the ancient capital of Scotland (by then North Britain) and the capital of England (by then officially South Britain) took a week, sometimes longer, and was intermittent. The place was cut off from the official Government in the South, and this severance encouraged individuality. Scotland retained her national Church and her own legal system. Then there was the matter of language, of how people communicated with each other. Here, too, there were strong differences which held 'North Britain' and 'South Britain' apart.

Until the failure of the last Jacobite Rising of 1745, and the consequent emigrations and evictions, Gaelic was widely spoken north and west of the Highland line and was often the only language there. But the difference lay not only between Gaelic and English. There were differences almost as wide between the English of London and the Scots tongue as spoken in Edinburgh and in the rising commercial city of Glasgow. Historic Lowland Scots was akin to English but no more than that; some would say that, though akin to English it had different origins in the one-time various languages of 'Low Dutch', particularly in the Frisian Islands. Certainly there are countless differences in

13

pronunciation and word-meaning. Nor was this to be discovered only among the poorer classes.

Scottish lawyers, men of education and learned in Latin (which they did not pronounce after the English fashion), learned in French, German, Italian and other living European tongues, were at a loss when trying to express themselves in English—just because it was akin to but so different from their own language. The lawyers, for instance, were especially at a loss when they had to plead before the House of Lords in the new seat of Government in London. They struggled manfully but unsuccessfully to make themselves understood. They would have done better to have used interpreters.

All these outward visible and audible signs of national difference between the two Kingdoms now officially forming one nation, one state governed and largely administered from London, caused much distress in what once had been Scotland, and in what had been her capital, in the years immediately following the Union. Edinburgh was of necessity deserted for the new capital of Britain; the Members of Parliament, the administrators and many of the nobility cleared out of Scotland leaving the erstwhile capital to exist only as the headquarters of the Scottish legal system and the city where, once a year, the General Assembly of the national Church briefly met. So deserted was Edinburgh in the early eighteenth century that, in the 1720s and 1730s grass grew, it is said, between the cobblestones of the wide, lofty and impressive High Street of the Old Town upon the Castle Rock.

Then, after the failure of what was obviously going to be the last Jacobite Rising in 1745 a remarkable and an uniquely extraordinary thing happened, and one which was to affect the youth of Walter Scott by providing him with a stimulating and vivid background. Edinburgh, the deserted one-time capital of a Kingdom that had officially ceased to exist, pulled herself together and from the 1750s till the end of the century launched herself upon what has now been called her Golden Age. This was at its height in the year in which Walter Scott was born.

'Golden Age' is a facile phrase which could have been applied to other and earlier periods according to your temperament, your point of view or religious views. Certainly the court of James IV provided from the purely literary and poetic point of view a Golden Age more diverse

14

than any to follow it in Scotland. Whether Golden or not, there were, under the Bruce and later the Stewart monarchs, scenes of high drama enacted in Scotland and in Edinburgh which drew the attention of people far from Scotland and which laid the basis of a good deal of later historical writing whether of merit or merely fustian.

The 'Golden Age' of the latter half of the eighteenth century had this one unique quality. At a time when, for half a century the Kingdom of Scotland had officially been obliterated, the capital of North Britain became a European intellectual, literary and philosophical capital which exerted its influence not only on British but European thought. Some of the names of those who brought this about are now largely forgotten save by the learned. Let but two be mentioned that are still remembered, David Hume, the philosopher, and Adam Smith, the author of *The Wealth of Nations*. At the time there were many others, such as Principal Robertson, the historian, who were then universally respected (Robertson still remains highly regarded by fellow historians today). But whether remembered now as are Hume and Adam Smith, or largely forgotten, they were in their time so famous that Edinburgh became known as the 'Academy of Europe'.

It was at this time that Mr Amyat, the King's physician who had lived for two years in Edinburgh said: 'Here I stand at what is called the Cross of Edinburgh (the Mercat Cross by St Giles' Kirk in the High Street) and can in a few minutes shake fifty men of genius and learning by the hand'. The enthusiastic and warmhearted Englishman must have been putting it too strongly when he said 'fifty', but his attitude expressed a general European and even English point of view about Edinburgh at the time Scott was born in the latter half of the eighteenth century.

Then there were the physical, the architectural achievements which were just beginning in the year of Scott's birth, which were in their day outstanding and which remain, even in this age, though much invaded, spoiled and in danger, unique. The New Town of Edinburgh is the only example in Europe (therefore in the world) of a sustained piece of neo-Georgian town planning.

Scott was eventually to move into the New Town for his Edinburgh residence, but the Old Town on the hill was the scene of his birth and early childhood; and the southern extension of George (properly George's) Square, still a part of the Old Town, was the background of his boyhood and youth when he lived with his father while studying law and taking his first steps as a young advocate. It was in the Old Town on the slopes of the Castle Rock in the Edinburgh 'Golden Age' that, as a boy, he became strongly conscious of his own nationality and of his nation's past. To begin even remotely to understand the driving force of Walter Scott's powers, to know the stuff of which his dreams were made, it is essential to savour the taste of the town in which he was born and its standing at that period.

Much has been written about the Old Town in its eighteenth-century heyday and before its collapse when all the prosperous folk withdrew to the New Town. We do not propose to repeat these descriptions in detail. For those, however, who have never seen Edinburgh, or who have had only a passing glimpse of it, it is necessary to say something about its unique appearance and qualities.

The Old Town of Edinburgh, with wynds and closes off it, consisted mostly of the Royal Mile, which is the stretch of wide highway between the Castle on a volcanic rock 443 feet above sea level down to the Royal Palace of Holyroodhouse some 250 feet below. This Royal Mile consisted of three sequent streets, the Lawnmarket at the top, the High Street in the middle and the Canongate at the bottom. Protected on the north side by the Nor' Loch (once a swamp which had been converted into a lake-like moat in the reign of James II of Scotland in the fifteenth century), this steep rock-built city had once been protected against invasion from the south by the Flodden Wall.

Until the latter part of the eighteenth century there had been little inclination to breach the southern wall by expansion. At the same time, until the noble and bold plan of the New Town was put forward, it seemed impossible to build an extension on the other side of the Nor' Loch valley for the simple reason that it seemed impossible of access from the historic old Edinburgh in its lofty position.

The growing population had little power of gaining more room for itself save by extending upwards. Edinburgh's lofty buildings (made even more lofty by its high rock basis) provided the first skyscrapers in the world. Visitors were at once struck by the great height of these dwelling places.

And, though this was the age before the picturesque or romantic had come into fashion, many who came here for the first time were caught by the nobility of the ancient city's site. Seated upon the one manageably declining side of a precipitous rock, with the sea in the form of the Firth of Forth at its feet, with the near mountain of Arthur's Seat marking off its end behind Holyroodhouse, and with its mountainous range of the Pentland Hills at its back to the south, it was indeed a stirring spectacle.

Striking it may have been, and wide and spacious though many parts of the Royal Mile undoubtedly were (six coaches could drive abreast in the High Street) this confined and lofty position had its drawbacks and some human disadvantages for its inhabitants.

Its main disadvantage was the difficulty of getting rid of the city refuse. There are many tales told of the filth hurled from high windows into open streets or wynds to be carried away by the town cleansers in the morning. These again need not be repeated here. Let it suffice to say that Edinburgh, both before and after the Union, and until the building of the New Town, must have been one of the most insanitary cities in Europe.

In the year of Scott's birth the Town Council had tried to forbid the habit of hurling all refuse, including the contents of the pot and the chamber stool into the streets, but they had only succeeded in modifying it. As late as the 1790s and at the turn of the century there still continued privately owned perambulating 'conveniences' carried by humble folk known as the 'Wha wants me men'. These were elderly citizens who prowled about the entrances of the closes and wynds uttering the mournful but urgent cry: 'Wha wants me?' They carried buckets, and possibly some cleansing paper, and were enveloped in huge cloaks under which their clients could hide as they took down their trousers to relieve themselves.

Insanitary this wide, noble, loftily built rock city may have been, but it had one human advantage or good quality which was largely dispersed when the spacious, gracious and sanitary New Town was built. This good quality was companionability. All Edinburgh then with its some 50,000 population was crowded on this rock and lived for the most part in the 'lands', or what we now call high-piled flats. These lands all owned a common stair; and on that common stair a Duchess, a Lord of Session, or a Lord of the peerage might meet their neighbours below them in the same building—shopkeepers, booksellers, cobblers, young aspiring lawyers, harlots, or possibly even a 'Wha wants me man' who might be living in the lowest and humblest hole in the whole huge towering structure.

Everyone knew everyone in the Edinburgh of the eighteenth century whether they spoke to each other or did not. But for the most part they did speak to each other and, be it noted and stressed, in the same common tongue of antique Lowland Scots. The Duchess of Gordon was particularly apt and expressive in this tongue, especially when she was bargaining with the fishwives whom she loved to beat down to the lowest price—and to be heard doing so.

No town in the United Kingdom and few towns in Europe had a more naturally striking situation, made more striking by sky-aspiring architecture. No town in Britain, few, if any, in Europe had such a wealth of intellectual and literary distinction at the time. Certainly in no town in these islands were the inhabitants less inhibited in their daily intercourse which passed between the powerful, the aristocratic and the humble. If English visitors such as Captain Topham are to be believed, the friendliness and individual good companionability of the Edinburgh folk were socially intoxicating to the incomer. The Edinburgh or Lowland Scots reputation for dourness and meanness had not yet begun.

Dr Samuel Johnson's attitude may be quoted in this context; his feelings about the Scots were ambivalent. He had many friends and colleagues amongst them, but he could never resist a gibe against them—often more good-humoured than it reads on paper two hundred years later. It is significant, however, that he never accused them of meanness, only of ridiculous pride and clannishness: 'No, sir: the Irish are a FAIR PEOPLE—they never speak well of one another' was a characteristic oblique buffet against the Scots, uttered, possibly with a smile, in Boswell's presence.

It is a fairly sound generalization that you find a people at their best not when they are abroad but when they are on their own soil. This is true of the Scots, Lowland and Highland, today. It was even more so in the latter half of the eighteenth century, and particularly in Edinburgh of the 'Golden Age' at its climax about the period of Walter Scott's birth and childhood. You could have seen the Scottish companionability at its best and least inhibited. But this companionability was to decline with the desertion of the Old Town for the New. The New Town was a noble and unique architectural development, but it began a way of living which later in the nineteenth century was to disseminate and draw away this gay friendliness. It was to become a city which later R. L. Stevenson was to rebel against despite his ineradicable love of it:

> Ye fine religious decent folk,
> Flaunting yourselves in gold and scarlet,
> I sneer between two puffs of smoke.
> Give me the publican and harlot.

This was a specimen of his tinkling, but none the less deeply felt, juvenilia.

There were publicans and harlots in the mid-Victorian Edinburgh of R.L.S.'s youth, but they were hidden for the most part in the obscurer streets of the New Town and only displayed themselves obviously in the rotting slum which the Old Town had become.

There were also plenty of publicans and harlots in the Edinburgh of the 'Golden Age', but life upon the high-pitched swarming Castle Rock was far too constricted for them to be hidden away. All society, male and female, used the inns and oyster cellars kept by what we now call publicans; and the harlots inhabited the lower rooms of the soaring buildings in the upper levels of which lived the peerage, the judges, men of international renown and other gentlemen or ladies. This fact was recognized by all, the high-born as well as the low. The Edinburgh of the latter half of the eighteenth century, the Edinburgh where the 'Moderates' held sway in the Church and the pious Evangelicals had not yet emerged, the Edinburgh in which judges on the bench used the coarse speech of the people to enliven their legal dicta ('Fare ye weel, ye bitches,' was Lord Kames's public goodbye to his brethren on the bench), was a realistic as well as a gay, social, companionable and intellectual city. Hypocrisy and inhibition (the Doctor Jekyllism of Victorian Edinburgh) were well over the horizon in the Victorian age which was yet to come.

Realistic, intellectually and socially stimulating as was no other city in the United Kingdom, this was the place in which the boy Walter Scott was born. Immensely inquisitive about all that went on around him, remarkably acquisitive of knowledge, deeply imbued with Scottish patriotism, the boy, the youth, the growing young man Scott found this the most vivid background he could have chosen for his birth, expanding childhood and youth.

'At length they approached Edinburgh.' This simple sentence when read in its context in *Old Mortality* sounds like a warning bell—a bell to denote that a crisis is to occur in the story. Again and again in his finest Waverley novels, in those set in his own land, Edinburgh is the stage of crisis on which the drama is played, the place where the storms boil to their culmination, or where puzzling knots are untied. It is, too, against the stormy or pawkily placid background of eighteenth- or seventeenth-century Edinburgh that Scott sometimes begins his stories, thus to hold the reader's attention and to sink the anchor which shall hold to the end, no matter how far the characters may wander under Scott's guidance. Yet it is to Edinburgh that they return.

Scott was haunted by the city of his birth. As has been well said: 'Edinburgh made him and Abbotsford ruined him'. He may have been made and haunted by Edinburgh, but he was capable of rebelling against the Edinburgh that grew up in his youth and his maturity.

For many of us who were born in the Edinburgh of the early years of this century, who have wandered far and have returned to our and Scott's native city, the New Town— or what we are allowed to retain of it amidst the wheels of the juggernaut called 'progress' and the venality of modern civic affairs—the New Town stands for all that is gracious in Edinburgh. We have but to think of its noble, ample streets, squares and crescents and places when we are far from it to gain a cooling refreshment of the mind. Moreover it is a part of our past, of our heritage. Thus we look upon it—sad for its violation yet grateful for what we have of it.

Not so Walter Scott. A child of the uneven, disordered companionable Old Town, the fruit of Scotland's history, he shrank from what was to him the 'ordered severity' of Georgian Edinburgh. As he wrote to Joanna Baillie in 1816, and in obvious reference to the New Town:

> I have always had a private dislike to a regular shape of a house . . . the cat-lugged bandbox with four rooms on a floor and two stories rising regularly above each other.

20

Yet it was in just such a house in Castle Street in the heart of Craig's splendid New Town—a plan as yet uninterrupted by Victorianism and the age that was to follow—that he lived so much when he was in Edinburgh. As soon as he had married and gained independence in the profession of law it was in Castle Street that he settled down to write and to work in Edinburgh.

How often must he have looked up to the Old Town on the Rock with the Castle as its culmination. Yet now he knew that he could do no more than look up at it through autumnal mists or the illumination of summer. He had to go there to attend the Court of Session but he well knew that he could no longer live there. By the time he was at the height of his fame, even by the time the first of his Waverley novels appeared in 1814, his own Edinburgh in which he had been born was a rotting slum from which socially he was forever disbarred.

The Royal Mile upon the far hill there had been given over to the swarming and proliferating slum dwellers. They now occupied the painted courts where the judges and the great folk had once 'gloried and drunk deep'. The companionable closes and wynds where Scots folk eminent in lineage, learning or the law had bandied words with the humblest of their compatriots and fellow citizens were now falling into decay, and the old life had gone from them. But the shell of it was there for him to look at like a drop-curtain scene against the southern sky whenever he cared to raise his eyes from Princes Street or any of the regular intersections of the New Town in which he was now compelled to live. He could not escape from the reminders of Edinburgh's great past.

This attitude of Scott towards the Old Town of his birth strongly tinged his approach to his native land. How much was going, how much irretrievably lost? He expressed himself in this theme in 'A General Account of Edinburgh' in his *Provincial Antiquities and Picturesque Scenes of Scotland* published in London in 1826. This is what he said:

> The tardy cry of '*Gardez l'eau*' (the warning shout given by householders about to throw their refuse into the streets) was sometimes like the shriek of the Water Kelpy, rather the elegy, than the warning, of the overwhelmed passenger. Want of cleanliness was frequently accompanied by its natural attendant, want of health . . .

The same narrowness of accommodation had its effect on the morals of the men. All business, especially whatever concerned with the law, was necessarily transacted in the taverns, and in taverns also were held all festive meetings; the necessary consequence of which was deep and constant drinking. Each inhabitable space was crowded like the under-deck of a ship. Sickness had no nook of quiet, afflication no retreat for solitary indulgence. In addition to these inconveniences it is scarce worth mentioning that every drop of water used in a family had to be carried up those interminable stairs on a porter's shoulders; that the hearing was constantly assailed by the noise of neighbours above and below; that many of the rooms were dark even at noon-day, or borrowed but a gleam from some dark alley; and that in ordinary houses there was scarcely space enough for the most necessary articles of household furniture.

Still, with all its inconveniences, this style of living was long looked back to with fond regret by many who survived that great change, which might be said to commence about sixty years ago. The close neighbourhood into which they were previously formed, gave the Scotch, a proud and poor people, the means of maintaining frequent and genteel society, without incurring much expense. All visits were made in sedan-chairs, and even a large circle of acquaintance could be maintained at a trifling expense. The ladies entertained only at tea; for dinner parties, except on extraordinary occasions, were confined to near relations. Much is said, and no doubt with truth, of the display of fashion and elegance, which assembled on these occasions; and wealth having comparatively little means to display itself, birth and breeding claimed and obtained more general respect than is paid to them in the modern more public and promiscuous assemblies. In society of a class somewhat lower, the closeness of residence had also its advantages. Neighbours were so dependent on each other for mutual comfort and assistance, that they were compelled to live on terms of kindliness and harmony, which soon became habit, and gave a tone of social enjoyment to the whole system, which perhaps conduced as much to general happiness as do the feelings of sturdy independence and indifference, with which the owner of a 'house within itself' usually regards his next neighbours. In an Edinburgh *land*, a sort of general interest united the whole inhabitants, from the top to the bottom of these lofty tenements. Love and friendship might communicate through ceilings no thicker than the wall of Pyramus; and as the possessors were usually of very different ranks, charity had not far to travel from home ere she found fitting objects of her regard.

Such are the advantages which the poor and aristocratic gentry of Scotland used to ascribe to the old system of Edinburgh manners, when they found that new wants, and a different set of habits rendered it difficult for them to maintain their ground in that by which it was superseded. But the progress of society cannot be suspended, and while it moves on, must display new advantages and inconveniences as the wheel gradually revolves.

The wheel gradually revolves. As a child he had met or seen old people who remembered Scotland as an independent kingdom. As a youth we know that he met and talked with Jacobites who had been 'out' in the Jacobite Rising of 1745. His heart warmed to them and to his country's past now slipping away. Yet reason told him to accept the present situation as unavoidable. It was as unavoidable as the necessity for living in the, to him, unsympathetic New Town with its regular 'cat-lugged, bandbox' houses after the 'English style'.

This led to his much discussed 'dual personality'. That is not a phrase which would have meant much to him. Despite all the power of his mind, his wide learning and reading, he was no 'intellectual', he did not discuss the finer points of philosophy, psychology or religion, though he was able to portray those who did. He was neither an optimist nor a pessimist but a meliorist who loved the past, particularly of his own country, yet found it best to accommodate himself to the present, uncomfortable though he may have found it. He might have laughed at the verbal witticism of Wilde's profoundly Christian aphorism: 'The past is the history of what ought not to have happened; the present is the story of what ought not to be happening', but he would not have agreed with it. He was at once too homesick for his country's past and too practical about living in its present.

Stronger, however, than his dual 'personality' which he may not have been aware of, stronger than the politics in which he was compelled to be involved, stronger than any speculations or philosophy or religious attachment which he may have occasionally allowed himself were his powerful and consuming imagination and his capacity to express it.

That imagination, that expression of it in his books, were stimulated, more potently than by anything else, by the contemplation of the past of his native city and of his country. That past faced him each day in the sight of the Castle and the Old Town wherever he turned southward from his house in Castle Street, wherever he wandered in the fields and moors, the towns and villages round Abbotsford in his well-loved Borderland; it sprang at him from the Highland hills. He heard the voice of that past amongst the poor folk in town of country, and in Border speech and in the still-living Border ballads, in the Gaelic speech or Celtic-tinged English of the North and West.

All these sights and sounds at once trouble the exposed nerves of his patriotism and of his unsleeping imagination; he could not have resisted them even if he had wished to do so. They drove his willing pen to express that imagination as soon as he was in its grip, and in expressing his imagination he was consummately able (to use a trite phrase) to make the past live. He made it a real thing, not the mere summoning up of 'the remembrance of things past'.

No one who is not familiar with the Scottish scene and the Scottish tongue can appreciate to the full how much he made it live, how real was his seizure and presentation of it. It is primarily to his fellow countrymen and his fellow citizens that Walter Scott addresses himself in his greatest work. This surely was and is still undeniable. Yet his influence on the world of his age and well after that age was enormous. However inadequately translated, as we shall see, however mutilated his plots may have been upon the stage of drama or of opera, he made his deep influence felt everywhere.

How did he achieve this world-wide recognition? By his extraordinary imagination and power to express it. But perhaps most of all by his power to make the past a living, vital thing—a thing that went on. In this he satisfied his own imagination and his own homesick Scottish longings, but he also (and this is important) satisfied a craving amongst his readers, many of whom were wholly ignorant of Scotland past or present. He satisfied that craving because it is universal and because his imagination and potent expression allowed him to do so.

Childhood: a Dream and a Reality

This chapter deals in its larger part with the child Walter Scott's first conscious memory of his surroundings. These were placed in and around his paternal grandfather's hillside sheep-farm in lower Tweeddale. They were surroundings of great moorland beauty and full of historical Border significance. They indeed formed for the precocious little boy a 'dream and a reality' from which he was never to escape or wish to escape during all his life. They are fundamental to an understanding of him.

Before coming to this Borderland one must pause upon his birthplace—a spot, even for the Edinburgh of the eighteenth century, of unusual, if not unique squalor, insanitariness, and what we might now (holding our noses) look upon as picturesque!

Scott could not remember the wynd in which he had been born when his father and family lived, or attempted to live there. Perhaps this was as well; for even his love of 'Old Edinburgh' might not have allowed him to support such a recollection without disgust.

The Old College Wynd, where Walter Scott first opened his eyes, had been known in Pre-Reformation days as the Wynd of the Blessed Virgin Mary in the Fields, 'The Fields' where nearby Darnley, Queen Mary Stuart of Scots 'langleggit' husband had been blown up and killed in a deliberate explosion of gunpowder. Queen Mary's connivance in or complete innocence of this deed is still hotly debated.

Today the wynd has been cleaned up and is known as Guthrie Street—a part of the architecturally dull, grey but necessary slum-cleansing of the first half of the nineteenth century. It keeps, however, its tortuous shape and is still constrictedly louring. Any native-born citizen of Edinburgh who really knows his town and its past can feel, and, in the nostrils of his mind, remotely smell the one-time overripe and polychromatic decay of this still obsequiously narrow thoroughfare.

An impression of its uncleaned appearance shortly after Scott's birth there can be gained from a rare coloured print in the Edinburgh Public Library. The rotten old dwelling houses, liquescently coloured in a way which never obtained in the old and important Royal Mile, lean towards each other closely. People might well have been able to shake hands with each other from the windows across the street. All 'houses' or apartments, often inhabited by very well-bred folk, were upon 'common stairs' sometimes used as common repositories for domestic refuse.

College Wynd was, and is, tributary to the main street, the Cowgate, which runs directly under the Royal Mile and the Castle on the southern and English side of the Old Town, but within the old Flodden Wall. The Cowgate in the eighteenth century must have been as insanitary as any part of the old capital of 'high stinking and high thinking', but it cannot have been as unhealthy as the College Wynd which fell and twisted its way into it from the College Hill above.

The Cowgate, running due East and West, was a comparatively broad street open to both of Edinburgh's prevailing and cleansing winds. Not so Old College Wynd, which was a protected nest of dirt.

We know indeed that germs flourished. Six of Walter Scott's nine elder brothers and sisters, born before him in this place (and the children of healthy parents) died in infancy. Walter as a small child was taken out of it only just in time, when his father, also Walter Scott, moved to the salubrity of George's Square, a fine Scottish eighteenth-century suburb just outside the Flodden Wall.

It is astonishing now to think that a well-doing and well-connected lawyer like the elder Walter Scott could have settled in and tried to bring up a family in such a festering spot as Old College Wynd. But that was the Edinburgh way of it then. Reputable lawyers neither knew nor cared much about germs; and Old College Wynd had for long been a respectable warren, all the more so for being antique. It is possible, however, that the move to George's Square had been suggested by young Walter's maternal grandfather,

Dr John Rutherford, Professor of Medicine at Edinburgh University, a man of science ahead of his time. As we shall see later, Rutherford was to give some helpful advice about the effect of fresh air on his young grandson, even after George's Square.

Walter Scott the elder not only moved to George's Square then arising by the common land of 'the Meadows', but also built himself a house there (number 25) on the west side. It still stands; for the west side of this unique experiment in native Scottish pre-Adam Georgian architecture has not yet been violated by the modern Edinburgh University which has recently indulged in a fit of *trahison des clercs* in George's Square.

Looking at number 25 which has scarcely endured any alterations from the day it was put up, you can gain evidence of the elder Walter Scott's means and, for a lawyer, ample circumstances. It is a good-sized eighteenth-century house which, though now in urban circumstances would, in the country not have disgraced a small laird or reputable landed proprietor. It is difficult to understand how he could ever have suffered for himself and his family, not only the antique dirt but the uncomfortable narrow circumstances of the Old College Wynd when he could have afforded to build a house such as this.

When the boy Walter Scott was eighteen months old at George's Square, he fell victim to a 'teething fever'; and three days later they found he had lost the use of his right leg in some kind of infantile paralysis. This was thought to have had some connection with the teething fever. But this is medically unsound. Teething fever does not lead to infantile paralysis.

As a grown man of six feet he always limped, but had forced himself to have such control over the stricken limb that he used it in riding, walking large distances, and even dancing with the lassies on public ballroom floors. Until late middle-age he must have exercised his damaged limb with greater vigour than did most of his friends their two unaffected legs.

But the family at 25 George's Square were not to know this and were seriously alarmed. The uncouth medical devices of the time used by surgeons and physicians had no effect. Then, with his native common sense, grandfather Dr Rutherford suggested even cleaner and fresher air in the countryside. The child was sent off accordingly to Sandy Knowe, the sheep-farm on lower Tweeddale cultivated by his paternal grandfather, Robert Scott.

This protracted sojourn on the moorlands not only probably saved his life and more certainly prevented Walter from growing up a helpless cripple, but also influenced his mind deeply when it was passing through its most retentive period of childhood.

His grandfather had been born before the Union of the Kingdoms in 1707. He may have remembered little or nothing of the Kingdom of Scotland in her days of independence; but both he and Walter's grandmother, born Barbara Haliburton, now the farmer's wife, were steeped in the lore and traditions of Border warfare—that warfare which had produced some of the greatest ballads in the old Scots tongue. The effect of this and of the company of the shepherds on the boy Walter Scott, the future poet and novelist of Scotland, cannot be exaggerated.

Robert Scott was no more than a tenant farmer inhabiting with his wife a small farmhouse on the hillside; but he was a man of proud family connections. American readers will not be surprised at such a combination. All over the United States there are simply-living folk in the countrysides and sometimes in the towns who are related to the greatest citizens of America, and who take the fact of that relationship for granted.

It is to be hoped that most Scottish readers with any knowledge of their country's past will also not be surprised at such a thing. But, maybe a word of explanation is needful to remind the English reader of Scottish traditions in such matters.

A Highland clansman, even in the latter half of the eighteenth century when the suppressive laws after the Jacobite Rising of 1745 had officially abolished the Highland system, was also his chief's kinsman. He nearly always bore the same surname and thought of himself, however humble, as cousin to the great man. Even now, when the Celtic Highlands and Islands have had to put up with destroying forces more potent than were the Hanoverian laws passed in remote Westminster, they preserve much of this kinsman-clansman tradition.

In Walter Scott's day the great border families of which the Scotts were amongst the most powerful kept up the same kind of tradition. Robert Scott of Sandy Knowe was kinsman to Scott of Harden—a chief, some would have then said, and some still say, superior in lineage to the great Duke of Buccleuch who, by courtesy and through the female line had been allowed to retain the name of Scott. In the seventeenth century Anne, as the only surviving child of the second Earl of Buccleuch, was his heiress. She had married not very reputably (at least in Scottish and Border eyes) a bastard of Charles II—the Duke of Monmouth. Upon Monmouth's execution she kept the surname of Scott and the large Buccleuch lands in Scotland *and* the estates of her executed husband in England. Robert Scott of Sandy Knowe was officially a hill farmer in no great style. Yet he was akin to Harden. Scott himself, in a well-known passage of his fragmentary autobiography of his early days, has told of the loving care bestowed on him at Sandy Knowe. This loving care sometimes took such extraordinary forms as wrapping up the child's naked body in the bloodily wet skin of a newly-killed sheep—an age-old country remedy believed in for crippled children.

He tells of an early sympathy he acquired for the, by then, defunct cause of Jacobitism. He got this from the farm-hands and shepherds, some of whom had seen the barbarous cruelties practised on the Highland prisoners of the '45 at Carlisle. He grew to loathe the name of 'Butcher Cumberland', William, Duke of Cumberland, son of George II. After his massacre at Culloden, Cumberland had been welcomed to London with an ode composed in his honour by Handel, *See the Conquering Hero Comes*. For long the flower named in England after the Royal Duke as 'Sweet William' was called in Scotland 'Stinking Willie'.

Oddly enough this childish love of Jacobitism and loathing of Cumberland was combined with an eager and partisan following of the news of the American War of Independence which had then broken out. He longed to hear of Washington's defeat.

I set this down with regret. But 'Wattie', though increasing in health and precious understanding, was only a small boy then. Moreover there were Jacobite exiles in the Americas, including Flora Macdonald and her husband, who actively took the 'Loyalist' side there. My elderly great-great-grand-father of Charleston, South Carolina, was one of these. He suffered at American hands for his inexplicable obstinacy.

James Boswell in Edinburgh, and thirty-one years older than Scott, did not share these views; indeed he incurred some disapproval in respectable circles for taking the unpopular anti-English side about the American war. I was shown at Yale an as yet unpublished letter from Boswell to the Reverend Hugh Blair, a member of the literary Establishment then and Minister of St Giles'. Blair had complained of Boswell's continued absence from the family pew for some months.

Boswell replied in the most spirited and detailed way. He said that he could not bear to 'sit under' a Christian minister who used his fashionable pulpit to fulminate against the Americans in their struggle for freedom. Blair's eventual answer to this reasoned and strongly-felt defence of the colonials' cause was very feeble.

I owe the privilege of examining this correspondence to Professor Frederick Pottle, the eminent Boswellian scholar of Yale.

A partiality, or interest in the colour and drama of Jacobitism (a lost cause at that time not yet sicklied by the glucose of false sentiment) was to remain with Scott for all his life. A stronger influence on him from those Sandy Knowe days was his intense absorption in the old Border tales, particularly those about his own forebear, 'Beardie' Watt of Harden.

These he heard from his grandmother and aunts accompanied by recitations of Border ballads. He devoured them and instantly grasped many of them in his extraordinarily retentive memory. As shall be shown later, this powerful instant memory, not only for verse, but for long passages of prose was, even more extraordinarily, to remain with him until age. Visitors to Abbotsford loved to get him to display his power of memory on passages casually thrust upon him. Good-naturedly he nearly always obliged them.

As a child and later a growing boy, however, he cared to exercise his instant memory only upon verse or prose that interested him. He was, to put it mildly, deeply interested in what he heard of the past at Sandy Knowe.

Within sight of the magical Eildon Hills whose triple peaks were to haunt him for all his days, not far from Tweed which was for him *the* river of all the world, amongst the green and heathery-coloured moorlands of lower Tweeddale, within remoter sight of the Lammermuirs, he could not but have been entranced by his surroundings.

We know he absorbed with the greatest relish the old tales and verses about the one-time 'auld enemy' of England. Here was a partiality close to his own patriotism and to the patriotism of the older folk around him.

It was a partiality, a patriotism which was later in life to become a home-sickness for the free Kingdom of Scotland not so long vanished. For myself I believe that he expresses this home-sick patriotism in his first purely Scottish Waverley novels. He did not explicitly speak in the novels of his nostalgia but gave it colour (and what colour!) in the Scottish characters, admirable, absurd or even disagreeable which his abounding imagination created.

As shall be shown later when we come to the novels, he wrote them in secrecy, tried to conceal his authorship of them, giving a variety of excuses for this evasion. Later his imagination, his power to re-create the past led him to place the scenes of his novels in England and in continental Europe.

Constantly, however, he returned to Scotland, never more autobiographically than in the *Redgauntlet* of 1824, never more poignantly than in that novel about an absurd Jacobite rising and in its absurd failure—a rising which was supposed to have been attempted some twenty years after the '45. It was a rising, of course, which never occurred outside Walter Scott's imagination.

The concluding cry of Redgauntlet, however, when he sees all his plotting contemptuously dismissed by the British authorities as not worth bothering about is not easily forgotten—'Then the cause is forever lost'. There are, one suggests, undertones here. But this is to anticipate.

The farm of Sandy Knowe today stands on its sheep-farm uplands exactly as it did when the child Walter Scott was there. The grim medieval tower of Smailholm, so beloved of Scott when he was a grown man, is farther up the hill than the farm. The view from the top of it is scarcely changed. You see a great width of Scottish Border country, and can look ahead into the lands of the 'auld enemy' of England.

The 'auld enemy' of England may have appeared as a traditional enemy indeed to the child at Sandy Knowe; but all of a sudden 'Wattie' was to make the acquaintance of that 'auld enemy' in his most agreeable and kindly form.

In his fourth year 'Wattie's' parents and his relations at Sandy Knowe decided to exchange raw sheepskins as a

31

remedy on a sick child for the healing waters of Bath in Somerset. His Aunt Janet took him there via London (a sea journey from Leith lasting twelve days); and the child enjoyed himself vastly looking at the antiquities in London and later at Bath.

He stayed at Bath for a full year, but without much visible improvement to his leg. His mind, however, grew and enriched itself. His greatest experience was to see *As You Like It* at the Bath playhouse. He was quite overcome by it; and from this never-to-be-forgotten experience of the play, began his life-long veneration for Shakespeare.

He returned from Bath and London to Scotland with, what American readers may be amused to learn, was a pronounced 'English accent'. Soon, however, he re-acquired an educated Eastern Scottish voice which never deserted him. There is reason to believe that to the end he had that unmistakable gutturally 'burred' r which is to be found only in the coastal districts from Berwickshire and the Lothians up to Fife.

Coming back to Scotland he went first to his father's house in George's Square, Edinburgh, then for two years more to Sandy Knowe. But the old people on the farm were by now dying or dead; and between the ages of seven and eight he came back to begin his formal education in Edinburgh, based upon his parents' house in George's Square.

But Sandy Knowe and the moorlands of lower Tweeddale remained for him a dream and a reality. It was a dream and a reality which was to make his fame internationally and to lead to his near complete financial ruin in his own country.

4

Youth in Edinburgh: 'Makin' Himself'

It is a tribute to young Walter Scott's inborn power to charm that his days, amongst his schoolfellows at least, were happy when he entered the famous Edinburgh Royal High School in 1779.

The Royal High School was traditionally founded by King David in 1128, but the earliest records surviving of it are from 1496. It became then the Grammar School of Edinburgh subject to the discipline of the Provost of the 'Hie Kirk' St Giles' and of the Town Council. From then onwards until the early nineteenth century it was *the* school for the sons of the Edinburgh aristocracy and Establishment generally.

When Scott became a pupil at it, it had not yet gone across to the New Town fine and ample Grecian building later put up in the style of the 'Athens of the North'. It was still obscurely in the Old Town, not far from the place where Walter had been born, but in much less squalid circumstances. Obscurely placed it was still entirely a school for Establishment boys.

It is an unfortunate truism that the sons of the upper and ruling classes in these islands are, when at school, abominably cruel to each other. No 'working class' parents, the mother especially, would endure that their boys should be treated thus at their non-fee-paying schools. But the Establishment classes put up with it and even seem to encourage the tradition.

George Orwell has a painful story of life at his private school and at Eton. 'The strong were always right, the weak always wrong.' This is comparatively modern, but my mother told me of the outrageous bullying her elder brothers saw and endured at Eton in Victorian times. Long before that there was Shelley at Eton, and before him there were sufferers in the eighteenth and seventeenth centuries.

There are observers of the Scottish scene who hold that in our native Establishment schools the cruelty is worse than in England. This may well be so. I recall with revulsion my time at one of these bastard Scottish public boarding schools spawned in the early years of last century in imitation of the Rugby of Dr Arnold.

It is difficult to believe that the boys at the Establishment Edinburgh schools in the latter half of the eighteenth century were different from those who came before or after them. It is impossible to believe that so truthful and realistic a man as Walter Scott could have allowed himself to have become softened by false sentiment in recollection of his schooldays. He was modestly but surely speaking of facts when he wrote this in a fragment of autobiography:

> Amongst my companions, my good-nature and flow of ready imagination rendered me very popular. . . . My lameness and the efforts I made to suffer that disadvantage by making up in address what I wanted in activity engaged the latter principle in my favour; and in the winter play-hours, when hard exercise was impossible, my tales used to assemble an admiring audience round Lucky Brown's fire-side, and happy was he that could sit next to the inexhaustible narrator.

He was still obviously trailing clouds of glory from Sandy Knowe and Tweeddale; but it says much for him that he was able to use them so unconsciously and to such great effect amongst his urban fellow schoolboys.

Need it be added that, like most men born to greatness, he was in his schooldays and in his classes largely self-educated. He liked Latin and did well in it. He did not care for Greek and was pronounced a hopeless dunce in it. 'I was never a dunce,' he said in his autobiography, 'but an incorrigibly idle imp who was always longing to do something else than what was enjoined him.'

The something else was not always play or some other schoolboy diversion; it consisted of a love of history, of literature and of foreign languages. He now began to lay, largely by his own efforts, the foundations of his knowledge of German and other European tongues—invaluable to him in future years.

After the Royal High School he attended the Old College,

34

now University of Edinburgh; later he became a law student; for his father had determined that he should follow that profession. At fifteen he signed indentures as his father's apprentice.

The elder Walter Scott has sometimes been dismissed as an unbending Calvinist; though whether he upheld the preposterous and shocking doctrine of predestination for damnation or salvation is not clear; but he did enforce the rigours of extreme Presbyterian practices on his family and on the young Walter, who groaned under them, particularly on Sundays.

It will not do, however, to label Walter Scott's father merely as a dull, unbending Puritan. He had as a solicitor amongst his clients Highland Jacobites who had survived from 'the Fifteen' and the 'Forty-five', and dealt with them sympathetically. He had also a horror of those few among them who had betrayed their cause.

When Murray of Broughton, the well-known Jacobite turncoat, called upon him at George's Square on a business matter he dealt with him as a man of business, but could not bring himself to be sociable. Mrs Scott brought in some tea and tea-cups for refreshment. After Murray had left, old Walter Scott hurled the tea-cup from which his visitor had drunk into the square where it broke. He explained to his startled wife that no member of his family should ever drink from a cup that had been stained by the lips and tongue of a traitor.

On the other hand, he was genial as well as practical with the faithful Jacobite Stewart of Invernahyle who had 'been out' in 'the Fifteen' and 'the Forty-five'; and the young Walter was fascinated by him. The gentle, courteous, strict yet fundamentally romantic elder Walter Scott was a human paradox of a kind, one might suppose, could only have lived in the Edinburgh and Scotland of his era—but one may be wrong; perhaps some still do.

While training for the law and indentured to his father, and before it was decided that he should aspire to the higher branch—that of advocacy at the bar—young Walter was sent on various legal errands for his father.

One of these took him to Perthshire for his first sight of the Highland Hills. It is with genuine regret that one records that Walter's job here was to expel tenants of Stewart of Appin—thus helping in early 'Highland clearances'.

These unfortunate tenants, thrust out from Balquhidder where their ancestors had lived for centuries bore the name of Maclaren, McLaren, McLaurin or whatever Celtic or English orthography you care to use for that small but vigorous and loyal clan—a further cause for my regret in recording this venture.

Sir Walter Scott's attitude towards the remoter Celtic Highlands and Islands has been debated; but we shall come to that later. One thing is sure. Whatever task he may have been youthfully employed on at Balquhidder, this first sight of Perthshire and its mountains made a deep impression on him which was to last. It animated some of his most popular epic verse and touched some of his novels, particularly *Rob Roy*.

But these errands on his father's business as a solicitor ended at seventeen. The family at number 25 George's Square decided then that he should move higher up in the law and study to become an advocate at the bar—or what is known in England as a barrister. Three years later he was 'called Advocate'.

This was, in Edinburgh professional society a distinct move upwards. Walter now began to dress better and to conduct himself more stylishly. This custom amongst young advocates still prevails with us. The humblest Edinburgh advocate knows consciously or subconsciously that he has set his foot on a course that may lead him to being one of the Crown Judges at Parliament House.

As Lord of Session he will then be able to assume the honorary but resounding title of 'Lord', which he may carry with him into England or wherever he goes. And he may, to make it more resounding, take his title territorially from some place in Scotland with which his family has been associated rather than from his surname. James Boswell's father, for instance, had the title of Lord Auchinleck. This habit still continues though until recently, the wife of a judge with a territorial title remained simply Mrs X—his family name. This used to cause embarrassment when Scottish judges with their wives crossed the Border and signed the register when staying at hotels. All that is over now.

When the Court of Session 'skails' (dismisses itself for the day) and the advocates march down 'the Mound' from the Old Town to the New, curious members of the public may amuse themselves by trying to spot which amongst the confident and well-dressed young men are going to become 'my Lords'.

After all, the Edinburgh and Scottish legal society is, in comparison with England, small and concentrated. You are bound to make some lucky guesses. Are you inclined to plump for the pale and earnest-faced youths obviously devoted to the night-time study of briefs, or do you choose those rubicund ones who have already tasted the vinous pleasures of bar society? It doesn't matter; the Lords of Session spring from both types.

Of what type was Walter Scott? It is generally and rightly assumed that he was not of the pallid, brief-reading class. He was flushed, exuberant, friendly and eager to make friends. He joined in the social life of the more gay and extrovert of his young advocate companions, he joyfully became a member of dining and debating clubs. And Edinburgh being the Edinburgh that it was (and in legal circles still is) he did not shun the pleasures of the wine bottle.

He must have occasionally been youthfully and sociably drunk. But such tales of his conviviality as do come down to us testify more to the strength of his head than to his drunkenness. He was able to drink deep and long and some-times send under the table (while he was still seated and in command of his faculties) seasoned and usually victorious topers.

Later in life he kept a fine wine cellar from which he was highly generous to all visitors of all classes and all nations. He regarded fermented liquor as one of the gifts of God, and, in consequence, was distressed by those who misused it. He had a horror of what were known in those days as 'dram drinkers' by compulsion, or what we now call alcoholics. He was never openly censorious of them, but pitied them and avoided them when he could.

His capacity for deep-drinking in youth was restrained and offset by his extraordinary powers of physical exercise on foot (despite his lame leg) and on horseback—powers remarkable and remarked on even at that time. In his fragmentary autobiography he says:

> I had a dreamy way of going much further than I intended . . . my return was protracted, and my parents had some serious cause of uneasiness.

For example, I once set out with Mr William Clerk [his great friend in training to be Advocate, and of whom more below] and some others to fish the lake above Howgate [the other side of the Pentland Hills from Edinburgh] and fished the whole day. We breakfasted at Howgate [the inn is still there and well known] and while we were on our return next morning, I was easily seduced to visit Pennycuik House, [a fair number of miles out of the way back to Edinburgh] the seat of his family.

Here we were overwhelmed with kindness by the late Sir John Clerk and his lady, the present Dowager. The pleasure of looking at fine pictures, the beauty of the place and the flattering hospitality of the owners drowned all recollections of home.

In short he gave his fishing companions the slip—they may well have been sent back on horses or by some conveyance provided by the hospitable and wealthy Sir John Clerk —and walked his own way back to Edinburgh and George's Square.

Taking Edinburgh to Howgate, Howgate to Penicuik House with possible divagations and then back on his own to Edinburgh was a considerable trip for a lame man—over twenty-five miles, but Scott thought nothing of it, and often achieved longer lonely walking expeditions.

William Clerk was one of the greatest friends of Scott's youth and was to remain as such for all his life. Readers of Lockhart and other books on Scott may be puzzled by William Clerk (styled of Eldin) and his connection with the Clerks of Pennycuick now spelt Penicuik.

Without going into the complications of geneaology, the matter is quite simple. The Clerks of Eldin were a cadet branch of the Penicuik Clerks, and William, Scott's friend was in fact a cousin of the Sir John Clerk who entertained the party of young men described in Scott's autobiography, quoted above.

Before talking about the remarkable family of the Clerks of Penicuik, we may pause on one observation. Penicuik House is today one of the most beautiful, picturesque and astonishing 'ruins' in all Scotland, possibly in all Europe, therefore in the world. Any reader of this book who finds himself in Scotland, and particularly Edinburgh, should strive to see it. It is only twenty-five minutes' drive in a motor-car from the West End of Princes Street in Edinburgh.

But, one important fact must be made clear. Penicuik and its 'policies' (*anglice* domestic grounds) are private property.

You cannot just drive out and have a look at the place as you wish. The present and 10th Baronet, Sir John Dutton Clerk, is, however, generous and hospitable. He allows the people of Penicuik, the nearby small town, regular appointed access to his estate, and does not object to some visitors from Edinburgh joining them.

Should any visitors from America or England who are interested in the story of Scott and the Clerks of Penicuik write *well in advance* asking permission to see the estate, they are unlikely to be refused. They will then (apart from Walter Scott/William Clerk interest) have the pleasure of looking at one of the most staggeringly beautiful ruins that exist—and in circumstances of great beauty.

One might go on writing about the Clerks of Penicuik for chapters of this book, but must compress. The Clerks have been Scottish barons (too complicated to define that title here) since the days of Mary, Queen of Scots, whose cause they espoused. They came to Penicuik in 1615 and lived in an old Scottish baronial house there.

In the middle of the eighteenth century Sir James Clerk built, largely to his own design, a superb Palladian house decorated with importations from Italy. It was in this (by our standards) huge house that Scott and his friends were entertained.

In 1899, the last year of the nineteenth century, it was not so much burned down, as gutted so as to make it uninhabitable. In the early years of this century the family moved to the renovated stables of the old Palladian house (about the size of a small Oxford college) and it is here that the present baronet and his family live.

Though gutted by fire the front façade and walls of Sir James's house remain. Its beauty of design is still apparent, but to this is added the melancholy of broken windows and a smashed interior. Rooks and other birds fly in and out of the faceless windows and nest in the inside where once some of the most cultivated people of Scotland's efflorescent eighteenth century lived and entertained. This melancholy has its strong appeal. But its powerful beauty remains.

Anyone who is interested in the Scotland of the eighteenth and early nineteenth century, particularly anyone interested in Walter Scott's place in that period should try to see it. *But*, let it be repeated, you must receive permission before you go there.

Edinburgh's legal society and custom has not changed much since Scott's day; and this apparent digression does not lead us far from his position when he first took the gown and tried to hire himself out as a pleader on the floor of Parliament Hall.

Had Scott been content to stay in Edinburgh and confine his ambition there to the local path upwards, had he used what surely would have been his notable eloquence as a pleader in the Courts of Session, had he cultivated his family and friendly connections in high places he would most probably have become a judge—a Lord of Session. He might possibly have become Lord Kelso or even, had he wished it, Lord Sandy Knowe.

If he had done this we might have had from him some of his verses (he had once admitted that he saw no reason why a Lord President of Scotland should not also write poetry) but we should certainly have lost the Waverley Novels and much else besides.

We were saved from the loss by Scott's fundamentally restless and inquisitive character which would never have allowed him to tie himself to a round of ambitious duties in Edinburgh alone. There were two other factors that entered.

First: Scott immediately began to spend his holidays from Parliament House not in cultivating the great ones in Edinburgh but in travelling about Scotland. Especially he moved to the Borders which he now looked at from the English as well as the Scottish side. A man of whom Walter Scott was very fond, who accompanied him on the Scottish Border jaunts and illuminated them for him, was Robert Shortreed, Sheriff-Substitute of Roxburghshire. American, and possibly some English readers are asked to await a definition of the Scottish legal meaning of Sheriff in a more relevant place below.

Shortreed was a man after Scott's heart. A Borderer of the Borders, he was known to everyone, the peasantry as well as the gentry, in his wild and wide domain which covered some of the 'Debatable Land' in Liddesdale. He had good knowledge of Border lore, and some knowledge of Border ballads. Though his scholarship on the subject was inferior to Scott's his enthusiasm was not less. He knew where the ballads were still remembered and spoken, and could lead his younger companion to them.

From 1792 and for the seven ensuing years Scott and Shortreed made these 'raids', as they called them, into Liddesdale.

As Lockhart puts it:

> To these rambles Scott owed most of the materials of his *Minstrelsy of the Border* [the first of Scott's great literary achievements] and not less of that intimate acquaintance with the living manners of these unsophisticated regions, which constitute the chief charm of one of the most charming of his prose works. But how soon he had any definite object in his researches seems doubtful. 'He was *makin' himself* a' the time,' said Mr Shortreed, 'but I didna ken maybe what he was about till years had passed. At first he thought of little, I dare say, but the queerness and the fun.'

'Makin' himself' . . . 'the queerness and the fun'. The Sheriff knew how to express himself very well. Scott was indeed, and on foundations laid more deeply in him than his delightful, eager little companion knew, making himself. He was making himself in a direction where his ambitions drove far more strongly than any that may have touched him as an advocate in Parliament House, Edinburgh. Today we are grateful for these ambitions which for us far outshine in their object any glittering prize he might have won in the law. We are grateful, too, to Sheriff Shortreed for accompanying him and joining in 'the queerness and the fun', when Scott was 'makin' himself'.

Of this there was plenty during these raids; and we are left in no doubt about it by Lockhart. There were no roads, tolls or inns in the raided country. The two men had to ride along tracks which were no more than beds of dry, or not so dry streams; at the end of the day they stayed in farmhouses or shepherds' 'cot-houses'.

Scott, at once, was on the friendliest terms with all whom he met. Advocates from Parliament House, Edinburgh, were seldom, if ever, seen in Liddesdale, and the young Walter Scott may at first have inspired some shyness. This soon vanished under his easy manner. 'He's just a chield like ourselves,' commented one shepherd who had approached him warily.

Apart from the wild riding over trackless moorland the pair had to put up with primitive accommodation, sometimes sharing one bed or even lying on the floor. Shortreed loved Scott's companionship in these circumstances:

41

Sic an endless fund o' humour and drollery as he then had wi' him! Never ten yards but we were either laughing or roaring or singing. Whenever we stopped how brawlie he suited himsel' to everybody! . . . I've seen him in a' moods in these jaunts, grave and gay, daft and serious, sober and drunk; but drunk or sober he was aye the gentleman. He looked excessively heavy and stupid when he was fou, but he was never out o' gude humour.

When Scott got drunk it was usually out of politeness. His hosts might have been offended by his abstinence especially when pains had been taken to supply the refreshment. There are some delightfully ludicrous and characteristic accounts of how this refreshment was supplied.

It is tempting to linger on these seven-year continued raids of 'queerness and fun' fortified by song, poetry and probing into the past. It is tempting because to read and to write about them is to be infected by the happiness of it all. It is all there in Lockhart and in excerpts elsewhere.

That we have lingered thus far on Liddesdale 'raids' is because they are relevant to Scott's strong feeling for his native country's past.

At Sandy Knowe and Kelso he had heard from his grandparents and relations stories of the Old Borderland, and had also had ballads recited to him. In Edinburgh he had heard tales of Jacobitism from those who had lived in the days of the now lost cause. But it was always *hearing* about the past, receiving it, as it were, at second hand.

Here, in the yearly repeated 'raids' into the wilderness of Liddesdale, in the 'queerness and the fun', the laughing, the roaring, the drinking, the endless talking and listening he was in the midst of a part of Scotland's past that was still alive, still lived by living people.

The shepherds and the peasant folk there no longer joined in raids across the Border into England. They had no need to, and, even if they had, they lacked leaders. But equally there was the fact that the great events of the Union of 1707 had scarcely passed these remote folk by, or had scarcely touched them. They spoke the old Scots tongue of their forebears, but at no remove, and using in their voices no hint of quotation marks. Their repetition of ballads may have been faulty, but they had heard them from the descendants of people who had lived those ballads.

No lawyer except their Sheriff and the young advocate from Edinburgh visited them, no business man, no modern man of affairs. Save for the cessation of Border warfare they lived the lives of the Scots folk who had come before them in the days of the independent Kingdom.

Here was richness for the youthful advocate, patriot and aspiring man of letters, Walter Scott.

It was about this time that Scott intensely enjoyed the experience of first love—indeed love at first sight—and suffered his failure in it.

This deeply felt experience is not a part of our theme, but, if it were, it has, in the writer's opinion been too much dwelt upon by biographers of Scott—Lockhart excepted. Scott became in the nineteenth century one of *the* romantic figures of his era; and what, in the eyes of the more romantic biographers, can be more romantic than the blasting of first love's hopes? Undeterred by the fact that the object of Scott's love bore the prosaic name of Williamina Belsches, they have luxuriated in his pain and deep distress over her.

It certainly was pain, and pain remembered by Scott for nearly all his life, but to claim that it had any ineradicable effect on his life and work is too much. At any rate he recovered from it soon enough to meet, love and marry Charlotte Carpenter (Charpentier), the daughter of a French émigré. She did enter into and have an effect on his life. She bore him children, kept house for him in his various homes, gave him love and a kind of understanding sympathy.

His lost love shall be but briefly treated here. Williamina was the daughter of a well-doing lawyer and, on her mother's side the granddaughter of the Earl of Leven. Belsches had no reason to despise Scott, still less dislike him, but he had larger ambitions for a son-in-law. These he satisfied when his daughter eventually married the wealthy Sir William Forbes of Pitsligo, thus killing Walter's hopes stone dead.

Biographers are constantly detecting portraits of Williamina in various heroines of the Waverley novels. The writer agrees with Hesketh Pearson in believing that there is only one—that is 'the most animated and attractive heroine, Catherine Seyton in *The Abbot*'.

This is not to say that Scott put her out of his mind or that he forgot the pain of losing her. But he did not in the romantic manner of Heine luxuriate in his pain, or make a verbal melody of it. He would never have addressed the shade of his lost love as Heine did in *Ich grolle nicht* from the '*Dichterliebe*' as '*Ewig Verlones Lieb*'. His good sense

43

would have made him ashamed even to consider doing such a thing.

Not much later he met Charlotte Carpenter in Cumberland and married her in Carlisle Cathedral. The approaching nuptials were celebrated by a stag party for two, composed of Scott and his friend Shortreed. Lockhart quotes Shortreed's account of this:

> His [Shortreed's] *Memorandum* records that the evening of the 30th September was one of the most joyous he had ever spent. 'Scott,' he says, 'was sair beside himself about Miss Carpenter;— we toasted her twenty times over—and sat together, he raving about her until it was one in the morning.'

His marriage, of course, prevented further long raids into Liddesdale, and he settled down at first near Edinburgh. Then came the second factor which clearly indicated his lack of ambition to become a Lord of Session. This second factor has been referred to earlier when we mentioned Scott's holiday travels as being the first sign that he was not bound to the step-ladder of success in legal Edinburgh. It was the offer to him and his acceptance of the post of Sheriff of Selkirkshire in 1799.

American readers may care to note that the Scots legal word sheriff bears no relation to the popular use of the same word in films and stories in the U.S.A. A Scottish sheriff does not wear a ten-gallon Stetson hat, nor does he mete out rough and ready justice by galloping round the countryside to 'shoot up' villains in village saloons.

He is, on the contrary, usually a quiet, studious man of the law who loves country life. Avoiding the historic complications of 'Sheriff Principal', 'Sheriff Depute' and 'Sheriff Substitute' one is content to say that he holds a Crown appointment and (*aut Culpam aut Vitam*) for life. *But*, if he does accept it and stays as Sheriff, he will be supposed never to aspire to be a Lord of Session. His position in Scotland is vaguely equivalent to, but not the same as that of a County Court Judge in England.

Scott's salary from the Sheriffship was £300 a year; this, combined with his wife's small but reasonable fortune and the various legal jobs which, in those days a country Sheriff was allowed to retain in Edinburgh, and some legacies that came his way made him financially comfortable. At first he intended to stay in Edinburgh at 39 North Castle Street, which was to be his New Town house for so long, and only drop down at regular intervals to Selkirk for the not very arduous task of dispensing justice there.

The Lord Lieutenant of the County, however, a man of strong local feeling, did not approve. He thought 'his' sheriff should reside near his shrieval work. After a time he made his wishes known and in 1804 Scott obeyed them. Keeping on his Edinburgh house he moved his officially permanent residence to Ashestiel in 'the Forest of Ettrick'. Here he was to stay until the itch to take and build Abbotsford and become a country laird mastered him.

Part farm, part manor, Ashestiel was a well-established Border house near the unbridged Tweed. It was accessible to the county town but was also a Border refuge. As such it was peculiarly suitable to Scott's literary activities.

He had already, a year and a half earlier, published his first widely successful book *The Minstrelsy of the Scottish Border*, of which we shall speak in the next chapter. Here, and in his house in the country south of Edinburgh he could ponder at peace, and in stimulating surroundings, when he required stimulus, on verse of his own making, yet deriving from the same source.

5

His Character Formed:
His First Best-Seller

Scott 'had now taken sasine of the Border, being the local justiciar of the shire which holds the upper waters of its most famous river—Tweed'. Before coming to his literary activities there and before dealing with his first big success, *The Minstrelsy of the Scottish Border*, which, in fact, had been published before his descent upon Ashestiel, we may consider what kind of a man he had become in his late young manhood.

Lockhart says: 'His figure, excepting the blemish in one limb, must in those days have been eminently handsome— tall, much above the usual stature [about six feet at a time when men did not grow to much of a height], cast in the very mould of a youthful Hercules, the throat and chest after the finest model of the antique, the hands delicately finished, the whole outline that of extraordinary vigour without as yet a touch of clumsiness.

This is laying it on a bit thick. His hands were very large and powerful—Scott himself said they were the largest North of Tweed—his mouth, though expressive, was big; and he had other physical peculiarities, though not unpleasing.

As for the blemished leg, he had long mastered this, at times, obvious disadvantage; he had forced his lame leg to do a normal job. He could outwalk, outride, outjump (on horseback) nearly all his companions, and, as has been mentioned, dance in the ballroom.

His physical activities now received further impetus. When the French Revolution broke out there was a general scare of invasion of Britain, particularly after Buonaparte's rise to power. Naturally the scare was largely concentrated on the Southern coast of England, but it sped up northward, and in no place more strongly than in the East of Scotland around Edinburgh. Scott could not join the infantry Volunteers of Defence because of his lameness. It might not have been too much for him to march, but his step would have interfered with the regular rhythm of his fellow Volunteers.

Instead, in 1797 he joined the Royal Edinburgh Volunteer Light Dragoons. He joined this body's arduous training and hard riding with gusto. It satisfied his longing for action and military action—if only in preparation for defence. And it satisfied his patriotic desire to defend the soil of his own native land of Scotland.

It may in a sense have satisfied his conservatism aroused by the news of the Revolution. But 'conservatism' is a word that must be used with provisos about Scott. He was conservative less in a political sense than in an inborn temperamental one. He was rational enough to see the need for a reform of monarchical France, but was repelled by the wholesale destruction of the past that went on in Revolution's name. He would never have echoed Wordsworth's famous lines about the Revolution:

> Bliss was it in that Dawn to be alive,
> But to be young was very heaven!

If he found any bliss in being young at that time it was that it gave him the opportunity to take action, to be a volunteer soldier of cavalry.

It was now, too, that we, looking back at him over close on two centuries, begin to feel that extraordinarily generous heart sometimes displayed humorously, sometimes with passion; he retained this to the end of his days. He retained too his fascinating talk with which he now, in an adult way, began to delight his adult companions of all ages.

There is a temptation in writing about Scott to overpraise his personality, but one must express the truth. He was surely one of the most agreeable and naturally good men of his time and circumstances. He was always extravert and entertaining; and he was, not foolishly, but with generous deliberation an outstanding giver-away of himself, of his

47

essential self. Outstanding! And all this in an Edinburgh and a Border Scotland when men had not yet cultivated the habit of dourness and of being 'buttoned up'.

Had he not been a genius or had he never expressed that genius for the benefit of the whole world, it is possible that 'the Shirra' of Selkirk might still be recalled in the memoirs of the time, such as Cockburn's *Memorial*, as one of the notabilities of a notable time in Scotland.

He shunned extremes in philosophy, a science in which he was not well grounded, and in religion, in which he had been overgrounded by his father and domestic tutors at George's Square.

He shrank from the then very definitely defined doctrine and disciplines of the Catholic Church but could describe with sympathy, if not acute understanding, those who supported them. He was a Protestant, but a Christian Protestant. That phrase, as anyone who knows the history of Lowland Scotland, is no paradox.

The extreme Covenanters, and a character such as his David Deans in his great novel *The Heart of Midlothian*, were passionately obsessed by the Old Testament at the expense of the New. One almost gets the impression that they deliberately avoided the memory of Jesus Christ and of his actions and were out of sympathy with his character. They can hardly be described specifically as Christian Protestants.

An obsessive devotion to the Old Testament has largely declined in modern Scotland, but it has left outside the Evangelicals an odd legacy in a lack of sympathy with the character of Jesus Christ.

Those who nowadays may seldom darken a church door, but who have learned in the rigorous school of modern Edinburgh conduct that man's first duty is 'not to give himself away' are out of sympathy with the historical figure of Jesus Christ.

The more extreme amongst them may, without being aware of it, distrust, dislike—or at best—not care to think about the story of the God-Man who was crucified at Jerusalem. He more than anyone on this earth, and in all meanings of the expression gave Himself away.

There was none of this pernicious nonsense about Scott. He was a Scottish Christian Protestant who at home worshipped indiscriminately at the two historic post-Reformation national churches, the Presbyterian and the Episcopal. If he had a preference (one which would have appalled his father had he lived to have known it) it was for 'the suffering Episcopal remnant'. When he was in Edinburgh for any length of time he attended St George's Episcopal Church in York Place, at which he was a pew-holder. And he did once say that the pleasure of entering a Presbyterian Church of Scotland kirk was the knowledge that you could come out again.

Yet, in his *Old Mortality* which some hold to be his masterpiece amongst the Scottish-based Waverley novels, he shows a rare and understanding sympathy with the Covenanters and their cause. It was a far more understanding sympathy than he was able to extend to the Catholics and their cause.

Yet, by paradox, his imaginative perception of life and faith in the Middle Ages was claimed by the early Anglo-Catholics to have helped their struggles. Newman prayed for him when he was dying; and some nineteenth-century Catholic converts looked back with gratitude on what he had done to make the Church understood by the ordinary people of Queen Victoria's reign.

He humorously defended the absurd amongst his acquaintances, if the humour took him (and it usually did) and if their absurdity had some grounds calling for sympathy. He also defended, as shall be shown, and to his own cost those who were in their behaviour absurd but yet had their own talents. The Ballantyne brothers whom he brought up from Kelso (memories of his early days there) to Edinburgh to print his works he defended, in Lockhart's view, almost obstinately. Yet they unwittingly, if wantonly and foolishly, were agents in his huge financial crash, which will be told later.

So too shall be told, when we come to it, Scott's passionate and morally courageous defence of those hounded by hypocritical society.

Lord Byron's expulsion from England was an example; and this was the Byron who, by then, had supplanted Scott as an epic poet. That Byron drove Scott from epic poetry to novel writing is something that all the world can be grateful for; but Scott did not know that then.

Scott may or may not have read Macaulay's aphorism: 'We know no spectacle more ridiculous than the British

49

public in one of its periodic fits of morality', but he certainly would have approved of it.

When Byron had been driven out of England by the malice of society gossip Scott, as we shall see, wrote: 'I have been too long accustomed to the sight of a noble staghound set upon by village curs', and compared Byron's fate to the staghound's.

Byron was deeply grateful for Scott's warmhearted and characteristic defence. But it was more than gratitude that animated the European wanderer's love for Scott the man and admiration for the Waverley novels.

This more than cordial relationship between these two great contemporaries, so unlike each other in some ways, so like in certain fundamental virtues, makes a fascinating story. But like the remarkable account of Scott's influence on North America (already mentioned) it too must wait its relevant place in the tale of Walter Scott's life. It is mentioned here while we are considering the character of Scott—already formed by the time he had come to Ashestiel.

Scott, as has been said, had launched his first best-seller *The Minstrelsy of the Scottish Border* before he had settled in the Border. But before that best-seller he had been dabbling in romantic horror productions of the then fashionable Matt Lewis school. Most of them were translations from the German with which Scott was familiar. But they were failures, scarce worth the paper on which they were printed.

Scott's pleasure in German came partly from the romantic spirit then stirring in it, partly from certain similarities in it to the old Scot's tongue. He outgrew this, but his interest in German literature was later and more worthily roused by Goethe. Goethe, who himself admired the Waverley novels, was for Scott a great European. He remains *the* European for many of us today—this despite Kaiserism, Hitlerism, two world wars and the tales we have heard from our elders of the rise of Prussianism in the 1870s. But Scott had no foresight of this.

Scott turned with gusto and surely with a premonition of better success to something he really did know about—not German fables, but the living ballads of his own land.

Scott had given up his 'raids' into Liddesdale with Shortreed after his marriage but had whetted his appetite for Scottish balladry. He continued to run around on ballad

50

collection and research in less remote places and on lower Tweed. His wife slightly complained to him of this running around. But Walter's good spirits set her right; and before long Charlotte was amused and pleased to act as hostess to some of the queer folk he brought back from his researches, first to their house at Lasswade, near to, but on the Border side of, Edinburgh.

There was Richard Heber, Member of Parliament for Oxford, a devoted and expert antiquarian, brother to Reginald Heber, the Bishop of Calcutta and hymn-writer. Scott liked Heber, though he was to receive a shock about him. Richard Heber was much later forced to 'run the country', having been detected in 'unnatural sexual practices'. He was, of his kind, not alone in this. Some of the higher clergy, those connected with them, and at least one other Member of Parliament were caught out just after the Napoleonic War had ended, and when peaceful sports could be enjoyed again. See, for example, the notorious case of the Anglican Bishop of Clogher, who was caught in 'flagrant delight' with a guardsman in a public house off Haymarket. The guardsman received the lashings of a regimental flogging in front of his comrades. The Bishop was only unfrocked. He later fell into a decline and became a butler in an aristocratic household in Edinburgh's New Town. But he lived long into Victoria's reign. His period of Episcopal servitude began before Scott's death. It is conceivable that Walter Scott (all unknowing) may have been waited upon by him at one of his friend's tables.

Heber's sad case much distressed Scott who was then in financial ruin himself. He noted in his *Journal*: 'These things—worse than loss of fortune or even loss of friends—make a man sick of this world scene'. Scott in the conversation of male society was no prude; but it would have been too much to have expected him, in his era, to have smiled at, and have been anything but saddened by the scandal of homosexual practices amongst his friends.

But there was no hint of forthcoming financial or scandalous ruin when Richard Heber began to help Scott on *The Minstrelsy*. Maybe the greatest assistance he gave was the discovery of that astonishing eccentric scholar, John Leyden browsing at the top of a ladder in an Edinburgh bookshop. He promptly introduced him to Scott.

Leyden, the scholar, is sometimes carelessly mistaken by

those who 'just know about *The Minstrelsy*' for a learned German or Dutchman. He was nothing of the sort; he was a highly characteristic Border peasant from Teviotdale of a kind which at that date could only have been found in the Lowlands of Scotland.

Names such as Leyden and Fleming, frequent in the Eastern Lowlands, are centuries-old relics of the days when Berwick, under the throne of Scotland, did much trade with the Low Countries. People acquired surnames from their connection with this trade.

Leyden, the son of a remote shepherd, was consumed from boyhood with a passion for learning. He would trudge barefoot over seven miles to school when he knew that lessons would be given there. Somehow he managed to reach Edinburgh University, to live on bread and water while attending lectures, and to show that he could learn languages faster than the professors could teach their grammars.

With this extraordinary apparatus of natural scholarship, he also had a native Borderer's knowledge of balladry *and* with all the scholar's insistence on getting his sources correct. He was of the greatest assistance to Scott; and Scott put himself out to help this strange youth in his personal affairs —gave him money, books and recommendations.

Another oddity was the antiquarian Joseph Ritson. He was an eccentric to the point of being unbalanced, and eventually died in a lunatic asylum. He attacked all other ballad collectors, but reluctantly gave his admiration to Scott and his young *protégé* Leyden for their accuracy. He gave the tribute reluctantly because of his strong dislike for the Scottish race. But Walter Scott got on with him and even managed to placate him when Leyden mercilessly teased him for his absurdities.

Other peculiar associates included Charles Kirkpatrick Sharpe, an antiquarian of knowledge, but one who had to be deflected from his love of digging out obscene old gossip rather than worthwhile material. Also there was James Hogg, the 'Ettrick Shepherd', of whom more below, and others.

Scott ruled and conducted the quarrelsome orchestra of experts, kept them in tune and got music out of them. How did he do it? By his imperturbable and all-forgiving good humour. A life-long quality of his, but one seldom, if ever, shown to great effect. How much we suffer now from the rarity of men with Scott's almost godlike forgiveness and infectious good temper!

The Minstrelsy of the Scottish Border appeared in 1802 to be followed by a third volume and second edition in London. It was reprinted several times; and Scott made a little over £600 out of it—nothing to what he was to make over his own epic poetry and novels later. But he had made his name and had great pleasure in the sociability attached to the doing of it.

It was 'the queerness and the fun', however, that had been animated by patriotism. As he was to write in his introduction:

> By such efforts, feeble as they are, I may contribute somewhat to the history of my native country; the peculiar features of whose manners and character are daily melting and dissolving into those of her sister and ally. And trivial as may appear such an offering to the *Manes* of a Kingdom, once proud and independent, I hang it upon her altar with a mixture of feelings I cannot describe.

Here was Walter Scott speaking from his heart, and as he was to speak again, but seldom so explicitly.

Scott, with Leyden's love of authenticity and wide personal knowledge of tradition to guard him as well as help him as was accurate with his texts as he could be. He was certainly more accurate than Bishop Percy had been with the *Reliques* on the English side of the Border. Walter Scott lacked, however, the modern editors' apparatus. He is not the equal of Professor Child of Harvard.

He did his best to present a text of literary, not scientific, standard, and admittedly added his own hand where his sources were obscure, conflicting or did not make sense. John Buchan, whose 1932 death-centenary book on Scott contains factual blemishes, had an impeccable ear for verse. He gives effective examples of where Scott had emended a line or two or even added a stanza. The emendations and additions are poetry worthy of their setting. As Buchan puts it: 'The versifier has become a poet'.

As I admitted in the Foreword, I have eschewed literary criticism here save where it is relevant or suits my purpose. It suits my purpose to quote one whole short ballad and to give it provenance.

Much of *The Minstrelsy of the Scottish Border* was action

poetry—about fighting, raiding, desperate voyages, and so on. Occasionally it relies on the pure pathos of sorrowful reflection. Here is *The Border Widow's Lament*:

I.

My love he built me a bonny bower,
And clad it a' wi' lilye flower;
A brawer bower ye ne'er did see,
Than my true love he built for me.

II.

There came a man, by middle day,
He spied his sport, and went away;
And brought the king that very night,
Who brake my bower, and slew my knight.

III.

He slew my knight, to me sae dear;
He slew my knight, and poin' his gear;
My servants all for life did flee,
And left me in extremitie.

IV.

I sew'd his sheet, making my mane;
I watched his corpse, myself alane;
I watched his body, night and day;
No living creature came that way.

V.

I took his body on my back,
And whiles I gaed, and whiles I sat;
I digg'd a grave, and laid him in,
And happ'd him with the sod sae green.

VI.

But think na ye my heart was sair,
When I laid the moul' on his yellow hair;
O think na ye my heart was wae,
When I turned about, away to gae?

VII.

Nae living man I'll love again,
Since that my lovely knight was slain;
Wi' ae lock of his yellow hair
I'll chain my heart for evermair.

54

The poem speaks for itself, without glossing any Scottish or antique words. They are none of them difficult; and, if you can bring yourself to read the poem aloud, the sound of those words will enforce their sense.

Americans who, in their shorter national existence, have thrown up anonymous ballads from their Middle West and West, would not care to be thought of as so foreign as to have their local and effective words explained in footnotes to English-speaking readers. They would expect us to feel for their meaning. We ask from them the same indulgence in this poem from the Old Scots.

Scott says that he 'obtained this lament from recitation in the Ettrick Forest' and adds that it was through the agency of James Hogg, the Ettrick Shepherd. Hogg was an attractive, repellent peasant, the 'boar of the Forest'. Alluring to talk with, he could be brusque and—unlike most Scottish peasants—ill mannered. He was highly extravert and was only too ready to play a role, when he felt he was called upon to do so for the Edinburgh gentry.

When he entered Scott's house and found Mrs Scott, who was not well, stretched upon a sofa he promptly took up the same position on another sofa. What was proper for the lady of the house was proper for him.

After Scott's death he was much taken up by the Edinburgh literati who would invite him to alcoholic junketings at Ambrose's Tavern—now the 'Café Royal' where generations of Edinburgh men have enjoyed themselves and continue to do so. Here he would play the Wild Ettrick Shepherd to excess and to the romantic, the condescendingly snobbish delight of his host.

'Are you thirsty, shepherd?' he was once asked. 'Thirsty? Bring in St Mary's Loch. I'll drink it dry.' These and other wild witticisms of his are included in *Noctes Ambrosianæ* by that rather tiresome romantic pedant and anonymous journalistic vilifier John Wilson who, when he was bold enough to sign a name to anything, did so under the pseudonym of Christopher North.

But for all the attitudinizing, ill manners and encouraged folly, Hogg was touched by native genius in some of his own verses. And never more obviously than in that horrific novel about the effects of the Calvinistic doctrine of Predestination: *The Memoirs of a Justified Sinner*.

If there was one individual of whose sharp tongue Hogg

was a little fearful, it was his formidable widowed mother, who lived in Ettrick. She had a splendid and authentic memory from her girlhood of the spoken Border ballads. There can be little doubt that it was from his introduction to her that Scott got many of the ballads, particularly the shorter ones such as *The Border Widow*.

When *The Minstrelsy of the Scottish Border* was published she spoke her mind on it to Walter Scott:

'There was never ane o' my songs prentit till ye prentit them yoursel', and ye have spoilt them awthegither. They were made for singing and no' for readin', but ye have broken the charm now, and they'll never be sung mair.'

Perhaps in her limited sense she was right. After *The Minstrelsy of the Scottish Border* had attained London success, had swept over Edinburgh, Glasgow and much of the Scottish countryside, maybe Border peasants would cease to sing or recite in the privacy of their own homes these immemorial ballads.

But, with the nineteenth century looming ahead, they would probably have done so in any event—at least by Queen Victoria's reign and with the arrival of the steam railway passing through the Border hills. The Scottish Border ballads would then have been lost or reduced to inaccurate insignificance.

That they were not lost, that they remain known in Scotland, England and America, that they are known over much of Continental Europe where their unique appeal can overcome the difficulties of language is due to Walter Scott.

We owe this to his patriotism, his unflagging zeal beginning in the 'queerness and the fun' of the Liddesdale raids. We owe it also to his serene good humour and temper, his abounding *bonhomie* and generosity of spirit which overcame the absurdities and quarrelsomeness of his eccentric expert assistants.

56

6

❈

Poetry. The Ballantyne Secret

Scott's first long poem containing his first published verses of repute, as apart from his poetic additions to or amendments in *The Minstrelsy of the Scottish Border* was *The Lay of the Last Minstrel*. It originated in a suggestion for a theme put to him in 1802 by the youthful Lady Dalkeith, wife of the son and heir to the Duke of Buccleuch.

He worked at it sporadically amidst his legal duties, house removes and volunteer soldiering; but when he did work he rattled on at great speed. It was eventually printed in Edinburgh by James Ballantyne and published in London by Longmans in 1805. It was an immediate success.

As Scott had sold the copyright to his publisher completely he only got £770 from it. The word 'only' is operative, and when one comes to think of it, startling. Even today, with the devalued and devaluing pound, a poet at the age of thirty-three who had, as far as the general public is concerned achieved no more than a successful collection of his native country's ballads would be deeply grateful to receive £770 for an unsolicited epic of 582 lines.

If we think of the modern poet receiving today the equivalent of what seven hundred and seventy pounds sterling was in 1805 (something in the nature of five to six thousand pounds—and no income tax), he would be more than grateful, he would be staggered.

Walter Scott was not financially staggered. Indeed he lent to, invested in, or contributed or whatever phrase you will to the printing business of Ballantyne the whole profits in the hope of future literary gains between the two of them. This was not the first, but one of the earliest and more significant moves in the Scott-Ballantyne financial connection which was to produce such a profit, such loss, such heartburning, such ruin, such posthumous dispute, but, in the end such lonely grandeur of effort by Scott. But no one foresaw this then, least of all Scott and Ballantyne. Poetry, amongst other literary commodities, was obviously paying well.

Now one pauses upon that statement with wonder. Great poetry, and even not so very great poetry is the prime product of the English genius. To a lesser extent, simply because there is not so much of it, it is the first product of the Scottish genius. Taking the two nations together, there is nothing else in the world of art in which they have become so famous. Not their music, their painting, their architecture and even their drama and their novel writing have so widely and so long-lastingly been recognized abroad.

From the anonymous Scottish ballads, and the anonymous early English verse, to the poetry of Shakespeare and many others including Burns and Byron, the poetry of these two nations has inspired and influenced the stream of international art from Russia to the Americas. Even Scott's epic verse, now not so widely recognized or appreciated, did in its day have much influence from Moscow to the newly-founded U.S.A.

Today the English and Scottish poet is (with exceptions so rare as scarcely to count) alone amongst our artists incapable of making a living wage directly from his art. His work may be assisted by Art Councils, charitable literary societies and the like, or be used ephemerally on mass-media; but only a few people read him, and fewer still go to the extent of buying his books—again with a very few exceptions.

The very name of poet as a man's profession has sunk in repute. A serious musician, painter, dramatist, novelist, yes. He is somehow reputable and is so regarded by tolerant businessmen. But a serious poet in these islands who is bold enough to call himself a professional poet is looked on with suspicion—a self-indulgent trifler, a *flaneur*. Yet, by calling himself a poet and doing his best he is striving to be the heir of those who produced the prime product of the English and Scottish genius.

In the early years of last century Scott, as we shall see, was to receive profits from his epic verse which made his £770 from the 'Lay' seem like chicken feed. They were profits which, if translated into the value of our currency today, might make a modern best-selling novelist gasp.

58

Nor was he alone in this; there were a number of others on these islands who found verse and poetry profitable. To name but one, there was the man who supplanted him in epic poetry and drove him from the field, whom, none the less Walter Scott liked, generously supported and defended —Byron.

All this happened at a time when our mass-media of communication was undreamed of, and when a large proportion of the British Islanders was illiterate. There are a number of reasons one can give for the profitability of verse and poetry at that time.

There were, for instance, the landed gentry; then more evenly distributed and far more powerful and rich than today, and the urban cognoscenti. Such men bought handsomely produced and expensive books which they had heard well spoken of for their massive private libraries. They looked upon such purchases as obligatory—an addition to their estate which they would leave for their descendants.

Taking this and all other reasons into account, the huge profitability of verse and poetry from 1800 until well into Queen Victoria's reign is a remarkable and an extraordinary thing to look back upon.

What pleased Scott far more than the £770 he got for *The Lay of the Last Minstrel* was the wide repute he made for himself. He was gratified by the praise he received from great names in England and Scotland, and, being the kind of man he was, admitted his pleasure freely. *The Lay of the Last Minstrel* had made him famous before his thirty-fourth birthday and he relished it. Lockhart says that 'its success at once decided that literature should be the main business of Scott's life'. The law now fell into second place.

It must surely be a strange experience for a reader who has never seen the 'Lay' to look at it for the first time. It is strange enough even for one who has only schoolboy or youthful memories of it, but who has put it at the back of his mind for many years.

To begin with there is the odd sensation of coming across 'quotations' which everyone knows, but which not everyone has associated with it. One has heard of the man who saw *Hamlet* for the first time and who was impressed by the play but objected to Shakespeare's over-use of common 'quotations'. So it is with the 'Lay'. But one of many examples is:

> Breathes there the man with soul so dead,
> Who never to himself hath said,
> This is my own, my native land!
> Whose heart has ne'er within him burned
> As home his footsteps he hath turned
> From wandering on a foreign strand!

Was it Walter Scott who wrote that familiar jingle—stirring jingle withal—in his first successful long poem? Yes, it was.

Then for Scottish children of all ages up to ninety there is the more familiar:

> [1] If thou wouldst view fair Melrose aright,
> Go visit it by pale moonlight.

and there are a number of other familiar lines and phrases which come upon one as a shock. But yes, Scott wrote them, or rather rattled them off in the 'Lay' and they still live.

The Lay of the Last Minstrel was, as Scott told Wordsworth, 'written with heart and good will, and for no other reason than to discharge my mind of the ideas which have rushed in upon it'. This is why it is fresh and appealing, and, apart from any casual poetic or versifying merit it may possess, is of interest to anyone who is held by the story of Scott's life.

Its plot and the timing of events in it are rather obscure. It is supposed to 'illustrate' as Scott said in his dedicated foreword to Lord Dalkeith 'the customs and manners which anciently prevailed upon the Borders of England and Scotland'. So far so good, but 'the poem was put into the mouth of an ancient Minstrel, the last of his race, who had survived the Revolution' [that is the departure or flight of James VII and II, the last Stuart King of Scotland and

---

[1] So universally known were these lines in my youth that I recall a ridiculous squabble over them. Earnest 'hikers' as they were then known, used to organize pilgrimages on foot to Melrose on moonlight nights. They were so disgusted by the crowds of motor traffic that got in their way, that they composed and published in their club magazine the couplet:

> 'If thou would'st view fair Melrose awrong,
> Go visit it by charrybong.'

This was widely circulated and often sung in the presence of motor-car visitors.

A well-known Scottish omnibus company took deep offence and even threatened legal action. But nothing came of it. This trivial and ludicrous incident is noted here merely to show how familiar were some of the lines in Scott's 'Lay' amongst Scottish tourists and visitors from abroad during the 1920s.

England, in 1688]. Here is the first inclination in the poem of Scottish Stuart patriotism.

The events told or sung in it happen about 1560, the year of Scotland's Reformation and when Mary Stuart, Queen of Scots, might be said to have her back to the wall fending off John Knox's tremendous verbal onslaught. Here perhaps is another use of Scottish Stuart patriotism; but Walter Scott, though he could perceive what the Catholic Faith stood for, had no intellectual sympathy for it.

To make matters more confusing, the age of general Faith (Catholicism) had long faded by 1560 and was as many centuries away as Michael Scott, the wizard. Yet the poem is full of Friars, Priests, Monks and even Michael Scott himself enters in a deathbed repentance scene. The aged Minstrel's memory of song and poetry may have been largely stretched, but he got his chronology a bit mixed. He could scarcely from 1688, the year of the 'Revolution', have recalled with feeling the age of general Faith.

But it doesn't really matter. Scott rattles along discharging his mind of 'the ideas which had rushed in upon it', and we rattle after him enjoying the vigour of his verse (unfair to call it facile) and its occasional genuine beauties. Yet nowhere are those sudden strange irruptions of pure brief lyricism which we find occasionally in the later epics, and more strikingly (because unexpectedly occurring) in the Waverley novels.

Scott, as has often been pointed out, had certain Shakespearian qualities—not imitations but qualities which he was almost certainly not aware of. He hated being compared with Shakespeare whose 'brogues', he declared 'he was not fit to tie'. Nevertheless these lyrics that float almost irrelevantly across some of his writings in the manner of:

> Take, o take those lips away,
> That so sweetly were forsworn;

from *Measure for Measure* are Shakespearian in their kind.

There are none of these in the 'Lay' though there are striking passages, none more striking than his version of the *Dies Irae* from the Latin Requiem Mass:

> That day of wrath, that dreadful day
> When heaven and earth shall pass away,
> What power shall be the sinner's stay?
> How shall he meet that dreadful day?

61

ending in the last verse thus:

> Oh! on that day, that wrathful day,
> When man to judgment wakes from clay,
> Be Thou the trembling sinner's stay,
> Though heaven and earth shall pass away!

Any Roman Catholic readers who can recall the *Dies Irae* or who can refer to their missals and read the Latin of this tremendous hymn—if such elementary scholars still exist in these days of the Babel of the vernacular—will recognize that this is a compressed, selected and personal version rather than a translation. To have made such a version in his first poem 'discharging his mind of the ideas which have rushed in upon it' shows how haunted he was by the Catholic past of his own country, even if he explicitly rejected the Faith as superstition.

Lockhart's account of Walter Scott's death, and some of the things he is said to have said has been questioned. It is unlikely, however, that Lockhart, who had no Roman Catholic leanings, would have made up the statement about Scott's partiality in his last days for 'some of the magnificent hymns of the Romish ritual in which he had always delighted'.

He adds: 'We very often heard distinctly the cadence of the *Dies Irae*; and I think the last stanza we could make out was the first of a still great favourite:

> Stabat Mater dolorosa,
> Juxta crucem lachrymosa,
> Dum pendabat Filius.

On 28th February 1829, Scott in his diary (and specially recorded by Lockhart) took a poor and superficially cynical view of the movement for Catholic Emancipation. 'Unopposed the Catholic superstition may sink into dust with all its absurd ritual and solemnities'. These words were written not for publication or for open controversy, but for his own eyes. But his own eyes may have been seeing contemporary events in the light of other people's opinions.

It should be remembered that when Pope Pius VI died at the turn of the eighteenth and nineteenth century of the 'enlightened opinion' of Northern Europe believed that there would never be another Papal election and that the Chair of St Peter would be allowed to crumble away or at most be preserved as an interesting relic of antiquity.

Scott must often have heard this kind of speculation and it may have influenced him. Yet, in his ending his half-conscious mind turned to the Latin hymn his own Scottish ancestors and the ancestors of all in Europe had sung or heard sung.

What would he have said if he could have foreseen that four generations of his immediate descendants were to become practising and devout Roman Catholics? And how would he have greeted the news that in the private chapel, especially permitted at his Abbotsford, the Blessed Sacrament is to this day preserved so that all visitors who wish to do so, may pray before it?

Quite certainly he and any of his contemporaries of his kind would, if they could have foreseen our age, have been distressed and appalled by so much in it two hundred years after his birth. Certainly he would be puzzled and distressed by much in his and our Scotland of today. But there are some things that are happening to us now and some things we are doing for ourselves that he might approve.

He would, I suggest, have been surprised to know that the Roman Catholic Faith has survived, despite so many buffetings in the Western world for two hundred years after his birth. Leaving aside the inrush of Irish Catholicism into Scotland after the dreadful years of the potato famine (leaving it aside simply because it is not relevant to our theme) he would have been astonished to learn how strongly indigenous Scottish Roman Catholicism has survived after his death in the Western Highlands, in many of the Hebrides and—most remarkable of all—in North-Eastern Aberdeenshire.

I do not think he would mind now (if we could pull him sentient and capable of thought out of his grave in Dryburgh) if he could know that four generations of his immediate descendants had become Roman Catholics and that they should have the right to preserve the Blessed Sacrament at his and their Abbotsford.

I suggest that, though puzzled maybe, he would prefer this to the indeterminate and certainly conformist 'nothing-arianism' of so many other Lowland and Highland lairds of today.

63

But to return from the Catholic Abbotsford of today to the strongly (if only poetically) Catholic atmosphere of *The Lay of the Last Minstrel*.

Lockhart was clearly right when he said that from the 'Lay' onwards 'literature was to be the main business of Scott's life'. But unfortunately for himself, and, for a time, for his reputation it was rather more than the literature of authorship alone. He foresaw, or thought he foresaw, the huge profits that could be made from printing his best-sellers and took steps to cash in on these profits.

At the beginning of this chapter it was said that James Ballantyne was responsible for printing *The Lay of the Last Minstrel* in Edinburgh. This is the place to say more about Ballantyne and his brother James. Scott had brought up from Kelso to Edinburgh a friend of his boyhood days, James Ballantyne, a fine printer and one whose printing work on the local paper Scott rightly much admired. Later James was to be joined in Edinburgh by his brother John. However excellent the Ballantyne brothers were as printers they had in business very slipshod method which Scott at first scarcely knew about, and subsequently chose to ignore.

Scott may be to blame for this later deliberate ignoring of their methods, and he may well be blamed for the way he made use of it—even though it cost him desperate over-work and trouble—but his first impulse towards the Ballantynes was kindly and loyal. He knew James to be a good printer and wanted to help him—one of his Kelso boyhood friends—by bringing his talents forward into the larger world of Edinburgh.

The real snag in his relationship with the brothers was that he concealed the fact that he had invested and went on investing or rather pouring money into their printing business. He made them conceal it too. The unfortunate result was that when Scott insisted that all his works should be printed by the Ballantynes, the booksellers and publishers just had to accept his insistence (taking it for loyalty from boyhood days) without realizing that Walter Scott, the increasingly famous author, was financially interested in their business.

Buchan, whose *Life of Scott* is not always factually correct but whose ear for verse was impeccable and whose moral judgments were sound, says this about the unhappy beginnings of the Ballantyne/Scott imbroglio:

On this matter much arrant nonsense has been written. It has been condemned as somehow discreditable and dishonest, incompatible with Scott's position as a judge [Sheriff] and a prospective Court official. A barrister [Advocate, surely, Mr Buchan, later Lord Tweedsmuir] it has been urged should not be a partner in a secret commercial enterprise . . .

He goes on to say that this did not apply in Scott's day, before the development of joint stock companies. An advocate or even a Court official, he implies, has the right to invest his money where he willed. The danger here lay in the feckless character of the Ballantynes, and in Scott's boundless and kindly optimism as a man of letters. But even Buchan burkes at the result of the secret agreement, and takes refuge in quoting a well-known passage from Lockhart.

Lockhart, as is now generally agreed, snobbishly disliked the Ballantynes, did not bother to conceal it and by strong implication was unfair to them—another instance of loyalty, but this time Lockhart's loyalty to the memory of his wife's father. His passage runs thus:

> It is an old saying that wherever there is a secret there must be something wrong. . . . It was his [Scott's] rule, from the beginning, that whatever he wrote or edited must be printed at that press; and had he catered for it solely as author and sole editor, all had been well; but had the booksellers known his direct pecuniary interest in keeping up and extending the operation of these types they would have taken into account his lively imagination and sanguine temperament as well as his taste and judgment.

And so on. Lockhart ends with the, for him, severe statement:

> Hence by degrees, was woven a web of entanglement from which neither Ballantyne nor his adviser had any means of escape.

Not even unremitting toil and hard work on the part of Scott and not the frentic, fantastic organization of what we would now call 'public relations' from the Ballantyne press in the Canongate could give means of escape. But there was another thing in which the printers and others concerned in the whole ramshackle state of affairs engaged themselves— one for which we, happily for us, have no cant phrase today, for it is scarcely allowed to exist openly amongst us.

65

This was the exchange of private bills of exchange, or what would now be known as I.O.U.s which were allowed to pass between a number of individuals (often scarcely known to each other) as if the paper on which they were written was the equivalent of real bank notes or even of real solid cash.

Both these commodities, cash and reliable bank notes, were rare in the Scotland of that time. This was happening at the beginning of affairs with which we are dealing, when all seemed sunny and hopeful save for the need for slogging hard work on the part of the most prolific author and editor of his time, and the evasions and postponements of those talented but evasively feckless men engaged with him in selling his work to the world.

All this was going on while Walter Scott founded his literary fame and while he was increasing it annually, one might say almost monthly. No one really foresaw disaster (and Scott is to be blamed here too). Though, when the complete and destructive explosion happened, with fore-warning rumbles, nearly twenty years later, it must have been easy for all to be wise after the event.

Wise after the event! They were in general kindly to each other too vocally in this now evident and inescapable tragedy of pretence exposed in a public explosion. We shall come to that explosion later on ('Much, much later on' as a famous but intolerably prolix advocate said in my hearing to a Lord of Session who, after three days of pleading asked the pleader when he was 'coming to the point'). For the moment let us linger in the anodyne of illusion cultivated by Walter Scott's increasingly crescent fame.

It is now that Archibald Constable enters the Scott story. Of humble country parentage in Fife he had, some years earlier come to Edinburgh as an apprentice in a High Street bookshop. He did not think much of the state of Edinburgh book-selling or publishing, and set himself to reform it.

He began by marrying the daughter of a wellish-off printer and using the money she brought him to start as a bookseller and publisher (these two businesses were often combined in the early nineteenth century) on his own account. He was a real book-lover, had a sense of business and a flair for what would go down well with the public.

He quickly prospered, became known in England and far beyond the borders of Edinburgh. There are those today who seriously hold that he was the most outstanding and remarkable publisher the United Kingdom has ever produced. Inevitably he was bound to approach Walter Scott, who was not only an Edinburgh man, and easily accessible from Edinburgh, but was clearly on the way to becoming a famous man of letters.

'Man of letters' is a phrase very apt for Scott at that time. True he was the author and (if we leave aside the somewhat vague suggestion for the theme of the poem from young Lady Dalkeith) the only begetter of the highly successful *Lay of the Last Minstrel*; but he made his name and fame with *The Minstrelsy of the Scottish Border* and though we know that he touched this collection with his genius and with some lines and stanzas of his own, he was *officially* no more creative than being known as the collector and editor.

It was as a man of letters interested in presenting with his own assiduity and style other men's poems and prose that Constable first approached him and first threw a publisher's fly over the nose of this promising Tweed Spring salmon. And what a huge and multi-coloured fly it was!

It was the preposterous suggestion that Walter Scott should edit, annotate and write biographical material for a hundred volumes covering all British poets from remote antiquity down to the early nineteenth century. It was fortunate that Scott, who rose easily to any publishing fly cast over him, had the sense to see that this one was too enormous, too polychromatic even for him. The fly sank within the river of literature never to be seen again.

There were other suggestions to the promising Mr Walter Scott; but the only one which he took was from William Miller of London (possibly in his name Scottishly derived). This was for an edition of the poet and dramatist John Dryden. It was to (and did) appear in eighteen volumes sold at fifty guineas a volume.

We have already commented on the extraordinary prices available for poetry and serious literature at the period of Scott's beginnings. What further comment is needed? Let the figure of fifty guineas a volume stand and speak for itself. To ease the labour of multiplication let it be casually stated that the full edition cost £945, and that in our modern currency that is the equal of at least between £5000–£6000. Scott was to gain larger and more extraordinary sums, particularly for his epic poems, but I shall avoid details about them even when I touch upon or consider them, for three reasons.

First, why exacerbate the understandably nostalgic cupidity of modern poets and men of letters. They are beset by public indifference, the demands of the Inland Revenue and by dislike of bureaucrats of any individual who tries to 'go it alone' or to be, as they describe it 'a self-employed person'.

Modern poets and serious writers will just have to accept the fact that they were not born early enough to be writing in the first decades of the last century, and that today they lack the force, vigour and contemporary genius to capture the literate public of the whole western world as did the still quotable giants of 1800 to about the 1830s. They may achieve sudden and surprising success; but it is ephemeral. With one or two exceptions (how tempting to name them) they are quickly forgotten.

It is a debatable point as to how much Scott, Byron, Wordsworth, Keats, Coleridge, Goethe, Heine, Balzac are read today. But they are not forgotten. Their creations of character and often their lines have entered the stream of modern consciousness, so that even those who have never opened one of their books have been touched by their genius.

To come to the particular instance of Scott, the second reason for refraining from giving detailed accounts of the astronomical sums he made is that one cannot be exact.

The Ballantynes' fecklessness, Constable's optimism (sometimes unfairly misjudged), the uncertainty of London publishers and booksellers, the lack of or half-managed foreign copyright, Scott's own land-hungry extravagance when he came to Abbotsford. All these and other factors make modern calculation in a currency at least five or six times the value of ours a very tricky business.

Finally, let it be repeated for any English or American readers that there was the rotten state of finance in Scotland of that era. There was much of intrinsic value in our country then as now—land, coal, increasingly well-managed agriculture, good fisheries and much human talent. Unfortunately there was just not enough hard cash or even risky bank notes to allow the flow of these valuable and Scottish things a regulated exchange. Idle to seek here the reason for this. The selfishness of some great men and the venality of some politicians? Who is to say? There it was, and it was lamentable.

American readers may have some idea of how lamentable it was, not by reminding themselves of the 'depression' of the late 1920s, but of thinking of a New York, today, yesterday, at any time when there just might not be enough dollar bills to go around. And worse still the fear that even those which were 'going around' might in one or two days become almost without value owing to unmanageable caprice.

Such a really serious state of affairs in modern New York or Washington is, even despite all their present woes, unthinkable. It was not unthinkable in the Scotland of Walter Scott's greatest activity.

When we come to the final explosion which blew him, his partner, his family into near ruin we shall have to face the human problem of how he and those around him got involved in this explosion, how he did manage to face disaster, how they did cope. This is more important than a balance sheet of pounds of imponderable and shifting value.

The seeds of the great crisis in Walter Scott's life were being sown in his early, his happiest and most active period as a man of letters—the greatest crisis of its kind ever to afflict a world-famous author. It is difficult not to anticipate that crisis by showing how it all began. But back now to the eighteen-volume edition of Dryden.

It is indeed a happy work—full of vigour, gusto and keen appreciation. Scott in the first volume devoted to Dryden's life, deals with insight and fairness about the vexed question of Dryden's apparently opportunist conversion to Roman Catholicism under the Catholic King James the VII and II. Scott, at that time certainly looked upon the Faith as 'superstition' and said so. But he is convinced of Dryden's genuine motives and pays tribute to the way he stuck by his convictions when James had fled the kingdom and when the Faith was being persecuted.

In the eighteen volumes of Dryden's works which he edited and annotated he refused Ellis's suggestion that he should cut out the lusty and gustful and indecent passages. Lockhart reports him as saying:

'I will not castrate John Dryden. I would as soon castrate my own father, as I believe Jupiter did of yore. It is not passages of

69

ludicrous indelicacy that corrupts the manners of the people. It is the sonnets which a prurient genius sings *virginibus puerisque*. It is the sentimental slang, half lewd, half methodistic that debauches the understanding.'

There is a general impression that Walter Scott was an excessively proper man. He was not. A son of the eighteenth century, he could talk bawdy, amusingly and could listen to it when it was amusing. 'Amusing' is the proper word here. The bawdy that he relished had no relation to our 'sick' humour of today. He would have been bored by the long contests of our 'smoking room' stories carried on and punctuated by the ritual phrase of 'Have you heard the one about . . .?' Being a man of his own century he would never have permitted bawdy talk in mixed company. But in male company and only on occasions he relished it, but not as a staple diet of converse.

One occasional use of it amused him much, and he employed it before the most solemn of his English visitors. He would quote the rich, salty, bawdy humour of the Scots peasant. And if the solemn Englishman did not follow it, he might or might not translate it (and therefore weaken it) for his guest.

There must be few country houses in Scotland and England where Scott's eighteen volumes of his Dryden edition are still preserved, bought by ancestors at £945 as an addition to their estates of culture. In my youth I must have stayed at some of these still surviving houses, but I lacked the curiosity at that age to seek out Scott's *Dryden*.

Recently, however, I examined a set of the eighteen volumes in the Edinburgh public library.

I could only spend a day or two with the volumes but I satisfied myself of their excellence. Informed, scholarly, tolerant, humorous, they give off on every page the infection of Walter Scott's happiness in this book.

It is pleasing that Professor George Saintsbury proclaimed it to be 'one of the best edited books in the language'.

Scott's next venture was the great epic poem of *Marmion* by which he became more than a Scottish and Border poet but a writer of international fame. It is mentioned here because its success prompted Constable to persuade him to undertake the huge task of editing the life, letters and works of Dean Swift of St Patrick's Cathedral, Dublin.

Constable offered him nearly double the sum he had received from Miller for his Dryden labours. But, by this time, it is impossible to be exact in knowing how much Walter Scott actually retained of the immense sum that came his way and how much was sunk in the Ballantynes' affairs and the affairs of those whom he generously, almost recklessly befriended.

Constable himself, as quoted by Lockhart, once complained: 'I like well Scott's ain bairns, but Heaven defend me from those of his fathering'.

Scott's edition of Swift took him nearly twice as long as his Dryden. This was not because Scott lacked admiration for the Dean of St Patrick's—the reverse, he admired him deeply—but because the complexities of Swift's nature required the modern psychiatrist's couch rather than the vigorous gusto of the Border laird and lawyer who had become a famous poet.

Scott discovered, however, much good straightforward sense in this editing work; and the first volume containing a memoir of Swift's life is full of good things.

It should be added that if Walter Scott refused to 'castrate John Dryden', he also refrained from defaecating (if one may use such a term) Jonathon Swift. Dryden's 'indelicacies' were of the jolly, bawdy, normal kind. Swift's obsessions were coprolitic and what we would now call lavatory humour —or more properly lavatory satire. But Scott refused to cleanse his great subject. He admired him too much. He took that strange, haunting, frightening, obscene genius of English prose as the man he was; he took and presented him entire and as a whole being. Scott would not bowdlerize.

This is a very different Walter Scott from the Victorian notion of him. He was essentially a man of the eighteenth century in his private speech in male company, but when it came to scholarly editing the eighteenth century in him took complete charge.

——◆◆◆——

7

Scott's Greatest Epic Poems—
and the Last

For all his life Scott's energy was unceasing and conducted with gusto. There is plenty of evidence of this, especially later on when he was to turn anonymously to the Waverley novels. These were so multifarious and frequent that many (even those increasing numbers in Edinburgh who were in the secret) doubted if it could all be the work of one man. Surely, they suggested, he must be working with one or even two other writers, making a kind of factory of authorship. They were wrong: his novels and poems—even those fragments of verse he put at the heads of chapters ascribed to 'old' sources—were by him.

He did, however, employ some researchers to help in his edition of Dryden and his less fortunate one of Swift; but the finished products were all his own, bearing his own manner, style and outlook on life. There were other labours which poured from him into the Ballantyne press, but are now forgotten except by the inquisitive antiquarian.

Yet while he was conducting all these editorial labours, some of which he conceived for himself, labours with which he was flooding the overflooding unbusiness-like Ballantyne press, he turned to one of his most famous epic or narrative poems. It was *Marmion*.

This style of long narrative verse is very much out of fashion today. Scott now, despite being a man of the eighteenth century, moved forward in his narrative poems into a new age.

Readers had grown tired of the dynasty of Pope with its inferior courtiers who made such effective play with the neatly turned heroic couplet. Walter Scott's vigorous, fast-moving story-telling long poems fulfilled a want; and *Marmion*, published in 1808, ran immediately through many editions.

The plot of *Marmion* is the defeat of King James IV of Scotland at the battle of Flodden, a defeat in which Scotland lost the most part of her chivalry, her fighting nobility and much of her army of plain soldiers.

Most Scottish readers will know that Flodden was our greatest defeat in the wars against England. Most Englishmen know of the fact of the battle and some from both England and Scotland well know about the causes that led to it and the character of the defeat. This book is intended for readers in America as well as in the British Isles. We ask forgiveness from British readers if we tell the story briefly again. The tragedy of Flodden was highly dramatic and was a tragedy that haunted Walter Scott's patriotism.

In 1314 Robert Bruce had utterly defeated an invading English army under King Edward II. He achieved this defeat, repaired Scotland, and refounded the kingdom by superb generalship. He lured the English enemy forces well into central Scotland and from a *ground of his own choosing* demolished them utterly at Bannockburn. Scotland was again a free and independent kingdom.

This freedom was all but thrown away by the courageous, chivalrous but foolish King James IV of Scotland in 1513. In order to assist his French allies against whom the English King Henry VIII was engaged in war, he invaded England but a short way into Northumberland, taking up, with his entire army, what he considered an impregnable position in the Flodden Hills not far from the Scottish border.

As Henry of England was engaged in the south he sent the Earl of Surrey to deal with this tentative invasion. Surrey brilliantly outmanoeuvred James down from his position, killed him and all but obliterated Scotland's fighting forces.

That Scotland's freedom was not obliterated too was due to the fact that Surrey had done the job he had been sent north to do—done it brilliantly and completely, crushing and slaying nearly all the Scottish invaders. And Henry, returning flushed with victory from France, had other things to concern him. He considered that the contemptible northern kingdom of Scotland had been so stricken and

73

enfeebled by Surrey at Flodden that she would never trouble him or his English successors again.

The internal plot of Scott's *Marmion* is complicated, but the great fact of Flodden obscures all these minor complications.

As in *The Lay of the Last Minstrel* the casual reader, looking at *Marmion* for the first time, will be struck by what seems to him familiar quotations:

> O Woman! in our hours of ease
> Uncertain, coy and hard to please,
> And variable as the shade
> By the light, quivering aspen made;
> When pain and anguish wring the brow,
> A ministering angel thou!

There are other lines in *Marmion* that leap out from one's half-conscious memory.

There is the noble, the inspiring description of the prospect of Edinburgh as seen from the Blackford Hill while King James is assembling his army. Well worth reading and reading aloud to yourself, it is too long to quote here. As its climax, however, there come the fine lines:

> Where the huge castle holds its state,
> And all the steep slope down,
> Whose ridgy back heaves to the sky,
> Piled deep and massy, close and high,
> Mine own romantic town!

Every Scottish child knows that the last line is about Edinburgh and that Walter Scott wrote it.

'Mine own romantic town' is widely known wherever English is spoken, but not everyone who has heard it and can recognize it knows that its subject is the capital of Scotland nor that the author of this fragment was Sir Walter Scott.

It is not literary criticism to point to the vigorous movement of *Marmion*, to the excellence of the battle scenes nor to the evocative power of scenic description, found more fully and more effectively in these epic or narrative poems of Scott than any that come into the Waverley novels.

Places and great deeds are the things that excited Scott in his longer poems. The characters (and what characters many

74

of them are!) of men and women are what moved Walter Scott's passionate or compassionate interest in the best of his novels in prose.

Another purely historical point is maybe worth mentioning. A story-teller in *Marmion* bewails the absence at Flodden of the great fighters who had assisted Bruce at Bannockburn when Scotland had been freed:

> Or well-skilld Bruce to rule and fight
> And cry 'St. Andrew and our right!'
> Another sight had seen that morn
> From Fate's dark book a leaf been torn;
> And Flodden had been a Bannockbourne!

Had Flodden resulted in as great a victory for the Scottish king and his chivalry as that at Bannockburn, the result in the end would have been as disastrous for Scotland as Bannockburn had been her salvation. If James had had the skill to outwit the Earl of Surrey's brilliant tactics and utterly destroy his army, *that* would not have been the end of it.

Henry VIII, still youthful, vigorous and filled with pride on account of his victories against the French, would have come back enraged against the impudent Scots. He would have gathered all his vast English forces, far, far greater than those which Scotland could command, not only to invade Scotland but utterly to subdue her.

He had even before Flodden declared to the Scottish Lyon King of Arms:

> But thus saye to thy master that I am the very owner of Scotland and that he holdeth it of me by homage.

This boast was utterly unfounded. It was based upon a claim put forward before Bannockburn by the English king but rendered meaningless by the great Scottish victory. It suited Henry to revive it even before Flodden. Had Flodden 'been a Bannockburn' Henry would have angrily remembered his boast and have marched in revenge and with all his mighty forces to subdue and take Scotland. The courageous, foolish King James IV was no strategist or even tactician. He was no Bruce; and he would have rushed to his and Scotland's destruction. The kingdom would have been lost.

As it happened Henry's contemptuous revenge was satisfied by Surrey's great victory at Flodden. Also Henry had a number of other things to occupy his attention.

There was his secret conspiracy to become Emperor in Europe. A little later there was the matter of his divorce from his Queen Katherine and his quarrel with the Pope. There was his foundation of the Church of England with himself as the head of it. There was all this business of marrying, beheading and marrying again. He was to become stricken with syphilis. He was to become slightly mad. He was to grow prematurely old, indolent and swollen in body. He who had married six women and had got rid of two of them by the headsman's axe was to end his days being henpecked by the sixth and last.

He had neither the time nor the inclination to bother about Scotland. The once sacred body of the King of Scots, killed at Flodden, was now in England where it was to lie above ground unburied for thirty years. Let it lie there, to rot! So much for Scotland! Henry had more domestic worries to concern him.

Scott, whose knowledge of Scottish and English history was deep, may have speculated in this way. But, if he had, he would know that a narrative poem was no place in which to introduce it.

He was poetically right to put into the mouth of one of his characters the lingering wish that 'Flodden had been a Bannockbourne'. It had long been a Scottish 'might-have-been' wish, therefore suitable for inclusion into a narrative poem written in Scotland on the theme of Flodden.

Marmion was written in Scotland with all Walter Scott's vivacity and speed. The last four cantos of it were printed sheet by sheet as soon as Scott had set them down on paper. Nothing in it was rewritten, touched up or toned down. The truth was that Scott so enjoyed composing and writing it that he went on with all the dash and gusto which was in his nature.

Earlier he had said to George Ellis: 'People may say this and that of the pleasure of fame or of profit as a motive of writing. I think the only pleasure is the actual writing and research, and I would no more work upon any other terms than I would hunt merely to dine on hare soup. At the same time if credit and profit come unlooked for, I would no more quarrel with them than with the soup.'

76

It is said that some of the most vigorous passages about Flodden were conceived or actually half-composed in his head when he was galloping on horseback on the Tweedside hills or with his volunteer regiment of cavalry.

Small wonder, then, that a new poem in a new fresh style, put out by a rising and well-known poet while enjoying himself, should communicate pleasure to readers. It ran into many editions for which he received a downright copyright payment on a scale which would make modern poets dream with envy. It also brought him much fame.

Walter Scott, despite physical pain which was later to strike at him savagely, and despite great financial difficulties, was an eminently happy man for all his life. It is probable that he was never more happy, more full of active content than, when at Ashestiel and with his family growing around him, he was pouring *Marmion* out of himself, that inexhaustible source—never more inexhaustible than at this time.

He attained even greater fame and even larger success in 1810 by the publication of his most celebrated epic or narrative poem *The Lady of the Lake*.

He had had the notion of producing a more northern successor to *Marmion*, and to that end went off with his wife and his eldest daughter to Loch Lomond and thence to Perthshire, the only Highland shire he was ever really to know well. It was Loch Lomond, its shores and islands that, in his own words, 'unchained the devil of rhyme in my poor noddle'.

The devil of rhyme led him over the short distance into the Trossachs in Perthshire. Even today the attention of passing motorists is fleetingly held by the wayside signs 'To the Trossachs'. The passing motorist may not necessarily associate the Trossachs with *The Lady of the Lake* nor even with the name of Sir Walter Scott, but he does vaguely know that here is a part of Scotland celebrated in poetry.

The celebrity at the time, of *The Lady of the Lake* upon its first appearance was fantastic for a long poem, even for an author of Scott's now rapidly rising fame. In a few months 20,000 copies were sold, and further editions multiplied. Lockhart says that 50,000 were attested 'legitimate sales in Great Britain' by 1836, and hints that illegal piracies both in Europe and in America may have vastly increased these numbers. Who can say what they reached? Perhaps even a hundred thousand?

Scott, always genuinely modest about his verse, was quoted by Lockhart in a reflective and recollected passage appearing in the introduction to an edition of 1830.

> It was certainly so extraordinary as to induce me for the moment to conclude that I had at last fixed a nail in the proverbially inconstant wheel of Fortune. But, as the celebrated John Wilkes is said to have explained to King George the Third, that he himself was never a Wilkite, so I can, with honest truth exculpate myself from having been at any time a partisan of my own poetry, even when it was in the highest fashion with the million.

This was no mock modesty. When Ballantyne asked him how he compared his genius with that of Burns, Scott replied: 'There is no comparison whatever—we ought not to be mentioned in the same day.' Scott venerated the native genius of Burns and admired the verses of others much inferior.

He was quite honest on these opinions, because he found writing narrative poems so easy and could dash them off at such a pace, he considered them inferior. Their very popularity may have increased his notion.

Though Scott told Robert Southey that he had studied the taste of the public as much as a thing so variable could be calculated upon, it is clear that his own taste was identical with that of the public. He had made the interesting discovery that people enjoyed reading a story in verse, especially when narrated in the rattling, galloping style which *he* enjoyed writing.

His own pleasure in producing *The Lady of the Lake* made him suspicious of its merit. In this he was genuinely mistaken. It is impossible to guess how many people today read or have read *The Lady of the Lake*; but anyone who cares to do so will soon discover that it has not lost the freshness that made its appeal on publication. It is full of exciting and vivid pieces of action—the stag hunt, the sending round of the 'fiery cross', the battle. It all sounds so well and so emotive—and not only to people in Scotland or elsewhere in Britain who may have seen or know about the Highlands.

In *The Lady of the Lake* as in the previous narrative poems there are a number of those strange, almost irrelevant snatches of lyrical melody which float across the scene. These irrepressible reversions to lyrical song were to appear again and again and even more strikingly in some of the Waverley novels.

It is an odd thing that Scott, who had no ear for music, who could scarcely sing or whistle a tune which could be recognized, should have had the musically lyrical gift in poetry. He certainly, by this gift, caused music in others.

> Soldier rest! thy warfare o'er,
>   Sleep the sleep that knows not breaking,
> Dream of battle fields no more,
>   Days of danger, nights of waking.
>
> Huntsman rest! thy chase is done
>   While our slumbrous spells assail ye,
> Dream not, with the rising sun,
>   Bugles here shall sound reveille.
>
> Sleep! the deer is in his den;
>   Sleep! thy hounds are by thee lying;
> Sleep! nor dream in yonder glen,
>   How thy gallant steed is dying.
>
> Huntsman rest! thy chase is done . . .

These and other lines from *The Lady of the Lake* were to act as inspiration to composers and singers who warbled them as melodiously as they did Tom Moore's popular lyrics frankly intended to catch the music-makers' attention.

Scott had no more intention of providing words for composers and singers than he had for promoting the extraordinary tourist-craze for the Trossachs which his most famous narrative poem aroused and continued to arouse for some time.

This tourist-craze and the money made out of it by local impresarios has so often been described that it needs no more than a mention here. What did Scott think of all this? We have no indication except that he was amused and perhaps pleased that people who knew little of Scotland and less of the Highlands should have their attention drawn to them so potently that they came to see for themselves.

This was all very well in the early nineteenth century; but the boosting of *The Lady of the Lake* as a popular attraction lasted into the early years of my boyhood. I recall that in 1913 at Christmas time at a large market in Princes Street,

79

Edinburgh, used for anything from cattle shows to popular entertainment, there was an enormous panorama entitled 'The Lady of the Lake'. This displayed Ellen's Isle on Loch Katrine containing life-like and life-sized wax figures. It always drew large crowds.

Boys at their preparatory schools in Scotland at the same period were sufficiently familiar with the more famous lines from 'The Lady' to make use of them if the occasion arose. In the same year of 1913 a new headmaster arrived to rule over us at our prep school near Edinburgh. His name was Stagg and this gave us our chance. We chanted behind his back one of the opening stanzas from *The Lady of the Lake*: 'The Stagg at eve had drunk his fill, Where danced the moon on Monan's rill' and added ribald lines about our headmaster's alleged addiction to the bottle.

These are trivial incidents to quote but the point is they continued to occur throughout the nineteenth century and well into this one—just over a century after the publication of Scott's poem. If he could have foreseen this perhaps he would have been as amused as he was at the tourist-craze for the Trossachs in his own lifetime.

Walter Scott never repeated the world-wide success of *The Lady of the Lake* in his subsequent narrative poems, nor came within any distance of it. Why?

The usual reason given is that greater epic poet, the young Lord Byron, whose *Childe Harold* was to appear in 1812, the same year which saw Scott's ambitious narrative poem *Rokeby*, drove Scott from the field of that kind of verse.

This is largely true, and Scott certainly felt the force of it; though, with his customary generosity and complete lack of jealousy, it did not detract from his admiration for Byron as a poet nor his affection for him as a man.

But there were other underlying reasons why Scott fell away, if reluctantly, from narrative verse. He was, it cannot be too strongly stated, realistic enough to accept the state of the world into which he was born. He also accepted the conditions of the Union between England and Scotland to form Britain which had come about sixty-four years before his birth.

What he privately thought of these conditions we do not know. He might well have wished that a Federal Union of the kind so strongly pressed by the patriot Fletcher of Saltoun had come about—or he might not. But the Federal

Union had not happened. The Union had continued to exist in the form originally agreed on in 1707.

Scott could see no reason for setting the clock back by sixty-four years. But he was jealous of the conditions that guarded Scotland's (North Britain's) identity and was constantly on the defence against English encroachments into our laws, religion or customs.

Lockhart describes an incident illustrating this at about this time:

> He regarded with special jealousy certain schemes of innovation . . . set on foot by the Crown officers for Scotland. At a debate at the Faculty of Advocates on these he made a speech much longer than he had ever delivered at that assembly . . . and with a flow of eloquence for which those who knew him had been quite unprepared.
>
> When the meeting broke up, he walked across the Mound to Castle Street between Mr Jeffrey and another of his reforming friends who complimented him on the rhetorical powers he had been displaying and would willingly have treated the subject-matter of the discussion more playfully. But his feelings had been moved to an extent far beyond their apprehension. He exclaimed:
>
> 'No, no—'tis no laughing matter; little by little, whatever your wishes may be you will destroy and undermine, until nothing of what makes Scotland Scotland shall remain.' And so saying he turned round to conceal his agitation—but not before Mr Jeffrey saw tears gushing down his cheeks—resting his head, until he had recovered himself, on the wall of the Mound.

Today you would be unlikely to see any advocate, young or old, weeping on the Mound on account of Scotland's decline or for any other reason.

Scott knew the Scottish national characteristics of the past as well as, if not better than, any men of his time. He had, as his writings abundantly show, a homesickness for Scotland's past. He could see its savage side, its absurd side as well as its most admirable side. For all that he loved it, he loved to think on it, to research on it and, above all, to write about it.

He had begun his serious literary career with his editing of *The Minstrelsy of the Scottish Border*. In so doing he had entered not only into the language of the Scottish past (he had heard that language spoken in his raids with Shortreed into Liddesdale) but he had also entered into the feel of the living past.

81

So strongly had he entered into the living language and the living past which was to live him enough to be sensibly perceived, that, when it was necessary for him to add lines or even stanzas to broken or obscure ballads, his own brief contributions in that kind were nearly always the equal of the original.

As we have seen in his remarks about 'The Minstrelsy' he had said:

> I may contribute to the history of my native country, the peculiar features of whose manners and character are daily melting and dissolving into those of her sister and ally. And trivial as they appear such an offering to the Manes of a kingdom once proud and independent I hang it upon her Altar with a mixture of feelings I cannot describe.

The phrase 'mixture of feelings' in this well-known passage is curiously indicative of the struggle in Scott's mind between his Scottish and his British patriotism—a struggle which, however painful to him, must have been subdued during the Napoleonic Wars when *The Minstrelsy of the Scottish Border* was first published and when Scott was serving as a volunteer cavalryman against the then very potent threat of a French invasion of all Britain.

In 'The Minstrelsy' Scott was able in a purely poetic and antiquarian and therefore uncontroversial manner to give vent to his Scottish patriotism. In his own original ballad-style long poem *The Lay of the Last Minstrel* he was able to continue in the same vein. The last Minstrel may have been a man who is supposed to have lived just beyond 1688 when the last Stuart King had fled the throne of England and Scotland, but the Minstrel's subjects are far back, as has been already noted, in antiquity, in the Age of Faith and even touching upon the times of Michael Scott the Wizard. This ballad-compounded poem could stand on its own artistic merits; and it stood very well.

In *Marmion* the complexities of the plot mean little; the real subject is the chivalrous folly of King James IV of Scotland and his utter defeat at Flodden. The battle of Flodden was at the time that Scott published *Marmion* still a wound in the memory of those Scots who were historically-minded. But no one's patriotic wounds were revived or intended to be revived by *Marmion*.

In *The Lady of the Lake* Scott plunged romantically,

dramatically, vividly, and with much exciting Perthshire Celtic detail into the private habits and personal disguises of James IV or James V of Scotland (he does not make it quite clear even in his introduction to the 1830 edition to which monarch he is referring). And the poem is purely and intensely Scottish. *The Lady of the Lake* was offered to the world on its poetic and Celtically charged (rather overcharged) merits; the world received 'The Lady' rapturously on her exciting beauties alone.

These three long narrative poems ending in the triumphant climax of *The Lady of the Lake* express Scott's absorbing interest in his country's past. They were the fruit of a deep sentiment of loyalty towards the Scotland that had once been before her 'peculiar manners and character' had been 'melting and dissolving' into those of England.

Perhaps some few of Scott's friends and fellow-countrymen may have recognized the impetus which drove Scott to choose the subjects of these three long narrative poems, but the majority must have accepted them as highly readable stories told in verse about Scotland. In England and in the rest of the world they were received on their novel and exciting merits. That their subjects were from the past of a small, remote Northern country 'once proud and independent' merely made them more romantic in an age when romanticism was just coming into fashion. Scott's fame was made.

But with *The Lady of the Lake* Scott must have thought that he had worked out the vein of such subjects. He could not but have been gratified, however, by the way all the English-speaking world (and not only the English-speakers) had excitedly applauded his powers in narrative verse. Why should he stop? Why should he not extend his field? He did.

Scott had by now made a great friend who was to remain as such for all his life, J. B. S. Morritt, the Squire of Rokeby in Yorkshire, a country gentleman of considerable artistic and literary taste. Scott decided to place his next long narrative poem at Rokeby and use the seventeenth-century civil war as his subject. He took great pains over it to get his English background right and called the poem *Rokeby*. It sold 10,000 copies, which for anyone else would have been a success; for Walter Scott, the author of *The Lady of the Lake*, it was a flop.

Though *Rokeby* has its merits the reasons for its lack of

success (by Scott's standard) are not far to seek. He did not pour it out of himself as he had done with *Marmion* and *The Lady of the Lake*. The very pains he took to get the background right are manifest. It would have made, as Lockhart wisely said, a good novel subject, but not a poetic subject in the Walter Scott impetuous style.

And, by the time *Rokeby* was issued, earlier in the same year the young Lord Byron whose epic verse had made him famous overnight had already taken the poetic world, and more than the world of poetry, by storm with the first two cantos of *Childe Harold*.

Scott must have realized that in this kind of narrative poetry he was now outclassed, but he felt he had one more shot to fire. This was *The Lord of the Isles*, chiefly concerned with the battle of Bannockburn which had set Scotland free again under Bruce; it was also a poem with a strong Hebridean background.

He fired this shot at his public in 1815. Only 15,000 copies were sold. As Scott admits in his introduction to the 1830 edition of his longer narrative poems, the subject was too big.

A taking title though well qualified to ensure the publishers against loss and clear their shelves of the original impression is rather apt to be hazardous than otherwise to the reputation of the author. He who attempts a subject of distinguished popularity has not the privilege of awakening the enthusiasm of his audience; on the contrary it is already awakened.

This is a trifle ingenuous. True the names of Bruce and of Bannockburn were known to, and proudly recognized by most Scottish people, but they did not know the facts of Bruce's life and career and very little of how the battle of Bannockburn had been so resoundingly won. Most non-Scottish, English-speaking readers had heard of Bruce and Bannockburn but no more than heard of them.

It is pitching it too strongly to say of *The Lord of the Isles*: 'He who attempts a subject of distinguished popularity has not the privilege of awakening the enthusiasm of his audience; on the contrary it is already awakened'. No, had it not been for another factor Scott might well have made another big success out of a poem on the subject of *The Lord of the Isles*.

84

Scott continues in his introduction to the 1830 edition:

> Although the poem cannot be said to have made a favourable impression on the public, the sale of fifteen thousand copies enabled the author to retreat from the field with the honours of war.

This military analogy about 'the field' and 'the honours of war' refers to Byron's overwhelming success with the first canto of *Childe Harold*—that is the 'other factor' which we mentioned in the previous paragraph.

In 1830 when Byron had been dead for six years Scott was clearly talking about his conquest by the younger man in this kind of long narrative poetry.

But this military analogy or metaphor does in no sense mean that Scott thought of Byron as an enemy. On the contrary, in the 1830 introduction to the earlier and even less successful *Rokeby* he openly mentions Lord Byron's name as his conqueror, but does so in the most characteristically generous spirit.

Byron was writing of the present, of his own travels in the then remote parts of romantic Europe. His subject was, if only from the point of view of time, within the grasp of some of his readers' experience, and within the imagination of all of them—especially the young.

Scott had not the experience to enable him to write a glowing and passionate narrative poem about *his* present time. Nor, if he had had it, it is doubtful if he would have used it in the vehicle he had made for himself—the long narrative poem interspersed with ballads and lyrics.

Scott fired his last shot in epic poetry for the reason that he had for some time been preparing it, and had been on Hebridean journeys where he had acquired background material, but he must have fired it with some misgivings.

A week after the book came out Scott went to see his printer, James Ballantyne, and asked what people were saying about *The Lord of the Isles*. Ballantyne seemed unwilling to speak. Scott broke the silence: 'Come, speak out, my good fellow. What has put it into your head to be on so much ceremony with me all of a sudden?' A pause, then Scott spoke again. 'But I see how it is; the result is given in one word—disappointment.'

Scott, still noticing James Ballantyne's silence, thought for a moment or two, then merely spoke of his surprise that he had been for so long a popular poet, and ended cheerfully: 'Well, well, James, so be it; but you know we must not droop, for we can't afford to give over. Since one line has failed, we must stick to something else.'

That 'something else' was, of course, the novel. The anonymously published *Waverley* had already appeared in 1814 and Scott was deep into the next one, *Guy Mannering*.

❖❖❖❖

8

Scott and Byron

The enormous international fame of the first cantos of Byron's *Childe Harold* is usually given as the prime cause of Walter Scott's withdrawal from the writing of epic or long narrative verse. It certainly was *a* cause, or rather an event which precipitated something that was bound to happen.

Scott was close on thirty-four when he published *The Lay of the Last Minstrel* and not far off forty when he stormed the literate world with *The Lady of the Lake*. It was the impetuosity, ease and obvious enjoyment with which he composed *The Lay*, *Marmion* and *The Lady of the Lake* that gave him his hold over so many readers.

Could he have kept this up? Could he have, as middle age closed upon him poured forth canto after canto of long narrative verse, scarcely turning the pages back to see what he had written before? It is unlikely. This kind of self-generating poetic energy on the large scale usually departs with youth. The wonder is that he was able to make so ambitious and so successful an outpouring of this kind as *The Lady of the Lake* in his late thirties.

It was at this period that he said: 'My poetry has always passed from the desk to the press in the most hurried manner possible, so that it is no wonder that I am sometimes puzzled to explain my own meaning'. A splendid, spontaneous, sustained singing gift! But could it have survived his forties?

The short melodious or poignant lyric was another matter. He used these lyrics in his three long narrative poems, but he used them to even greater effect in the Waverley novels, sometimes to carry the story on, sometimes decoratively. To the end of his days his gift for the short lyric was never quenched.

But the lyric lay deeper in him, in his mind and in his heart than did the power to rattle off stanza after stanza, canto after canto of narrative verse. His mind and his heart were never silent till death; but it is difficult to believe that even Walter Scott could have kept beyond forty the galloping pace he had set himself in his first three successful narrative poems.

Even Walter Scott! With the exception of Shakespeare, about whose working and private life we know very little if anything, there is no great writer in our language who has shown such prodigious energy in expressing himself. Deflected from long narrative verse in which he was once held to be pre-eminent, he turned to the novel and made it, re-made it, fashioned it as he would, achieved world-famous successes, and banal failures.

But he kept working and expressing himself to the end. He loved hunting as we have seen, not to have hare soup for supper but just because he loved the chase. He loved working and research and literary work for its own sake— not disdaining the hare soup of profit when it came his way. But his first love was the work itself.

There came a time in middle life when, through illness and weakness he could not sit a horse well enough to hunt. But he was never too ill or too weak to stop trying to work and to express himself when he was all but on his deathbed. He had returned from Italy to die at Abbotsford, and only just before the end reached his home.

> Presently he fell asleep in his chair, and after dozing for half an hour, started awake, and shaking the plaids we had put about him from his shoulders, said—'This is sad idleness. I shall forget what I have been thinking of, if I do not get it down now. Take me to my own room and fetch the keys of my desk' . . . His daughters went into his study, opened his writing desk, and laid paper and pens in the usual order, and then I moved him through into the spot where he had always been accustomed to work. . . . He smiled, thanked us and said—'Now give me my pen and leave me for a little to myself.' Sophia [Lockhart's wife] put the pen into his hand, and he endeavoured to close the fingers upon it, but they refused their office—it dropped on the paper. He sank back among his pillows, silent tears running down his cheeks.

It was his last effort to write and express himself. Within a few weeks he was dead.

'Even Walter Scott!' Even a man capable of this extraordinary dying effort might well have lost in middle age the ability to write easy, galloping narrative verse. And even had Byron never written a line, he would have turned to other media than narrative verse for self expression—particularly about his native Scotland—for such a thing he had to do so long as he could hold a pen.

Indeed we have evidence that he was turning towards the novel as far back as 1805. In that year, the one in which *The Lay of the Last Minstrel* appeared, he wrote seven chapters of a novel which was later to come out anonymously, *Waverley, or 'Tis Sixty Years Since.*

This, the first of all the novels, 'By the Author of Waverley' was published in 1814. Scott had by that date intended to 'retreat from the field' of narrative verse with 'the honours of war'. The unfinished manuscript of *Waverley* gave him a suitable, if officially anonymous, escape route.

In this chapter it is sufficient to note that Byron, while not the only cause of retreat did open up the way to it.

What is more to the point is Scott's conduct when he found himself publicly beaten at his own game, his own kind of verse by a young, fashionable Regency nobleman seventeen years his junior. He showed no resentment, no jealousy, no sulky silence. And this despite the fact that when their paths had indirectly crossed a few years earlier Byron had included Scott (whom he had not met then) with a number of writers whom he had lambasted in a satirical poem.

The result of Scott's attitude at the time of Byron's immediate success with *Childe Harold* was that the two men corresponded amicably, later met and took to each other strongly, admired each other's work genuinely and, when they separated never to see each other again, set up an affectionate friendship which was only to end with Byron's death in 1824. But the relationship between Scott and Byron is worth pausing upon. It was one of the happiest friendships between two great men engaged in literature—not a profession noted for friendly and affectionate sympathy. It is pleasant to recall and reflects credit on them both.

George Gordon, sixth Lord Byron, half English, half Scottish, represented in his blood two characteristically eccentric strains in the two nations which had made him. On his father's side the Byrons, ennobled in 1643 were ruined by the Civil War and the defeat and execution of King Charles I. Returning in 1660 at the Restoration with

Charles II they nearly ruined themselves with their own eccentricities. The poet's father had been known as 'Mad Jack Byron'.

The poet's mother was the unlucky thirteenth and last of the line of the Gordons of Gight, an Aberdeenshire family which showed a record of violence unusual even in Scottish lairds.

Byron, then, from his mother's side had something in common with Walter Scott. Scott used to claim for his landed Border ancestors that, despite their high fame in their own part of Scotland, they came from Border raiders who obeyed no law but their own. In their Border fashion they had been as violent as Byron's maternal ancestors, the Gordons of Gight.

Did they ever touch upon these ancestral traits they had in common when they met at John Murray's, the publishers, in London? John Murray III, the publisher's son, recalled seeing 'the two greatest poets of the age—both lame—stumping downstairs side by side . . . nearly every day, and that they remained together for two or three hours at a time.'

It is possible that Scott may have brought up the subject of untitled Lowland raiding lairds. It was a subject he was very interested in; and he had once seen Byron's mother in the theatre before her marriage reacting to the melodrama in a highly emotional, extrovert manner.

It is possible, indeed probable. We do know that, after meeting Walter Scott, Byron grew more proudly conscious of his maternal ancestry and in his journal wrote that, at the phrase Auld Lang Syne, all Scotland flew up before him. In his verse he was to proclaim: 'But I am half a Scot by birth, and bred a whole one . . .'

This was a distinct change from his Harrow and Cambridge days when, except for a few sentimental memories of persons and scenery, he had put behind him all his childhood days in Scotland. But this brings us back to the first and unfortunate time Byron had crossed Walter Scott's path.

In 1808 *The Edinburgh Review* had, in its most characteristic and condescendingly sneering manner, not so much attacked Byron's first volume of poems *Hours of Idleness* as waved it aside as juvenile trash—and this after some very good notices by the London and Southern papers. It was a notice calculated to wound, and it did wound the twenty-year-old Byron.

He had his revenge in a highly readable and amusing

satire showing the promise of the poet's powers to come. It was the well-known *English Bards and Scotch Reviewers*. It ran into five editions and amused many readers in both Scotland and England. Parts of it must have amused Scott, for much of it even today is irresistible. But he did not much relish the uncalled for reference to himself.

Byron at that time was not sure who had written the sneering review of his poems. So he lashed out all round, including not only Scottish reviewers but Scotch poets and English ones for that matter who did not conform to his standards based on Pope and Dryden. There is an extremely funny passage on Wordsworth, which one can still read with a smile.

Whatever Scott thought of the lines on his friend Wordsworth, he did not like to be accused of writing 'stale romance' for money, and the phrase 'Apollo's venal son' got under his skin sufficiently to irritate. He wrote to Southey:

> It is funny enough to see a whelp of a young Lord Byron abusing me, of whose circumstances he knows nothing, for endeavouring to scratch out a living with my pen. God help the bear if, having little else to eat, he must not even suck his own paws. I can assure the noble imp of fame that I was not born to a park and £5,000 a year.

Understandable, but not very like Walter Scott who was nearly always immune to hostile criticism or abuse, or, if he was compelled to comment on it, never, except on this occasion, let personalities intrude into the contest.

All this was back in 1809, but when in 1912 the first cantos of Byron's *Childe Harold* appeared he was deeply impressed, and all was put to rights. Scott wrote to Byron praising *Childe Harold* and mentioned the circumstances in which he had written *Marmion*—Byron's chief target of abuse.

Byron at once replied and passed on some very laudatory remarks that the Prince Regent had made on Scott's poetry with which he, Byron, had agreed. It was the kindliest letter.

After this all went well. As we have seen, the two men met in Murray's in London and talked much and long. They met each other once again before Byron's flight from England, but continued to correspond.

Byron in exile was much touched by a perceptive and warm-hearted review in *The Quarterly* (the rival to *The Edinburgh Review*) which Scott had written on the third canto of *Childe Harold*. We have already spoken of the astonishingly large payments poets received in the early decades of the last century. Almost as surprising was the amount of space given to reviewers in literary journals. Such reviews of *Childe Harold*, Canto III, and a few other of Byron's poems were close on fifteen thousand words in length. Byron wrote later to Scott in 1822 to express his gratitude.

Beginning by apologizing for the 'tardiness of his letter' he goes on:

> I owe to you far more than the usual obligation for the courtesies of literature and common friendship; for you went out of your way in 1817 to do me a service, when it required not merely kindness but courage to do so: to have been recorded by you in such a manner would have been a proud memorial of any time, but at such a time when 'all the world and his wife' so the proverb goes were trying to trample on me was something still higher to my self-esteem.

The younger man was referring, of course, to his enforced exile on account of his quarrel with his wife and the scandalous rumours attached to it which were sweeping over Great Britain.

The older man, the kindly generous-hearted Walter Scott replied in a well-known letter, only one sentence of which is usually quoted. We give below the whole of the part that is relevant to the matter Byron raised in his long letter.

> . . . I would have done a great deal—had anything been in my power—to prevent the unhappy family misunderstanding which preceded your departure from this country, and, if I had been a father, cousin or uncle, I have no doubt I should have sung out the old time doctrine of Bear and Forbear. But when such a break as this had taken place I felt indignant at the clamour [here Scott speaks of the 'pretenders to genius' in London seizing upon family disagreement to 'blacken and defame a man of true genius'. He concludes with this sentence referred to above as the only one usually quoted.]
> I have been too long an advocate for fair play to like to see twenty dogs set on one, were that one an equal—much less to see all the curs of the village set upon one noble staghound who is worth the whole troop.

This generous letter reached Byron not long before he left Italy on his voyage to aid the liberators of Greece—a voyage which was to end in his self-sacrificing death. Byron, already devoted to Scott (he had earlier paid Walter a

92

handsome compliment in the fourth canto of *Childe Harold*), was completely bowled over by this letter.

His voyage to Greece was filled with talk about Scott and particularly about the Waverley Novels. This is recorded in a strange book *Medora Leigh* by Charles Mackay which contains chronicles of Byron's last voyage, noted by an observer 'Mr S.':

> Byron's delight in the Waverley novels was so great that he never travelled without copies of them, and *Quentin Durward* was one of the last books he read. Dr Henry Muir, a resident of Cephalonia, happened to receive a copy and at once lent it to Byron, knowing that he had not read it. He [Byron] immediately shut himself up in his room, refused dinner, and merely came out once or twice to say how much he was entertained, returning to his room with a plate of figs. This was the day before he left for Missolonghi [where he died] and not having finished the book, took it with him.

It is tempting to quote the many, many times he spoke of Scott's goodness of heart and of character.

> I say that Walter Scott is the most open, the most honourable, and the most amiable of all men. He is as nearly a thorough good character as can be. I say this because I *know* by experience it to be the case.

Byron also spoke of his genius as a novelist (perhaps he was pleased at having been an instrument in turning Scott to his true vocation), but one must content oneself with only these lines quoted by an observer in *Medora Leigh*:

> At Vathi the liquor they were now enjoying was the product of Scotland in the shape of whisky chiefly from the distillery of mine ancient friend James Haig of Lochrin. This communication seemed to qualify the noble drinker, and led to a recitation in the pure Lowlands Scotch of Burns's petition to the House of Commons the line beginning 'Scotland my auld respectit mither'. He spoke these lines in pure Lowland Scotch, and said again that he was more than half Scotch.
>
> The conversation then turned on the Waverley novels. Lord Byron then spoke of *The Bride of Lammermoor* and repeated by heart some lines which he had held in his memory.

The passage that Byron remembered was one that made a special appeal to him; it was about the protection of an only daughter. These two are in Scots and Byron spoke them in that tongue which he had recalled from his childhood. The last reference to Scott we shall give here is:

He was handling some books in some small open shelves and said—'Pope's Odyssey—h'm, that is well placed here undoubtedly; Hume's Essays—then *Tales of my Landlord*. Ah, there you are Wattie!' He seemed much content.

The observer 'Mr S.' whose ancient friend was James Haig, the distiller of Lochrin, says that in all Byron's conversation at Vathi which continually returned to Scott, Byron always spoke of him as 'Wattie'.

It is strange and pleasing to note that when Byron was going on his last voyage towards the freedom of Greece and his own death (he had a strong premonition of this) his mind returned to Walter Scott and to Scotland. It was as if something elemental in him had been stirred into recollection, speech and action. For this, it is not too much to say, Walter Scott was entirely responsible.

He was responsible by the impression he had made on the younger man at their meetings in London and by the earlier and Scottish Waverley novels which Byron devoured so voraciously. He devoured them also, perhaps, with some homesickness for his own childhood in the North, before London, world-wide fame and the tumultuous joys and hates of his affairs with women had complicated life for him.

Homesickness for his own childhood. Indeed he says as much in a postscript to the letter quoted above in which he thanked Scott for having the courage to defend him. He speaks of that childhood here with a kind of yearning, and says that it makes him certain that the (then anonymous) 'author of the Scottish Waverley novels' was Scott.

Does it seem strange, this affectionate friendship between the man of fashion, libertarian young poet and the middle-aged to elderly Scots lawyer laird whose life lay almost entirely between Edinburgh and his Border homes? Surely not; they had certain deeply felt things in common.

A love of fair play, a hatred of pretentiousness, a love of poetry and of the art and action of writing with imagination. These and other qualities allowed the two men to see each other clearly through their differences, and to talk with each other as if they had no differences. Both, incidentally, were generous, humane and excellent company.

They both made it easier for each other. Byron's latest and most scholarly biographer, Mr Peter Quennell, puts it thus:

> Byron, as was usual when he entered wholeheartedly into a friendship, sensed the points at which their mutual interest and

philosophy collided and suppressed without any intention of deception, much in his character and opinions that would have been incompatible with those of the kindly but more conventional Scott.

Scott perceived Byron's character with astuteness and knew when to fall silent. He said afterwards to Moore:

He was often melancholy, almost gloomy. When I observed him in this humour, I used either to wait till it went off of its own accord, or till some natural and easy mode occurred of leading him into conversation.

This was the way to treat the young and prickly Byron, if you liked him, and this Scott certainly did straight away at their first meeting.

It was after their meetings and when they had separated never to see each other again that this mutual liking deepened into a warm and understanding affection.

It was this affection that came from the depths of his mind to the top when he was going to his death in the cause of Freedom in Greece.

When the news of Byron's gallant death in Greece reached Scotland, Scott wrote in *The Edinburgh Weekly Journal*:

Amidst the general calmness of the political atmosphere we have been stunned from another quarter, by one of those death-notes, which are pealed at intervals, as from an archangel's trumpet, to awaken the soule of a whole people at once. Lord Byron, who has so long and so amply filled the highest place in the public eye, has shared the lot of humanity. He died at Missolonghi, on the 19th of April, 1824. That mighty genius, which walked amongst men as something superior to ordinary mortality, and whose powers were beheld with wonder, and something approaching to terror, as if we knew not whether they were of good or of evil, is laid as soundly to rest as the poor peasant whose ideas never went beyond his daily task. The voice of just blame, and that of malignant censure, are at once silenced; and we feel almost as if the great luminary of Heaven had suddenly disappeared from the sky, at the moment when every telescope was levelled for the examination of the spots which dimmed its brightness. It is not now the question, what were Byron's faults, what his mistakes; but how is the blank which he has left in British literature to filled be up? Not, we fear, in one generation, which, among many highly gifted persons, has produced none who approached Byron in *originality*, the first attribute of genius. Only

95

thirty-seven years old—so much already done for immortality—so much time remaining, as it seemed to us shortsighted mortals, to maintain and to extend his fame, and to atone for errors in conduct and levities in composition—who will not grieve that such a race has been shortened, though not always keeping the straight path, such a light extinguished, though sometimes flaming to dazzle and bewilder it.

Since this sketch first appeared the author has had an opportunity of learning, from the very first authority, that the importance of Lord Byron's life to the Greek cause was even greater than he had ventured to suppose it. His whole influence was turned to the best and wisest purposes; and most singular it was to behold an individual, certainly not remarkable for prudence in his own private affairs, direct with the utmost sagacity the course to be pursued by a great nation, involved in a situation of extraordinary difficulty. It seems as if his keen and hasty temper was tamed by the importance of the task which he had undertaken, as the war-horse, which prances and curvets under a light burden, moves steadily as well as actively under the armed warrior, when he guides it into battle. His advice and control were constantly exerted to reconcile the independent and jarring chiefs with each other, and to induce them to lay aside jealousies, feuds, and the miserable policy of seeking each some individual advantage; and to determine them to employ their united means against the common enemy. It was his constant care to postpone the consideration of disputes upon speculative political maxims, and direct every effort to the recovery of national independence, without which no form of government could be realized.

To the honour of the Greek nation, they repaid with warm gratitude the wise and disinterested zeal with which they beheld him undertake their cause. Had he remained to uphold their banner, it had not, perhaps been in the present danger of sinking under their own disunion, rather than the force of their barbarous enemies. Greece and the world, however, were to be deprived of this remarkable man. And surely to have fallen in a crusade for freedom and humanity, as in olden times it would have been an atonement for the blackest crimes, may in the present be allowed to expiate greater follies than even exaggerating calumny has propagated against Byron.

With these last words, so ended a friendship compounded of affection and admiration, between two generous men whom the world thought different, but who had so much in common—not the least their love of Scotland.

9

His True Vocation—the Novelist

When Scott left the field of narrative verse he retreated to another field in which he was to be victor until death and for long after. The novels which he wrote with a speed and facility equal to and often greater than that with which he had composed verse were of a kind that had never been seen before. He changed the course of fiction, and though he was imitated, nobody reached him at his best—and much though by no means all of his best came first.

It was an astonishing achievement in which energy, gusto for living, observation, self-expression (let alone the capacity to change his medium in middle life) has never been equalled since. Had it been equalled before him? All we can say in answer is that it is difficult, if not impossible, to name any author in any language of international fame who, before Walter Scott had at the age of forty-three changed from poetry to prose and conquered the world all over again—conquered it even more decisively than he had in verse.

This change, which first advanced itself (though anonymously) in his novel *Waverley*, had, as we have seen, been planned, projected, or tentatively felt for a few years earlier. The change, when it came, roughly coincided with changes or developments in his life. They are worth noting, for they had much effect on Scott as a man and as an artist.

First, in 1811 his lease of Ashestiel ran out, and he bought for his Border home that property, now one of the most celebrated in Scotland—Abbotsford.

Second, he became a Clerk of the Court of Session, thereby moving up in the Scottish legal world and augmenting his reliable income.

Third, the printing and bookselling business of James Ballantyne, now joined by his brother John, having been launched into publishing (booksellers and publishers at that date often combined) began to show signs of muddle and loss.

On these events which came round about the greatest revolution in his working life—his retreat upon the novel—we may make these comments.

The Abbotsford property when bought by Scott did not then possess its high sounding and now famous name. It was then called 'Clarty Hole'. Clarty is the old Scots or Lowland word for dirty. Hence that rather odd Scottish proverb which speaks for one side of our national character—'The clartier the cosier'.

It was a proverb or saying which Scott, a son of the extremely clarty Old Town of Edinburgh, probably knew well, and it may well have amused him. But he was not in search of clartiness or cosiness when he bought the farmhouse with a filthy duckpond in front of it from which it got its name.

He saw in the property, which stretched along an undulating strip of land on the south side of Tweed between Melrose and Selkirk and in beautiful surroundings the basis on which he might found a country estate. It had historical association with a famous Border battle between various noble families mentioned in the Border Minstrelsy. Just by it was a ford of Tweed; and as the whole property had once belonged to the Abbot of Melrose, Scott decided to call the place Abbotsford.

We have no record of whether Scott in the privacy of his family of young growing children amused them and himself by continuing to call the farm Clarty Hole when they had taken possession of it. He might well have done so when they were all struggling to get into the place, for the 'flitting' to it aroused his never-sleeping sense of comedy. He wrote to a friend describing how the miscellaneous historical assortment he had already gathered round him was moved:

The neighbours have been much delighted with the procession of my furniture, in which old swords, bows, targets and lances made a conspicuous show. [He does not mention Rob Roy's gun nor the sword Charles I gave to Montrose, which were already a part of his collection.] A family of turkeys were accommodated within the helmet of some *preux* chevalier of ancient Border fame; and the very cows, for aught I know were bearing banners and muskets.

He ends by saying that the whole proceeding was like the movement of gypsies from one camp to another.

Somehow they got there, somehow they squeezed into the diminutive farmhouse of Clarty Hole. But the surroundings, the prospect then as now were enchanting, and filled Scott's head with dreams for the future.

Before the house Tweed, in one of its most characteristically noble stretches rolled on its way to Melrose and the sea. Behind and farther east down river there were the magical triple peaks of Eildon. *And* all around on this southern side there was land *waiting to be bought*.

It was *the* place in all Scotland to allure Walter Scott to build a house, to found and extend a country estate worthy of his forebears, his family and himself. It was an allurement, which from the moment he had seen Clarty Hole and the surrounding land, he could not resist. It was an allurement that was to inspire him and help to ruin him.

Whatever your views may be on the curious hotch-potch of architectural styles that goes to make the Abbotsford of today, you cannot but be touched by the splendidly preserved and living (in the sense that they are lived in) remnants of his inspiration and his ruin.

Becoming a Clerk of the Courts of Session does not sound as if it were an occasion to affect his life and his powers as an artist—but it did. Before we go further we may as well define what was the position of a Clerk of Session in Scott's day. This is usually passed over.

A Clerk of the Court of Session early in the last century had to sit in Court just below whatever Lord or Lords of Session he might be assigned to. He sat below the judicial seat but was separated from the open Court. His duties were quite simple but important. He had to record the judgments passed by the Court in the person of the Lord of Session or Judge so that the official result should be always available for consultation in future cases in the years to come.

To make this record for the future unassailable Clerks of Session were chosen not by hazard or convenience from members of the Scottish bar, but from men of property and a certain distinction in the Scottish legal system.

The duties of a Clerk of Session lasted a little less than six months in the year, and never meant more than four to six hours a day. It was (however intrinsically important) all but a sinecure. Owing to the importance of this position during Scott's day, the salary for this sinecure was £1300 a year. Today the Clerk of the Court of Session has a number of assistants, and is a Civil Servant. He is an important individual in his own right. He is, as was put to the writer by a learned Lord of Session, the man whose work it is to see that the business of the whole Court of session runs smoothly.

At first Scott had to do this task for nothing, as he was merely a 'stand-in' for 'an old friend who was obviously on the way out, but who had not retired or died'. After the old friend had retired or disappeared in any other way, Scott would get the job for the rest of his life. This made his combined income from the light Sheriff duties at Selkirk, plus some private family money, £1600 a year. Multiply that by, at least, four and you will get an approximate idea of his income in modern currency.

This notable increase of an assured income allowed Scott to dream about the extension of his property at Clarty Hole —the Abbotsford to be.

But the position brought Walter Scott the novelist another strong but intangible advantage.

Scott was immensely interested in human character. Scottish human character, in those days, was far more individual, and full of foibles and oddities than it is today, and it was to be seen to advantage in the Courts of law. Sitting just below the Judges (the Lords of Session) and face to face with the open Court with all its teeming life of lawyers, litigants and accused people brought before the Court, he was in a favourable position to note each day all the richness of the Edinburgh and Southern Scotland character.

There it was, all laid open to him each day, and with all its characteristics heightened by being on show in a Court of law.

Except at the end of the case when he had to record the results of it, Scott had nothing to do but to sit still, watch, observe and listen. He was therefore in a privileged position as a spectator of Scottish life and character.

With his superb and all but unique powers of memory

he did not need to take notes, but to pile up in his immensely absorbent mind the fruits of what he had heard and seen. He did this to some purpose. It was *the* job for a novelist in the making. That novelist was to be the supremely successful man of letters of his time. Yet the seeds of his financial ruin were already beginning to be sown.

The Ballantyne business had by now more than begun to show signs of its utterly unbusinesslike methods; it was completely given over to them. James Ballantyne, a fine printer, had no business sense. His brother John had been brought up from Kelso precisely to fill that want in the firm. He did nothing of the kind. He assumed great airs of business management but did not practise what his airs and mannerisms promised. He used to tell Scott what he thought their great author *wanted* to hear. When the truth was convenient, he spoke it; when it wasn't he avoided telling it straight out.

Scott himself is also to blame for this state of affairs. He liked the eccentric Ballantyne brothers for the richness of their humorous characters and appearance.

James was short but immensely fat and had a great air of being a successful man of the world. John was as thin as his brother was fat. He was as loquacious as his brother was portentous. The business was supposed to have been divided among three men each holding equal shares—the Ballantyne brothers and Scott. In fact (as Walter Scott provided the capital for the other two) the business should have been called 'Walter Scott Unlimited'.

This, then, was the state of affairs when Walter Scott turned novelist. A new estate purchased by the banks of Tweed and waiting (or rather, in Walter Scott's land-hungry eyes calling out) to be exploited and developed. The acquisition of a profitable and regular position in the Court of Session—and a failing business to back it all. It was failing not so much from the capacity to produce money as from the unbusiness-like treatment of their only source of money (Scott himself) and the inability to get rid of unwanted printed stock such as the *Edinburgh Annual Register* which Scott had insisted the firm should print and publish.

It was an ominous position, but none of them thought of it as ominous at the time. Unwilling to cut their losses on obviously unprofitable printed matter in their house, they relied entirely on the fame of Scott's genius which had, so far, never let them down. But could that genius go on being so enormously profitable even while Scott lived? And, even if it could do so, one thing was sure; Walter Scott could not live for ever.

Scott's imagination and genius can never have been more potentially vigorous and strong than during his period of change from narrative verse to the novel. He did not need the successful rivalry of Byron to spur him to energy on the new field which he was not so much to retreat to, as to capture with world-wide fame.

The Lord of the Isles apart (the material for which he did not want to waste, and with a subject which allowed him a graceful farewell to his old medium), he must have known that he had worked out the vein suitable for that medium. Scottish history is full of drama, but by the time he had toured the Hebrides and made his respectful salute to Bannockburn, he knew he had come to the end. All other episodes in his native country's story were too recent, too obscure or too controversial for narrative verse.

But the novel was another matter. Here he could take subjects out of Scotland's immediate past without choosing sides in his account of these subjects. As his material he could reflect the living Scotland he saw and heard all around him—in the law Courts, down on the Borders where he lived or in Perthshire, the only Highland county he really got to know well.

He could take these subjects and illuminate them, as only he could do, with the true speech of Scotland which he had heard so plentifully in his boyhood and his youth. It was a speech indeed which still existed, still sounded in his ears, if not so widely as once it had done.

The 'manners and character [of Scotland] might be daily melting and dissolving into those of her sister and ally', but they were still sufficiently alive to vitalize a host of fictional characters which his genius could now call into being. He might have exhausted what he could use in narrative verse, but a whole new world was now open to him awaiting only the energy of his pen for exploration and conquest.

The novel of *Waverley* was the first to sally into the new world. We must not, however, let ourselves be confused by the various accounts of its origin, of the discovery and re-discovery of the opening chapters in a drawer containing fishing tackle. Nor should we let ourselves be perplexed by

its patently inaccurate sub-title of *'Tis Sixty Years Since.*
All we need to know and consider is this:

No sooner had Scott scored his first and considerable
success in narrative verse by publishing *The Lay of the Last
Minstrel* in the first week of 1805 than he wrote the opening
seven chapters of the novel *Waverley*, subtitled (according
to Scott in a later general preface in 1829) *'Tis Fifty Years
Since.* Two questions for consideration at once arise.

Why, when he had proved to the world, and to his own
delight that he was a master of highly popular narrative
poetry, did he break off to write seven chapters of a prose
novel?

Second, as the novel's subject was the last Jacobite Rising
in Scotland (the famous affair of 1745) why did he get his
dates wrong in the subtitle when by 1805 it ought to have
been *'Tis Sixty Years Since?*

Let us take the second question first for it is one that has
puzzled many—including me long before I undertook this
book. That puzzlement or confusion is only increased by
the fact that when Scott did finish the novel for publication
in 1814 it bore a new subtitle *'Tis Sixty Years Since*—still
all but ten years out.

Scott is often accused of carelessness owing to the impetuosity of his writing. But this, at first sight would appear
to be a major error which he above all men would naturally
have avoided.

In the history of most countries there are events so
closely associated with their dates that a general knowledge
of those dates is taken for granted. Every educated Englishman, for example, knows that the Norman Conquest
happened in 1066. Indeed '1066 and All That' by means of
a popular book has passed into the language.

In Scotland the last Highland Jacobite Rising in favour of
the Stuart monarchs under Prince Charles Edward Stuart
(rather regrettably described as 'Bonnie Prince Charlie') is
so strongly associated with the year 1745 that it is simply
called for short 'The Forty-five' and everyone knows what
you mean. How could Walter Scott writing in 1805 have
made such a blunder as to speak about 'Fifty Years Since'?

The answer is that he did. He had set out in the opening
of the novel to deal with the huge national changes which
had occurred in Scotland as a result of the failure of 'The
Forty-five'. In these opening chapters he had let his mind

103

go back to his boyhood when he had met Jacobite survivors and, in particular, in the mid-1790s when as a youthful lawyer he had to enforce some of these changes in Perthshire. He just *thought of himself* in 1795 and consequently thought of 'The Forty-five' as being fifty years since. It was an error in notation due to an active imagination which he did not pause to explain. There seems no other reason to account for it.

Then what about the changed subtitle to the novel when it was eventually published in 1814—'*Tis Sixty Years Since*—still wrong?

The writer is indebted to an eminent scholar of Scott's life and work for this explanation of the second printed error. Ballantyne had seen the original seven chapters as written in 1805; he would have pointed out the mistake of 'Fifty Years Since'. Scott agreed to change it to 'Sixty Years Since', but failed to bring it up-to-date for publication in 1814. In that year it was sixty-nine years since—near enough to seventy for seventy to pass.

Is this too trivial a point to be elucidated at such length? I hope not. *Waverley* begat the most famous series of novels known to literature. This apparent bad error on the title page of the very first 'Waverley' has puzzled generations of Walter Scott's compatriots to whom 'The Forty-five' is an unforgotten and unforgettable year.

Of more general importance is the first question put above. Why, when he had the ball of narrative poetic verse at his feet, did Walter Scott break off to write seven chapters of prose fiction—and pretty factual chapters too? In his *Minstrelsy of the Scottish Border* he had magically brought to light a whole world of his native country's poetic past. This was for him a profoundly moving experience. It was more than moving, it was inspiring.

Under the inspiration he had received he had tried to make that poetic world live again, this time through his own composition from his own pen. A bold thing to attempt, but he had attempted it and offered the result to the world in *The Lay of the Last Minstrel*. The world of England as well as Scotland had loudly applauded the result. He must have been gratified by this.

Maybe he thought he had found his literary vocation; and we know that in the next year he set to on *Marmion*, with *The Lady of the Lake* not far behind. He could not have foreseen that the world would applaud, would be even more vociferous. He could not have known that from Russia to the Atlantic literary circles who could read English were to speak of him as the greatest poet of his age. Byron had not yet appeared as his conquering rival and his friend.

All the same he must have been filled with confidence and with the pure pleasure of composing poetry in a manner which he had made his own. Otherwise he could not have poured out the cantos and the lyrics at the rate he did, passing straight from his 'table to the press' so early as 1805. Why then did Scott interrupt this pleasurable outpouring to feel his way tentatively along the first seven chapters of *Waverley*?

The answer—soon to be made abundantly apparent to the world—was that he was emotionally intensely interested in a number of episodes in his native country's *recent* and *almost immediate* past. It is not too much to say that, realist though he was, he was made homesick by reflecting on Scotland's recent past in a way he never could have been by the great traditional and almost legendary peaks of her remoter history—feats which he had sung in verse.

All this made it obvious to his clear-thinking and judicial mind that he could not (dare not) throw the subject of Scotland's immediate past into the emotional vehicle of narrative poetic verse. Hence *Waverley* and a number of *Waverley*'s immediate successors.

In *Waverley*, the first but far from being the greatest or the best of the series to bear the famous name of 'The Waverley Novels', he had certainly chosen a ticklish subject from Scotland's recent past. It was an event which had inspired, lacerated and torn his native country only twenty-five and twenty-six years before his birth, an event the aftermath of which he could remember from his own childhood and youth.

It was the last Jacobite rising in Scotland in favour of the legitimate but exiled Stuart monarchs in 1745 and 1746, that is to say 'The Forty-five'.

I admit that I find myself in a difficulty when I have to deal with the 'Forty-five' in a book intended for American as well as British readers.

Every Scot knows about it, and is still (difficult though it may be to believe) ready to argue on it. Most English people have heard about it, but have only a peripheral interest in it as something that once briefly disturbed their monarchial succession. They recognize, maybe, the high drama of the event but it is all in the past.

It is, of course, for all Scottish people in the past from any practical point of view. But its significance is not entirely dismissed. It does (however much we may argue about it as something from the past) still mean something to us.

This is all very well for us Scots, and perhaps English, but it is too much to expect Americans to know about, still less to care about, a remote dynastic struggle in Europe and the British Isles. A struggle, moreover, which happened not long before the Americans attained the liberty of their own once 'British Colonies', and freed themselves forever from the shackles of warring monarchies.

Here, however (for the purpose of discussing Walter Scott's great artistic evolution or revolution from triumphant poetry to even more triumphant prose), is an attempt to explain the background of *Waverley*.

It is a compressed attempt to say what Stuart Jacobitism was all about, and why its last fling in the rising of 1745 in Scotland was a bold subject for him to tackle as his first flight from verse upwards into the prose of the novel.

The Stuarts, before the French influence in spelling known as Stewarts, were descended from the daughter of Scotland's great hero, Robert Bruce, who freed Scotland at Bannockburn and refounded the nation of Scotland *as it still exists*.

That I and all my compatriots who still call themselves Scots and not English (not even 'Britons', despite the Union of 1707, when we are abroad) is a direct legacy from Bruce and from many of his descendants who were our Kings and Queens.

They were amongst the most remarkable line of monarchs ever thrown up in European history. In their personalities some of them were unforgettably remarkable and belong in story and legend to the world, not only European history. One has only to mention as an example Mary Stuart, Queen of Scots, one of the most alluringly controversial figures of history. It would seem that a new book is written about her in a number of languages nearly every year—and many by Americans. But she was not the only Stuart of her kind.

The fate that overcame every one of the whole fifteen of them was, as Voltaire pointed out in a celebrated passage, extraordinarily unfortunate, often romantically so. One of them, amidst much popular lamentation, was executed by their English Parliamentarians—one driven forth. An unusually large number died violent deaths in warfare or by assassination. Only one spent a peaceful reign and died as he had lived. The rest either had to endure exile and poverty in youth before regaining their throne. The last three of these undoubtedly legitimate monarchs in unquestionable succession from Bruce were exiled for life.

Controversial in the drama of their own lives, they were the cause of bitter controversy in their own Kingdom of Scotland. Again, as an example we cite Mary Stuart, the Catholic Queen of a largely Protestant country—the Queen who outfaced the implacable John Knox.

Her son, James VI and I and Charles I, by then, through the accidence of succession, Kings of the *separate* realm of England as well as of Scotland (a dual monarchy like the later Austria-Hungary), gave much offence to their country of origin. They tried to enforce Episcopal worship upon Presbyterian Scotland. But Scotland would have none of it.

When Mary's great grandson, James Stuart Seventh of Scotland and Second of England, went one better (or, if you will, worse) than his Episcopal forebears, and became a Catholic, he had to flee both his Kingdoms.

Yet . . . yet (and this is a highly characteristic Scottish qualification) though the Stuart monarchs could deeply offend Scotland, the Scottish people could not bear others, particularly the English, to abuse or ill-use them. They were their own Scottish Stewarts.

When Cromwell brought Charles I to trial in London and chopped his head off, all Scotland, Calvinist, Catholic or Episcopal, was appalled, and gave shelter to his son. When James VII and II was turned out of England there was a strong feeling in his favour in Scotland.

It was a feeling which was to burst out in an insurrection in Scotland when James died in exile, leaving his son and heir the *de jure* James VIII and III. This insurrection broke out in 1715 and, through mismanagement, only just failed. It was then that the words Jacobite and Jacobitism, drawn from the Christian names of these two James, came into common use.

It was used to distinguish the Stuart supporters from those politicians in England who had imported the foreign German and Hanoverian monarch, George I, of the by now United Kingdom. He could not speak any tongue but German, and was contemptuously referred to in Scotland as 'the wee, wee German Lairdie'.

When 'the Fifteen', as it was to become known, failed, men thought that Jacobitism was finished, and resigned themselves to grumbling. But they were wrong.

Thirty years later in 1745 the young Prince Charles Edward Stuart, son of the exiled and dead James VIII and III, landed in Scotland to launch the 'Forty-five'. It was an astonishing achievement which some historians still believe could, if pressed home, have succeeded and restored the Stuarts.

Much nonsense has been written about the 'Forty-five' and, in much later years, when Jacobitism was completely dead (in that there were no Royal Stuarts left alive), it also engendered much false sentiment. An heroic historical fact was turned into a 'greensick tale for greensick drawing room girls'.

Passing over that nonsense and that false sentiment (sometimes called 'Bonnie Prince Charleyism'), a false sentiment which one may in passing state did not yet exist in Walter Scott's day, no one can deny the dramatic and extraordinary qualities of the 'Forty-five'.

The young Prince Charles, almost unaccompanied, without arms and little money, set out on his own initiative to sail from France to Scotland to lead the rising. He arrived in the late summer of 1745 in the West Highlands.

He met, even from stuanch Highland Jacobite chiefs, much discouragement. How could he, how could all those loyal Highlanders, defeat the might of the English without any of the sinews of war?

His Stuart charm *and* his Stuart determination conquered them. The Jacobite standard was raised. The Prince announced that he had been appointed Regent by his father. A considerable Highland force swept south, overwhelmed Perth and captured the capital city of Edinburgh. This after a resounding defeat of the English troops to the east of the city. The defeat (the battle of Prestonpans) was one of the shortest in the history of warfare—five minutes!

Charles, having captured Scotland, wintered in Edinburgh, holding Court at the Palace of Holyroodhouse where his ancestors had once ruled.

In 1746 the Jacobite army reached deeply into England and, by a series of brilliant manoeuvres, reached Derby. The Prince was for going on to London, but was overruled by his generals, and in bitterness retreated. Had his advising generals and chiefs known it, the Hanoverian George II had already packed his baggage, including the Crown Jewels, for a flight home to Hanover. Had they known it, would they have advised advancing? And if they had . . .? Prince Charles and his army won one more victory at Falkirk in Scotland, but were eventually utterly defeated at the bloody battle of Culloden near Inverness in the Northern Highlands. The Jacobite cause was forever lost, and the power of the Scottish Highlands broken in the ensuing massacre conducted by the German-English Royal Duke of Cumberland.

But the heroic tale was not yet quite over. The Prince, forcibly led from the field by his followers, escaped to the West Highlands and the Hebridean Islands. Here remote Celtic clansmen refused to betray his whereabouts despite the enormous reward offered by the Goverment of George II. Celtic Highland loyalty proved utterly unbreakable either by grievous threats of danger or by huge bribery.

After some months the Prince escaped to France and died in despair and frustration in 1788 in Italy.

But the story of the long months during which simple Highland folk had protected, in so dramatic a manner, him whom they believed to be their lawful Prince made a strong impression all over Scotland when it became known.

Even those in the Lowlands and in the capital, Edinburgh, who had opposed the Prince's landing and who had deplored Jacobitism could not withhold their admiration for the young man's courage while he was being 'hunted in the heather'. *Moreover*, as fellow Scots, even though not of the Celtic North-West, they were filled with pride when they learned how their remote compatriots had refused English bribes and had suffered much danger to protect their Prince.

Once again, and for the last time, a Royal Stuart had known the deep dichotomy which could exist in individual Scottish hearts at the mere mention of the name of 'the auld Stewarts' as they were then almost universally known.

Having now set down the compressed story of the Stewarts (the Stuarts), the Forty-five and eighteenth-century Jacobitism the writer does not regret the divagation towards American readers. Some of what has been briefly described here may be new to English readers. And, even if it is not new to many Scots, there is no harm in reminding them of it.

There is particularly no harm in reminding them of this Jacobite history because of the strong relevance to Walter Scott's first flight into the world of the novel—*Waverley*.

When Scott began to write *Waverley* in 1805 a Jacobite revival was unthinkable. But, in the minds of older Scottish folk it was still a ticklish subject. And it is worth remembering that though poor Prince Charles Edward Stuart had by 1805 long been dead, his younger brother, Prince Henry Stuart, now Cardinal of York in Italy was still alive.

He, the very last of the male Stuart line in succession, was to live till 1807. Though he had long relinquished the claim to the Stuart throne, there were a few followers of his in Scotland and in Italy who obstinately went on calling him by the Royal title of King Henry the First of Scotland and Ninth of England. And this while the first chapters of *Waverley* were being written!

Yes, Walter Scott, so deeply and emotionally interested in his native country's immediate past, may have found the Forty-Five indeed an alluring subject for his first novel. But he must have known that some readers would look upon it as still a controversial and embarrassing subject.

The 'Waverley novels' are the most celebrated source of fiction bearing one generic title. Not even Balzac's *Comédie Humaine* surpasses them in universal fame. And this is still true however much or little (a debatable point) people read and enjoy them today.

In their own time they were a revolution in world literature. No sooner was a new novel bearing on its title-page the simple statement 'By the Author of Waverley' (or known to be by the Author of Waverley) published in Edinburgh or London than the effect was internationally immediate.

In that pre-copyright era it was at once 'pirated' in America in its own tongue, and nearly always pirated in Europe by being translated into every language read by a literate public. 'The Author of Waverley' was sufficient advertisement for any enterprising publisher.

At first Scott made a genuine attempt to conceal his authorship, certainly of *Waverley* and of 'that novel's' immediate successors, the Scottish-based novels culminating in the splendid *Rob Roy*, and in the even more outstanding achievement of *Old Mortality*.

By 'genuine' I mean that it was a secret he may well have intended to carry with him to the grave. But even he, even after the success of the first 'Waverleys' could not foresee the world-wide fame in store for them nor the inevitable and, in the long run, unconquerable curiosity of the world as to who was the real author.

He told his wife and a very few of his more intimate friends, binding them to the strictest secrecy. He did not even admit Byron to a knowledge of the facts. Though, as we have seen, he was, by the time the Waverleys were coming out, on terms of mutual admiration and affection with his rival poet. Byron did his best to extract the secret which he had guessed, but his friend Sir Walter (or in private 'Wattie') would not be drawn.

Of course his fellow citizens in Edinburgh, his Scottish compatriots and a little later the London literary world began to guess the secret. Later this guess, amounting almost to an accepted certainty, spread over Europe and America. But it was not until 1827 that he all but casually admitted his so-called secret to the world and in public.

I shall deal later with the long-drawn-out official secrecy and the reasons put forward for it. Here we are concerned only with the first novel, *Waverley*.

The many reasons given for the continuing secrecy over the later novels (the impropriety of a Clerk of the Court writing novels, his 'humour', his desire not to flood the market with his products, his sense of fun, of secrecy, etc., etc.) may certainly have been operative in the concealment about *Waverley*. It is my contention, however, that added to these reasons was the *subject* of Waverley—the Forty-five. The reasons for this I have given above.

There are critics who deplore the most celebrated series of novels literature has ever known should have begun with one they say was 'inferior' to those that followed. They say that there are readers who, feeling it a duty to assimilate Scott's novels, begin with the first one, *Waverley*, and are so put off that they do not continue with the rest.

Who are these gallopers over the Walter Scott course who

fall at the first fence never to rise again, get up, gallop and jump with increasing exhilaration over what lies before them? Have they admitted it publicly? Are there any potential lovers of Shakespeare who have begun with the atrocious *Timon of Athens* and stopped there? Is the parallel just? Is *Waverley* so markedly inferior?

It is not. Goethe late in life re-read *Waverley* and said he would place it 'amongst the best things that have ever been written in the world'. That should make one pause respectfully—but, from our later age, and having read so much more than *Waverley*—only pause. It *is* inferior to much that follows in the Waverley novels, but it is unique.

It is unique not only as being the first novel of one of the world's most famous writers of fiction, but as a vivid (sometimes over-vivid) presentation of the clash between the old world and the new all contained within the microcosm of our small passionate Scotland. It is therefore, with all its faults, much more dramatic a novel than would have been one about a similar clash in the very different 'walled-in garden of England'.

It is unique in that it is the first novel about the last Jacobite rising of the Forty-five. It is unique in that it is presented by a man in the flush of his powers, well after the Forty-Five yet one who could remember from his childhood its aftermath, one who had talked with those who had fought and suffered in it.

We may smile at many things in the author's style of talking *about* things (when he wasn't reporting vivid Scottish speech, Highland or Lowland). We may recognize his laborious efforts to see both sides of an impassioned question. We may smile at the overcoloured romanticism of some (only some) of the dialogue he used to push the personal part of the story forward. Those of us who are Scottish may be amused to note how he compresses the whole Jacobite rising into Perthshire. But we ought to recognize its unique quality in being so near to the event.

It is said that Scott took as a model for his house in that shire the once famous Perthshire Grandtully. A Stewart of Grandtully about the time of Scott's boyhood was the prime mover in the most famous piece of litigation in Scotland— one of the most famous in Europe. Had Stewart and his wife, the heir to the Duke of Douglas (well on in life) 'bought' two French orphans in Paris pretending they were the fruit of her womb? Almost certainly yes. But all Scotland was split in violence over 'the Douglas Cause'. Did Scott think of this when he chose Grandtully for his 'Tully-Veolan'? Surely he did.

Waverley is as if we had come across a readable, vivid, well-constructed novel about Bannockburn by someone who had known and talked with men on both sides—about Crécy, Agincourt, or any other major event of change in history.

There have not been many novels about Crécy, and only one play in English about Agincourt. But there have been far too many works of fiction in all kinds of media about the Forty-five and Scottish Jacobitism generally. Some have merit, most have not. But there is only one that is by comparison approximately authentic—*Waverley*.

Stilted high English dialogue, yes. But plenty of real, vivid and often amusing as well as moving Scottish dialogue —the sound of things to come in later novels. Yes, the 'hero', Edward Waverley, is the stock Walter Scott young Englishman used as a mirror to reflect far more real Scottish characters. But he is less 'stock' than Frank Osbaldistone in the later and greater *Rob Roy*.

The Perthshire Highlanders! Some say that Scott never understood the real Highland character and merely observed its picturesque externals. Maybe Scott himself recognized this, and hinted as much in his postscript to the novel when he apologized for 'much bad Gaelic'—an apology that may have been meant for no more than merely getting Gaelic phrases wrong.

Maybe, but at the end of the novel Scott atones for this by lifting some of his Highland characters clean out of picturesqueness and giving them, chieftain and humble clansman, heroic stature.

He achieves this at last by showing us the captured Highland Jacobites standing their trial for high treason against the German Hanoverian King in London. He places this trial at an English Court in Carlisle, the Carlisle Scott knew so well.

In an often quoted passage he makes the poor clansman, Euan Maccombich offer to give his own head and the heads of six of his kind if only the Government will let their Chief Fergus McIvor go free to live in France and never trouble the English again. At first this uncouthly spoken offer provokes laughter in the English Court. But, in the end (though the offer is refused) the simple dignity of the man makes the spectators at Carlisle fall silent.

Less well known are the words uttered in prison at Carlisle to Edward Waverley who was given permission to visit him. Talking of English law and the hideous butchery imposed by it on those found guilty of high treason, he speaks a farewell to his friend. This is what Scott makes him speak:

'This same law of high treason' he continued, with astonishing firmness and composure, 'is one of the blessings, Edward, with which your free country has accommodated poor old Scotland— her own jurisprudence I have heard was much milder. [Here speaks Walter Scott, who knew Scots' law.] But I suppose one day or other—when there are no longer any wild Highlanders to benefit by its tender mercies—they will blot it from their records as levelling them with a nation of cannibals.

'This mummery, too, of exposing the senseless head—they have not the wit to grace mine with a paper coronet—there would be some satire in that, Edward.'

Then he speaks from his heart *and for his head* so soon to be cut from his butchered body—cut and exposed upon Carlisle's city walls for all to see:

'I hope they will set it on the Scotch gate, . . . that I may look, even after death, to the blue hills of my own country which I love so dearly.'

'The blue hills of my own country.' Here speaks a Highlander, with a Highlander's natural Celtic grace—but he speaks for more than his own Highlands. He speaks for his own ancient and 'once independent Kingdom'. Here, perhaps, and through the mouth of a Scotsman made real by his own creative imagination in his first novel, spoke Walter Scott too.

We have seen how warm an affection Byron had for Scott. We cannot resist quoting some celebrated lines from his *Don Juan*, Canto X. But it is not for their celebrity but for their possible relevance to 'the blue hills of Scotland' that we quote them. Byron admired and knew much of *Waverley* by heart. Here is the snatch of quotation:

> But I am half a Scot by birth, and bred
>   A whole one, and my heart flies to my head
> As Auld Lang Syne brings Scotland, one and all,
>   Scotch plaids, Scotch snoods, *the blue hills* and clear streams.

Was Byron's 'the blue hills' an echo from this moving speech in *Waverley*? It is possible.

This is mere speculation. Many of us, however, believe that it is more than speculation to say that later Walter Scott spoke for himself, and about himself, in the novel of *Redgauntlet* published in 1824.

That is a novel about something that never happened—a Jacobite, a Scottish rising that wasn't placed in the Highlands, but in the Borders and by the Solway Firth. It wasn't placed 'Sixty Years Since' but at some not exactly defined period in the latter half of the eighteenth century. It ends with the sad significant sentence: 'then the Cause is forever lost'.

Here is a purely imaginative work in which Walter Scott is not fettered by historical facts, but is free to fly in his own fancy—in his own private dreams.

We shall later examine *Redgauntlet* in detail.

10

The First Waverleys—
Scott's Anonymity

It has been well said of Scott that his paradox as a writer
is that, though in outlook and literary reputation he was a
romanticist, his greatest and most lasting achievement was
the creation in his Scottish Waverley novels of people
apparently without an ounce of romanticism in them—not
the creation of knightly figures or airy splendour.

We think of Walter Scott's name and do our minds turn
to Ellen of Loch Katrine's island, to Marmion (even to that
real figure, James IV of Scotland), to the Last Minstrel? No.
In their place there rises up before us so visibly and audibly
that we can see and hear them a very different assortment of
men whom their author knew so well that he presented them
to us in fiction.

At once before us a ridiculously likeable Glasgow mer-
chant torn between city commerce and the knowledge of
gentle (savage but gentle) Highland blood in him from his
mother's side—Baillie Nicol Jarvie. We see and hear the
Scotch pedant Oldbuck from *The Antiquary*, Davie Deans
from *The Heart of Midlothian*. We savour again the nearest
approach to the Sancho Panza of Don Quixote—Andrew
Fairservice from *Rob Roy*.

The imaginary stage is filled by and is resonant in the
voices of unforgettable Scotch characters (none aspiring to
romance) throughout the first six novels and including
Waverley. In these characters, too numerous to mention by
name, Walter Scott has created his world, a world far more
tangible, real, credible than those from his narrative verse.
He did this because he knew and loved such people—knew

116

Edinburgh : the Old Town as it was in Scott's youth

Edinburgh : the Old Town

Edinburgh : the building of the New Town, 1801

(Edinburgh Central Public Library)

The Raeburn portrait of Walter Scott in his thirties
(*Copyright Mrs. Maxwell-Scott of Abbotsford*)

'Clarty Hole', the decayed farmhouse, the site chosen by Scott
for the building of Abbotsford

(Copyright Mrs. Maxwell-Scott of Abbotsford)

Sir Walter Scott in later life, by Landseer
(*National Portrait Gallery*)

The newly-built Abbotsford according to Scott's design

(Copyright Mrs. Maxwell-Scott of Abbotsford)

Edinburgh, from the Castle, showing the newly-built Scott monument

them far better than the airy persons who inhabited his melodious verse. He had seen their originals and listened to them. They were his 'ain folk' of Scotland. And with the new world of the United Kingdom of Britain that was being created, it would seem that they were disappearing. He would create, catch them and preserve them on the printed page before they were in life gone. They have not gone yet.

In the many reasons put forward for Walter Scott's disavowal of the novels which he began on with such secret fervour as soon as he had acknowledged his need for retreat from the field of narrative poetry this gustful passion for portraying the real, touching, ridiculous, amiable living characters of his seemingly passing nation is oddly neglected. May it not have been one of the causes which began the, in the end fruitless device of Waverley authorship which he was to continue under many guises and disguises?

Let us once more grant and weigh the force of other reasons commonly put forward for his sudden secrecy.

The making and even publishing of poetry was a gentlemanly diversion for a man in a respectable profession. Yes, but the large sums Walter Scott drew from such a diversion by the time that he had got to *The Lady of the Lake* showed that it would be a very profitable diversion—we have used the term a 'pop art' for arresting narrative verse in the early nineteenth century. And, however privately Scott may have kept his literary accounting books, the informed world must have had a fair notion of what money he would be making from narrative poetry, or 'pop art'.

The composing and publishing of novels in Scott's era was admittedly not so respectable a literary diversion for men so well placed in the legal profession as Scott had attained by the time he launched *Waverley*. But Edinburgh is, and always has been, a small but resonant world. How could he hope to keep and retain such a secret beginning and spreading all out over the world from such an inbred spot?

If he was to have known what was to come he would have hesitated to practise this personal concealment—concealment rather than deceit. He did not know what was to come, however, and when it came upon him he was too deeply involved in a pretence.

The most potent of these reasons given for the secrecy of the novel-authorship seems to us now, with our hindsight, to have been his connection with the firm of the Ballantyne brothers. This was an uneasy connection which was halfway between private and secret. By and in involving the Ballantynes in the business of the Waverley novels, Scott was taking a purely private step. He wished to keep it from the world (at least the world of Edinburgh); so he chose anonymity.

Neither the printer James nor his fecklessly dishonest brother John could afford to quarrel with or even admit the true state of affairs to the source from which their blessings flowed. James, uneasily covering up for John, concealed things until the last possible moment and depended upon the pernicious system of 'accommodating bills', then generally the practice, but nowhere more virulently than in Scotland where cash was scarce and the value of the native Scottish banknotes fickle.

The Ballantyne brothers, including the excellent printer James, have been the subject of acid criticism in Lockhart's *Life of Scott*. And as this 'Life' has generally been acknowledged as one of the greatest in our language it must have been very wounding to the Ballantyne family to have been so prominently, and it might have seemed permanently, denigrated.

In fact Lockhart's sneering remarks are mostly based upon social grounds rather than upon nefarious deeds. Both Ballantynes were characters and often socially absurd. That was what drew Walter Scott to them and repelled the socially less secure but more prickly Lockhart.

At any rate the toll of the Ballantyne firm in Walter Scott's ruin has, in fact, been correctly put right and recorded again and again since Lockhart's work. No one nowadays goes to Lockhart for an unprejudiced view of the Ballantynes.

Scott's patronage of James Ballantyne and his family sprang from a generous and characteristic impulse. In its beginnings there was nothing you could have said against it. If you did not like Walter Scott the worst criticism you could bring about it was very like Scott's clannish and Border youthful habits. But nine-tenths of Walter's Edinburgh and Scottish acquaintance *did* like him and warmed in and felt the better for his company. They recognized only the generosity of Walter Scott's dealings with Border friends of his boyhood. So far it would have been criticism, but there was another and more private element in Walter

Scott's relationship with the Ballantynes' firm which he did not wish to bring out for all to see.

This leads us to the second thing that must be stated. In all Walter Scott's support and private financing of 'Walter Scott Unlimited' the Ballantyne firm which could not have lasted a year in Edinburgh without Scott's financial help and influence there was nothing that was dishonourable, still less illegal; but it was unwise.

Walter Scott, when he began to make big money as an author, and particularly when he saw the practical possibilities of founding an estate on the Borders at Abbotsford, began to have ambitions to touch the other elements of the then highly profitable business of book-printing, book selling and publishing—the tradesman's side, in short. Why should he not invest his author's earnings in such a venture, make it profitable and incidentally help a friend of his boyhood days and his friend's brother? There was no reason that he should not save his suspicion that men as well-placed in the Scottish legal system as he should refrain from such personal involvement in trade.

That was what he suspected, so he was, by the time he had turned novelist, already leaning towards concealment of his intimate financial connection with the Ballantyne firm. The writing and publication of *Waverley*, in a manner entirely different from his previous work, gave him what must have seemed an ideal chance to slip out of the scene by anonymity.

This very anonymity, closely guarded though it may have been, soon burst its intended bonds. Long before the first half-dozen Waverleys had appeared and taken the world by storm all Edinburgh, and consequently nearly all Scotland, was either partially or completely in the secret. It was of little avail that Scott got up at four in the morning, made his own fire and got down to Waverley novel writing in the privacy of his own home or homes. There was only one man in all Scotland it was generally believed who could write or be responsible for a team producing such multifarious work—Walter Scott. His baronetcy was not given to him for his poetry. The 'Great Unknown' was not unknown in Scotland, London or Europe. The only question that people asked themselves was *why* Walter Scott chose to conceal his authorship of the Waverley novels.

The Border between Scotland and England was soon

penetrated. The big publishing houses in London soon got on to the facts and took them for granted. As we have seen, Byron more than suspected Scott's authorship of *Waverley*, the very first novel, and the Prince Regent, a fervent admirer of the narrative poems, followed suit. Society, including that know-all, Lord Holland, scarcely bothered to argue the question. It just said that the anonymous author of *Waverley* and the novels that succeeded it, under whatever guises assumed, were by Walter Scott.

Abroad, outside the British Isles, where the fine points of authorship were not closely studied, the novels were universally attributed to Walter Scott. This was particularly stressed in the fairly new-born United States of America, where, through the fact that the narrative poems, openly proclaiming the name of Walter Scott, had been voraciously bought and pirated from source—no need of translation for ordinary folk there—were avidly Walter Scott conscious.

The Americans were not puzzled or put off by the vivid Scottish speech of the 'characters' in the first Waverleys, as were some English readers. Having broken loose from Europe and particularly England, American readers and writers were anxious to establish a truly American style in realistic dialogue in novels. They saw, or thought they saw, an example for their ambitions in the speech of the ordinary characters in the first Waverley novels. The translations into European tongues made little if any attempt to convey the real life-giving quality of Scottish speech in the novels which marked them off from the poems.

This life-giving quality made a direct if chauvanistic appeal to American readers, and the founders of early American literature. They may not have understood every word of the Scottish speech as it reached them on the printed page, but they *wanted* to understand it, and were from the beginning sympathetic to it. In America, free of copyright obligations, free of formal acknowledgement of authorship, there was no attempt to pretend in private or in public that Walter Scott had not been responsible for the novels. But, again this shall be mentioned in greater length in 'Scott and America'.

Scott twisted and turned to avoid as well as he could the factually accepted rumours spreading everywhere in his own city and country, and all over the world. He prevaricated, he all but lied to some of his best friends. He seized upon the amazement of the literary world that these novels succeeding each other so quickly could all be the work of one man. He even went to the length of reviewing a Waverley novel in an Edinburgh review as if it had not come from his own pen.

But, he must have realized, he was up against more than he could control. Maybe in the end he would have to give way and admit the truth. In the meantime, while he officially clung to his secret, he could give full play to what has been described as the 'foxy' side of his character by enjoying the freedom of saying what he would about the Waverley novels and joining in free discussions about them as if he had nothing to do with them.

Doubtless there were other reasons for his initial struggle to avoid admitting authorship of popular fiction in which officially highly unromantic characters continued to express themselves in a once distinguished tongue used long ago at the Scottish Court but now degraded to peasant or common use.

A number of these have been touched upon or mentioned in the lives and studies of Scott. In these mentions, time and again the critics and writers have commented on this vividness and the reality Scott attained in this speech, so different from that of his heroes, heroines and eminent people through whose eyes we see and hear these common folk.

The Scott hero or heroine (too often the mere story-telling medium) inclines far too much to use stilted and artificial dialogue. This is so much so that when a person of character, independence, as well as of breeding, such as Diana Vernon does enter a novel such as *Rob Roy*, the critics seized upon her as an example of Walter Scott's true feelings breaking through against his self-admitted predeliction for writing about rogues, vagabonds and old-fashioned Scottish eccentrics. But none of Diana Vernon's most ardent admirers would put her as a subject for readability on a level with her social inferiors in the tale.

The fact is self-evident to any reader of Scott's novels from *Waverley* to *Redgauntlet* that their author, when he used the still-living speech of Scotland (still living, yet practised for the most part outside polite society), he felt free. He was writing with all the gusto he had put into his long poems, but with an intoxicating freedom which drove him on and urged his patriotism; he was creating and writing about *real* people whom he had seen, heard, met or only noted from his silent seat as Clerk of Session. This was enough to make him spring into true life, and in springing into life, speak for the old independent Kingdom of Scotland which Walter Scott had never known, but in which his immediate forebears had been born. It was also a truer Scotland than even he had summoned up from a remoter past in his narrative poems.

In a word he was in his earlier novels free to write and create about the real country of his birth. It is impossible not to rejoice in that new-found projection as we read him exercising it. As we read it too, it is obvious that the supposedly anonymous author was enjoying that long pent-up freedom as much as we are.

But, giving all weight to these reasons for his concealment of the author of *Waverley* quoted at length above, admitting that if we put all of them together there have been sufficient reasons for his concealment, might there not be one stronger, more intimate reason which would weigh with Scott? How would the respectable public take to this unmistakably ardent true patriotism about the *real* Scottish character?

Walter Scott had been born in a Calvinist Scottish home which had accepted the union of Scotland and England as not only inevitable but as something to North Britain's advantage. From his childhood he had learned to look upon the remnants of picturesque Jacobitism of the Forty-five as only being all the more picturesque because they had utterly lost their force and could not, by the wildest stretch of imagination, be looked upon as 'dangerous' again.

He had but touched on the inner force of a moribund Jacobitism in his first essay into fiction, *Waverley*. And though, in the pre-execution scene of Hector the Highland chieftain, he had undoubtedly touched it with poetic feeling, he had never pled its cause.

It was just a part of the old world of Scotland inevitably on the way out in the eyes of progress. It was no more relevant to the age in which Walter Scott lived and wrote than were the Augustan splendours of the largely Hanoverianly-named New Town of Edinburgh (in which he had his residence in Castle Street) to the rotting and decaying mediaeval Old Town straggling down the east side of the Castle Rock.

How then could he justifiably defend his most forcible

122

revocation in the pages of the novels that followed *Waverley* of a host of characters that drew their so-fascinating read-ability from the fact that they were citizens of a free country now swallowed up and officially absorbed?

It is my contention that this unanswered (this never openly-spoken) question did weigh with Walter Scott; it did provide yet one more reason for official secrecy as to his creation of these characters.

It is impossible to argue about this contention, for I have no evidence on it. I can only speculate. But once having speculated, it is haunting.

It haunts one because of the great pleasure, not only Scottish readers but those from all over the literate world took from Scottish characters in the Waverley novels. Haunting too is the undeniable gusto and pleasure which their officially anonymous author pushed them forward with on to the world's stage.

Walter Scott, at least and at last potently relished his new-found freedom—even if he had to go through the rapidly thinning pretence that he had not found it and chosen it for his very own. He had at last come into his own—albeit concealing his own name while doing so.

11

---···---

The First Novels Continued:
Scott's Illness

The novel of *Waverley*, despite the anonymity and the
mystery of its origin, was a surprising success in Edinburgh
and Scotland. Nor did its theme of Jacobitism, and the
pure Scots speech of some of its characters act as a bar to
it in England. This contributed to making Walter Scott's
visit to London in 1814 with his wife and daughter Sophia
one of the happiest and most fruitful he ever enjoyed.

Napoleon, who for twenty years had been the menace of
Europe in general, and the United Kingdom of Britain in
particular, had been defeated, laid down his arms and, as
far as the world could foresee, had been successfully and for
ever banished to his minute island kingdom of Elba in the
Mediterranean. He had ceased to be Emperor and a
European scourge. His escape from Elba, the Hundred Days
leading to that 'damned close thing' but decisive battle of
Waterloo were events no one dreamed of. The Congress of
Vienna was set to refashion Europe to its pre-Imperial
design. A nightmare had seemingly been swallowed up in
sunshine—and nowhere with greater relief than in the
recently threatened and besieged South of England and
London.

This exhilarated the incoming Walter Scott on his 1814
visit. It should be firmly stated here (if it needs any stating
or underlining) that for all Scott's homesick patriotism for
the seemingly vanishing nation of Scotland and for the
disappearing Scottish individual character, he had also a
strong feeling for the more successfully surviving England.
For proof of that *Woodstock* need only to be referred to.

The 'Auld Enemy' had ceased to be an invading and destroying foe. Walter Scott recognized and took pleasure in the easy continuity of her unshakeable individuality under the 'essential Union' of two nations sharing the same sea-girt island. He was only sorrowful, deeply heartsick that his own smaller, less powerful nation of North Britain or Scotland should have to lose so much in a Union, at that time regarded as universally benevolent to all who partook in it. Walter Scott's generosity of heart was particularly untouched by what might have passed to observers as parochial chauvinism. To sum up, he accepted the Union of England and Scotland as necessary, was sorrowful that this inevitably meant the decline of Scottish national character and customs, but relished the continuing strong individuality of England—in his great character, and particularly in great affairs there was no meanness.

In this happy and fruitful 1814 visit to the relieved London he may well have been surprised that the fame of his changeover to novel writing had preceded him from Edinburgh amongst influential and knowledgeable people. Byron, when he tackled him with the authorship of *Waverley*, said that anonymity was probably essential to avoid giving offence to the reigning House of Hanover in a work of fiction about Jacobitism. This was nonsense.

Walter Scott had little, if any difficulty in consequence in pooh-poohing the notion of *Waverley* offending the reigning House to his new friend Byron. His fellow poet may have accepted this uncontrovertible argument but he was not persuaded that Scott was not the author.

The Prince Regent, at a fairly well-attended banquet twitted Scott in a toast as being 'the Author of Waverley'. Walter did his best to evade this Royal assumption, saying that he would make sure that the author would learn of the Prince's compliments—but it was a poor best, easily penetrated. So it was whenever he went to literary and learned London. People who had known the name of Walter Scott might be amazed at his versatility in turning to prose fiction about his own living country, but they admired the results, and no one 'in the know' in the South seriously questioned his authorship of *Waverley* or eventually the equally successful *Guy Mannering*, or took his evasions at more than their face value.

Walter Scott's arrival in literary London after the seeming

release from the threat of the Napoleonic invasion was a part of the general euphoria of the time. His versatility was accepted in London as just one more marvel of a marvellously released age.

It is doubtful whether Walter Scott, much more on guard with the English literati at home, did more in London than set up a token evasion rather than all-out denial of his authorship of the novels. What need had he to do more than stick to the outward display of anonymity? In his new and anonymous vein as a writer of fiction about his own land he was doing very well. Let it rest at that. Let the faulty walls of the Ballantyne firm be shored up by this new venture, and let him dream of hopes for his land-hunger at Abbotsford and go on in his own dream world. Thus he dreamed in pleasure, enjoyed new company and was actively happy in his family visit to London. He would seem to have had reason for being so.

And the novels which did follow directly on *Waverley*, with one exception, *The Black Dwarf*, did succeed wherever they were on sale. His *Guy Mannering* (nothing to do with Jacobitism but with the deep South West of Galloway containing smugglers, an immortal spae-wife or old woman with second sight *and* the constant Scott theme of a lost heir restored to fortune) did more than catch the public fancy in both England and Scotland. It aroused their appreciation of novelty in fiction and set a large public clamouring for more.

And that more was what Walter Scott, increasingly harassed by the difficulties into which the Ballantyne firm was sinking, was eager to give. The future, by his changeover to officially anonymous fiction writing on a scene and on characters he loved, ultimately now seemed bright.

Let it be enough to say that James Ballantyne lost his position as bookseller-printer and was retained solely as printer of Scott's works by that extraordinary, talented, over-optimistic man of affairs in the Edinburgh and London literary world, Archibald Constable. Constable, whose imperial grand airs did not please Scott, was eventually in 1826 to be one of the means of Walter Scott's final and all-but conquering ruin. He was nevertheless one of the greatest and most visionary publishers produced in Great Britain, but these very qualities were to be his undoing in the end. He reached out on a grand scale for more than he could cope with.

126

Walter Scott must, however much he personally shrank from 'the Emperor's' ways, have been glad of his rescue from the comparatively minor but potentially dangerous Ballantyne muddled crisis of 1815–16. He must have been especially glad of it not only for his dream house and estate of Abbotsford—but because he now felt in him the irrepressible urge to write novels that were genuinely novel in the sense that the world had never seen their kind before, and for which they would be perpetually and assuredly hungry.

But now, out of the blue, came a blow that struck Scott at his return home to Scotland when he was so confident of his own ability, and by his own pen to overcome all difficulties. This was a thing entirely new to him—deep ill health accompanied by excruciating pain.

His body which, crippled though it had been from birth, he had driven so hard and mastered so well by his own willpower and determination, turned upon him and would not take no for an answer.

It came to the surface for all to see (though he had been suffering preliminary pangs from it before) when he was at the beginning of the great Scotch successors to *Waverley* and *Guy Mannering*. As a host to a merry and friendly dinner party in his home at Castle Street, Edinburgh, his endurance, alas, could put up with it no more.

He leapt from his chair and, astonishing his friends and guests, ran out of the dining-room howling in deep physical distress. The agony he suffered from was, in those preanaesthetic days, deadly and unendurable.

He had inherited from his mother's side a tendency to stones in the gall-bladder. He did not know of this possible inheritance and when it struck him, it did so all the more alarmingly. He did not know what was happening to him and so, like a wounded dog which does not know why or who has wounded it, he gave vent (even though he was host) to howling and flight.

At first this public display of uncontrollable pain must have been a deep social and physical blow to his pride. But more weakening and lowering things were to follow. He fell into the hands of the doctors of the time.

They could not or would not operate on his gall-bladder, and sought merely to touch the surface of his body, weakening his physical powers of resistance without destroying his unconquerable will.

127

They bled him so copiously that he had scarcely energy to move about his bedroom or library. At the height of his paroxysms they applied salt in hot water to cover his stomach; this burned the fabric of his shirt and agonized his outer skin without drawing away from the more deeply seated pain arising from the source of all his physical distresses. He was blistered all over, and his natural courage was further weakened and assailed by the depressing diet which was enforced upon him—nothing but toast and hot water.

The stiff, silent upper lip of Victorian suffering had not yet come into fashion, nor, if it had, would that most natural and individual of men have seen much use in recourse to it when at the height of his bouts. Either in Edinburgh or in Abbotsford he would howl so that they could hear him all over the house and beyond.

There was nothing his wife and family could do for him save send for more doctors. These, to quieten his symptoms, forced laudanum and other opiates into him, which temporarily gave him relief.

Fortunately for him and for us his mind and body (particularly his body), while recognizing the use of passing relief, strongly reacted against opiates and he had an unconquerable revulsion to their after-effects. This was no pose, but a built-in part of his character of mind and body. At one time the doctor made him swallow enough opium to have killed a horse, yet never, like other contemporary sufferers, including not only de Quincy but, oddly enough, the great pastoral and respectable poet Crabbe, did he even show signs of addiction when he was not actually in extremes of pain.

The worst it did was to cloud the memory when he was in the act of composing a novel—dictating it when he did not have the force to drive a pen legibly across the page. The most celebrated instance of this act of creation and oblivion occurring at the same time is to be found in that dark and unrelieved tragedy *The Bride of Lammermoor*. This terrible tale, in which Scott's mind faces the spirit of pure evil— facing it with his subconscious rather than his conscious mind—was no sooner out of him and got somehow on to paper than his slowly convalescent mind began to reject the details of it. This rejection was so strong that when the proofs were returned to him for correction, he not only found the theme and manner repellent and grotesque but forgot the shape of the story and even the quality of some of the more malevolent characters in it.

Scott could hardly contain his impatience for the next set of proofs of *The Bride of Lammermoor* to come in. He genuinely wanted, as much as the ordinary reader who made up his public, to 'know what was coming next'.

He wrote to the Duke of Buccleuch and to Southey: 'I have been very ill. If I had not the strength of a team of horses I could never have fought through it and through the heavy fire of mediaeval artillery, scarce less exhausting—for bleeding, blistering, calomel and ipepecachuana have gone on without intermission, while, during the agony of the spasms laudanum [tincture of opium] became necessary in the most liberal doses, though inconsistent with the general treatment. I did not lose my senses, because I resolved to keep them, but thought once or twice they would have gone overboard, top and top gallants . . . My life has been in all its private and public relations as fortunate as ever lived, up to this period. . . . Fear is an evil that has never mixed with my nature, nor even has unwanted good fortune rendered my love of life more tenacious.'

Walter Scott's illness lasted for close on three years and reduced him from active middle-age to a scarcely recognizable elderly man in outward form shrivelled in shape and height, unable without assistance to mount a horse and scarcely able to sit it unless it was the most dependably easy-going in nature. He had in his appearance and movements become an old man while still in his forties. He was to recover his flesh, if not all his physical strength—and there were country activities such as 'burning the water to spear salmon', or coursing actively and to the fore after hares which hc had to abandon for ever. But indoors he would eventually play the host as well as he had been wont to do, when immediate memory came back to him. Little more than the shock of white hair remained for his acquaintances and widely growing circle of friends to remind them of the three years' calvary he had endured.

It was a calvary which, as we have said, was to reach its height of physical and mental pain in the macabre composition of the half-consciously dictated *Bride of Lammermoor*. Will Laidlaw could not restrain his exclamations as the story was wrung out of his master's tortured lips—'The like o' that, sir! Eh, sirs! oh, sirs!' But as Scott, unable to keep silent during an excessive pang of pain in his stomach, cried out, Laidlaw begged him to stop. The only response he got was: 'Nay, Willie, only see that the doors are fast. I would fain keep well all the cry as well as all the woollen to ourselves, but as to give over work, that can only be done when I am in woollen'—that is wrapped in his last winding sheet.

It was in these extraordinary circumstances of pain and determination that he composed much of five Scottish novels of the 'broken years' period. The outpouring of 'The Bride' from the author's subconscious and his subsequent forgetfulness of what he had written and caused to be written forms a dramatic, almost a melodramatic, account of his struggles against acute physical pain at this time. But to generations who came after him his most astonishing feat was the fact that he was able, while gripped in recurring pain, to put on paper that sunny, humorous and exciting novel on Glasgow and the Highlands—*Rob Roy*. He indicates in a letter to a friend his belief that physical tortures were on their way to relieve him:

> The disorder is less in my stomach than in my bowels. At times they perform their duty imperfectly then resist medicure and then follows a fit of the cramp. I lie in agony for several hours, swearing I will take *no* opium and swearing like King Corny of the Black Islands. I am obliged to end it by taking sixty or eighty drops of laudanum unless I have a mind to let the pain proceed to inflammation when bleeding is resorted to . . . I am then relieved, and next day is spent miserably from the effects of the medicine which disagreed with my constitution. But the third day comes and Richard is himself again. After all, can a man with any decency complain who has enjoyed so many years of health as has fallen to my lot? So we must take the bad and remember the good that has gone before.

By 1819 it was not the doctors' savagery on his outer flesh that began to relieve his pain, but the course of nature fortified by his own determination. The spells of stomach pain became shorter and less violent. He attributed this to his taking of calomel, in which he may have been partly true. More potent in dissolving and expelling from his tortured bladder the evil stones were his absolute determination not to give in and to carry on the great plans he had laid for writing. Nature was not so much conquered by his will power as forced to recognize it. Nature retreated, but left him as he described the sight of himself on his pony as 'the very image of death'. 'The image' received a blow from which the outward show he gave to the world never recovered. This only displayed to those who really knew him the' strength and power that lay behind the image. His clothes hung loose upon him, his hair was snow white, and through the jaundice which had attacked him when he was at his worst, his face had become haggard and remained long yellow.

It is wonderful that this ghost-like body of a man could write with such courage and hope to his friends. And it is indeed wonderful that earlier, when the signs of recovery were still to await him in the future, he should have the strength at all to write the novels of these three broken years. What is even more wonderful is the sheer quality of much of these works proceeding from the darkness of his pain and from the harassment of his affairs. Their quality today is recognized as pre-eminent, and it is enough to say that they include *Rob Roy* and that novel dearest to his compatriots *The Heart of Midlothian*.

If Walter Scott had died at the end of his broken years and, in fiction, had never put on paper more than the works he had called into being while in the purgatory of this period, he would still be remembered as *the* novelist of Scotland of the early nineteenth century and the writer who was to point the direction of international fiction in the world to come.

The Miracle of the 'Broken Years'

Had Scott died at the end of these thirty months he would
have been remembered in Scotland. And, though his world
fame would not have been so great, he would have projected
his patriotism upon the world.

Indeed on one occasion he thought he was going to die.
Lockhart gives his wife's account of this:

> He then called his children about his bed and addressed them
> with solemn tenderness. After giving them one by one such advice
> as suited their years and characters he added: 'I am unconscious of
> ever having done a man an injury or omitting any opportunity of
> doing a man a benefit. I well know that no human life can appear
> as weak and filthy in the eyes of God.' Then he laid his hands on
> their heads and said: 'God bless you! so that you may all hope to
> meet in a better place hereafter. And now leave me so that I may
> turn my face to the wall.'

But he did not die. It was the crisis of his illness from
which he began his slow convalescence. But convalescence
could not obliterate the memory of pain. This he expressed
in his finest short poem 'Dreary Change'.

> The sun upon the Wierdlaw Hill
> In Ettrick's vale is sinking sweet;
> The Westland wind is hush and still,
> The lake lies sleeping at my feet.
> Yet not the landscape to mine eyes,
> Though evening with her richest dyes,
> Flames o'er the hills of Ettrick shore.
> With listless look along the plain
> I see Tweed's silver current glide,

And coldly mark the holy fane
Of Melrose rise in ruined pride.
The quiet lake, the balmy air,
The hill, the stream, the tower, the tree,
Are they still such as once they were?
Or is the dreary change in me?
Alas, the warp'd and broken board
How can it bear the painter's dye;
The harp of strain'd and timeless chord
How to the minstrel's soul reply!
To aching eyes each landscape lowers,
To feverish pulse each gale blows chill,
And Araby's or Eden's bowers
Were barren as this moorland hill.

These poignant lines were forced from him after the doctors had given him too much opium. Yet they came from him one beautiful autumn evening when he was standing on the high ground to the south of his beloved Abbotsford.

With the exception of one other short verse about this time it is the only example of Scott's giving way to dejection; but it did not kill the lyric spirit in him—nor yet the humorist. Not long after, near the end of *Rob Roy*, James Ballantyne called on him for 'copy' and was astonished at the sight of a clean pen and a vacant sheet. 'Aye, aye, Jemmy,' said Walter, "tis easy for you to bid me to get on, but how the deuce can I make Rob Roy's wife speak with such a curmurring in my guts?'

The Antiquary, *The Black Dwarf* and *Old Mortality* followed on these years of broken pain, and *Guy Mannering* (written in six weeks) which preceded them—once again on the theme of a missing heir—contains the celebrated spae-wife, Meg Merrilies, into whose mouth Scott delighted to put the eloquence of her kind:

Do you see that blackit and broken end of a sheiling? There my kettle boiled for forty years. There I bore twelve buirdly sons and daughters. Where are they now? Where are the leaves—where are the leaves there were on the auld ash-tree at Martinmas?—The West wind has made it bare, and I am stripped too. Do you see that saugh tree? It is but a blackened rotten stump now—I've sat under it mony a bonnie summer afternoon when it hung its gay garlands over the poppling water. I've sat there . . . and I've held you on my knees Harry Bertram [the missing heir] and sung ye sangs of the auld barons and their bloody wars—It will ne'er be green again, and Meg Merrilies will ne'er sing sangs mair, be they blithe or sad. But ye'll no forget her, and ye'll gar big up the auld wa's for her sake? And let somebody live there that's ower gude to fear them of another world. For if ever dead come back among the living I'll be seen in this glen mony a night after these crazed banes are in the mould.

This poetic outbrust from a spae-wife or humble creature, not of the upper or rich class, was something new to find in a novel, and its novelty as well as the excellence of the tale showed that Scott was now becoming the master of his new medium of novel writing.

The wording of the spae-wife's outburst is worth noting. Scott, though he introduces other characters speaking broad Scots, was anxious that the spae-wife's words should be comprehensible to English readers. There is only one word —'gar' (to make)—which is in Scots. The rest is a kind of English, but in a rhythm that proclaimed its origin in pure Scots. Should the English reader forget the meaning of 'gar' he has only to recollect a famous early nineteenth-century story. At the end of one of those huge dinner parties where talking lasted two days and one night someone said: 'What gars the Laird of Garschatten look sae gash [ghastly]?' Garschatten's neighbour at the table replied: 'Wheest man! He slippit awa' to his Maker two hours syne [since]. But I didnae like to disturb good company by mentioning it.' Scott would have relished this native tale.

Scott and his wife and daughter were allowed to sail for London in 1814 confident of the future. That future he laid in the splendid novel of *Old Mortality*—an objective view of one of the most controversial episodes in Scottish history —the covenanting period. This was published in London as well as in Edinburgh. John Murray, the London publisher, wrote to Scott to say that the author was either Walter Scott or the devil. Lord Holland had no doubt too. Someone asked his opinion. He never doubted that it was Scott's. As for his opinion of the work, he said: 'We did not one of us go to bed last night—nothing slept but my gout'. But Scott kept up his denial and his pretence.

Scott enjoyed himself during this London visit, but when it was all over, and when he was looking forward to working again in his own country, the shattering blow of pain and ill health was to strike him.

Lockhart gives a description of Scott's lamentable appearance at this time, but quotes him: 'The physicians tell me that mere pain cannot kill; but I am sure no man would live other three months, encounter the same pain, and live. However, I have resolved to take thankfully whatever drugs they prescribe, and follow their advice as long as I can. Set a stout heart to a stay brae is a grand rule in this world.'

In 1818 his body had almost recovered, and, of course, his stout heart had remained true to itself, and in February of that year his Scottish patriotism received a moving reward. At the Union of Parliament in 1707 there was a clause saying that the ancient regalia of the Scottish Kings should never be moved to England, but they had disappeared. Had this clause been disobeyed by the London authorities? True there was a dusty old chest in a room of the Castle which some believed *might* contain the jewels, once the outward and visible sign of her once independent Kingdom, but no one could say for sure.

Scott when in London had raised this problem with the Regent—he was probably the only living man who could have done so—and had extracted from him a promise to appoint a commission to investigate the contents of this mysterious all-but-forgotten chest.

Scott was head of the commission and took with him his daughter, Sophia, later to be married to Lockhart. Other commissioners also brought their womenfolk with them. Sophia later told Lockhart that her father's conversations had previously worked her up to such a pitch that when the creaking old dusty lid was forced open she nearly fainted and withdrew from the circle of spectators.

She need not have done so. There, in perfect order save for the accumulation of dust, lay the Crown and the Sceptre of James V of Scotland. With it was the splendid Sword of State presented to James IV by Pope Julian II, as well as the silver mace of the Treasures of Scotland.

At first Sophia was unaware of this, but she turned when she heard her father's voice proclaiming passionately, 'By God, no!' One of the other commissioners, who had not entered into the gravity of the occasion, had actually attempted to put the Crown of Scotland upon the head of one of the young ladies present. Scott's voice was enough to make him lay it down with an air of painful embarrassment.

Scott with his usual desire not to give pain or hurt to the offender said to him: 'Pray forgive me'. He then turned and saw his daughter deadly pale and leaning by the door. He immediately drew her out of the room, and when she had recovered a little in the open air he walked her across the Mound and thus to Castle Street. 'He never spoke all the way home,' she said, 'but every now and then I felt his arm tremble, and from that time I fancied he began to treat me more like a woman than a child. I thought he liked me too better than ever he had done before.'

Scott later wrote a memorandum on the chequered history of the Scottish regalia. At one time he thought of making it the theme of a novel. It is a pity he did not. The strange story of the regalia's movements is a good one and Scott, who more than anyone had a veneration for the outward and visible signs of the past, could have treated it splendidly.

Walter Scott was now easily the most famous of his compatriots and in November of 1818 the Prince Regent, who had loved his work and relished his company, offered him a baronetcy. At first Scott hesitated. He was pleased with the thought that he should be able to give his sons a heritable title, but wondered whether he would be able to support the expense. A lucky windfall to his estate and the sale of his copyright to Constable for £12,000 removed these fears. He accepted. He was glad that his ancient Border name should have a handle that it had often borne in history. He foresaw an obvious quotation from Henry VI: 'I like not such grinning honour as Sir Walter hath', and hoped to go to London at Easter to be received by the Regent, now King.

But, alas, his spasms of pain and cramp returned with increasing violence, and the journey had to be postponed. When he did go that astonishing achievement of the novels of 'the broken years' was behind him. Men have been ennobled for less.

------◆◆◆◆------

13

The Waverley Novels Abroad—
Particularly in America

The Heart of Midlothian which Scott's compatriots and not only his compatriots, consider to be the finest of his native novels, was published in 1818. Beginning with a rumbustious account of the Porteous Riots in the Grassmarket of Edinburgh which, as a protest against the recent Union in 1707, inflamed the capital of Scotland in the early years of the eighteenth century, and containing in the bygoing the description of an eccentric laird's death, known by many critics as 'the funniest deathbed in fiction', it moves to a humble family of peasants living outside the city by Arthur's Seat.

This family, Davie Deans and his two daughters, Effie and Jeannie, thereafter provide the substance of the novel. Davie, an old Scots Covenanter, is appalled at his younger daughter Effie's fate who had allowed herself to be seduced by a sprig of the landed nobility, and to be with child by him. Added to this there is for him the dreadful horror in the fact that Effie had told no one that she was expecting a child. Under a barbarous old Scots law this meant that when she did give birth to an illegitimate child, she would be due to be hanged. She had not even admitted her plight to her elder sister, Jeannie. Davie Deans clearly hints that she might say that she had, but Jeannie, an implacable Scots lover of truth will have none of it. Instead she decides to walk to London in the hope of putting her sister's sad case before the Queen.

This she does, and the centre part of the book is picaresque, taking up an account of her vicissitudes on the four hundred and twenty miles of the road. In London, and in the small society of Scots folk there she is introduced to the great Scottish nobleman, the Duke of Argyll, who is much touched by her fortitude. The Queen (whose knowledge of English is better than King George I's—he only spoke German) who, after one of the most moving pleas put into the mouth of a humble Scots peasant, promises a pardon for Effie with which Jeannie returns to Edinburgh in time to save her sister.

'If it like you, madam,' said Jeannie, 'I would hae gaen to the end of the earth to save the life of John Porteous, or any other unhappy man in his condition; but I might lawfully doubt how far I am called upon to be the avenger of his blood, though it might become the civil magistrate to do so. He is dead and gane to his place, and they that have slain him must answer for their ain act. But my sister, my puir sister, Effie, still lives, though her days and hours are numbered! She still lives, and a word of the King's mouth might restore her to a broken-hearted old man, that never in his daily and nightly exercise forgot to pray that His Majesty might be blessed with a long and prosperous reign, and that his throne, and the throne of his posterity, might be established in righteousness. Oh, madam, if ever ye kend what it is to sorrow for and with a sinning and suffering creature, whose mind is sae tossed that she can be neither ca'd fit to live or die, have some compassion on our misery!—Save an honest house from dishonour, and an unhappy girl, not eighteen years of age, from an early and dreadful death! Alas! It is not when we sleep soft and wake merrily ourselves that we think on other peoples' suffering. Our hearts are waxed light within us then, and we are for righting our ain wrangs and fighting our ain battles. But when the hour of trouble comes to the mind or to the body—and seldom may it visit your Leddyship—and when the hour of death comes, that comes to high and low—lang and late may it be yours! Oh, my Leddy, then it isna what we hae dune for oursells, but what we hae dune for others, that we think on maist pleasantly. And the thoughts that ye hae intervened to spare the puir thing's life will be sweeter in that hour, come when it may, than if a word of your mouth could hang the haill Porteous mob at the tail of ae tow.'

Tear followed tear down Jeanie's cheeks, as, her features glowing and quivering with emotion, she pleaded her sister's cause with a pathos which was at once simple and solemn.

'This is eloquence,' said Her Majesty to the Duke of Argyle.

Coming at the climax of the Scottish Waverley Novels it is a triumph. *The Heart of Midlothian* is Scott at his pure best. As such it is recognized by Scots readers not only in Scotland but wherever they may find themselves. It has been less popular in England, partly because of the essential Scottishness of the story, and partly because the wealth of broad Scots which English readers find difficult, or say they find difficult, to understand.

It was popular in translation in Europe where the language difficulty does not obtrude. From Russia to Spain there is no attempt to reproduce old Scots. The translators have either put the stories direct into their own language or have lapsed into local dialects. The Spaniards have not even attempted the use of Catalan, which would be a fairly reasonable parallel to Scots.

But in the United States of America it was different. Old Scots did not bother them there. Indeed, in their desire to break free of 'Mandarin' English in their own American writing, it set an example.

I was in the Eastern States of America in 1967 when beginning to prepare this book. I was so impressed by the evidence of Scott's one-time influence on the U.S.A. that I made notes of it then and, indeed, wrote a chapter included here as it stands for it is relevant:

Walter Scott's influence on the States of the North American Republic was for long so extraordinary that it deserves a full description. Influence is too weak a word; impact, strong impact, an impact which touched not only the literate and reading public of America but which affected American thought and the American way of life is a better description. The story of Scott and America during his life and for more than half a century after his death in 1832 is interesting, romantic, at times absurd, and at points moving. The comparison drawn earlier between Scott and an 'invention' such as radio or television which touches people of all classes and all tastes, whether devoted to reading generally or not, rises again in one's mind when scanning the accounts of the reception of his genius here.

Here. These words were written in the New York Public Library. Here it has been possible to examine from long defunct journals and from more recent summings up in essay form the story of Scott and America when his impact on the country was most forceful. Here too, and especially farther north in New England and at Boston, it has been possible to talk with learned Americans who know the story

139

and are deeply interested in it as a piece of history—'As exciting,' as one of them said to the present writer, 'and as romantic as a Waverley novel itself; and like a Waverley novel all in the past.'

'Has it no bearing on the present, then?' I could not help asking. 'None. It's a pity Scott has reached an all-time record low with us. No one reads him, no one even prints him. Oh, yes, there are the standard collected editions of his novels on the shelves of all public libraries, but who takes them out? The last novel of his to be printed here in recent times was *Ivanhoe*, and that only for the reason that it was sometimes set as a subject for school examinations. But they've stopped printing even *Ivanhoe* now. It's a great pity, but perhaps this bicentenary and the whole story of Scott, the extraordinary *story* of the man, as presented by your writers and ours here in America, may arouse public interest among us again. I hope so.'

With this information, given with kindness yet with the authority of learning sounding in one's ears, *and* on the spot here in America, it was even stranger to read from old sources and more modern comments of the mighty impact Scott once made in this country.

His epic poetry, *The Lay of the Last Minstrel*, *Marmion* and *The Lady of the Lake* formed for a time the favourite reading and source of recitation in America. These resound-ing verses, so full of imagery and a vivid sense of colour, had had their effect on Continental Europe, but there was always the difficulty of language which confined true pleasure in them to those who at least knew something of the English tongue. No such difficulty appeared even for the simplest readers in America. Nor were there any obstructions lying in the use of the old Scots tongue—obstructions which might have impeded (but did not) the success later in America of the Waverley novels. All was crystal clear, refreshing and invigorating, perhaps a little more than merely refreshing.

The American publisher, Samuel Goodrich, discussing the 'general intoxication' with Scott said:

These productions seized powerfully upon the popular mind. Everybody could read and comprehend them. One of my younger sisters committed the whole of *The Lady of the Lake* to memory and was accustomed of an evening to sit at her sewing while reciting it to an admiring circle of listeners. All young poets were inoculated with the octa-syllabic verse, and newspapers, magazines and even volumes teemed with imitations and variations inspired by the 'Wizard Harp of the North'.

But as at home, and in Europe generally, Byron's fame in this kind of narrative verse drove him from that field. As we have seen, he accepted this defeat from his friend with the utmost generosity and turned with gusto to the Waverley Novels, the first five of which were placed in his own country's past. Now began the mounting story of Scott's impact on America.

The earlier novels, particularly *Waverley* and *The Heart of Midlothian*, had their immediate appeal all over Scotland, and this appeal was partly echoed in England, but there is no denying that Walter Scott's liberal use of the old Scots tongue in the mouths of his peasantry, his aged eccentrics, his men of commerce such as the Baillie Nicol Jarvie did offer difficulties to English readers who thought of this ancient tongue as something no more than a strange, out-landish dialect of their own speech.

No such difficulties appeared for the American readers; or if they did, they relished overcoming them. According to an interesting article, 'The Romance Ferment after Waverley', by G. Harrison Orians in *American Literature:*

> The national features of Scott's novels made the strongest appeal to the ardent spirits of the age. The actors in the Scottish novels displayed their country in their speech.

He goes on to say how this speech inspired American writers to attempt truly national novels. They had a new and grow-ing tongue in which to express themselves. But they did not despise the old historic tongue of Scotland. They did not think of it as a dialect. It came easily to their ears and mouths.

The first purely Scottish Waverley novels made their immediate impact, which was followed by the effect, par-ticularly in the Southern States, of the old novels of chivalry such as *Ivanhoe*. We shall deal with this effect in the south later, for it was the subject of a long-lasting controversy which is not dead yet. But at the beginning it is important to stress the huge influence of Scott at that time all over the States—North as well as South.

Publishing, as apart from printing and bookselling in the shops, publishing as we know it was just beginning in America. And all publishers could, in these pre-copyright days in America, put out an edition of a Scott novel as soon as a copy fell into his hands, free of payment to the author and be sure of a sale. The operative phrase is 'as soon as'; the sooner the better, for the sale would be the larger. Extraordinary shifts (probably the most remarkable of their kind in the history of the printed word) were devised by keenly competitive publishers to gain first access to the pages of a Scott novel.

They had agents in Edinburgh and London to pounce on the first possible copies available of a new Scott novel. They also had agents in Glasgow to be ready for quick transportation across the Atlantic. One publisher was even said to have had the fastest sailing ship moored off Greenock waiting only for the arrival of a new 'Waverley'.

Even if by these means an enterprising publisher in New York, Philadelphia or Boston got a 'three days' edge' on his competitors, it was worth a good deal of money to him locally. He would not be in time, of course, to forestall sales in other towns. The only publisher who was able to achieve this was that remarkable character, Mathew Carey, a born Dubliner, a revolutionary in France and in Ireland and in the end a United States citizen in Philadelphia. He had all the fire, the impetuosity and ingeniousness of his Celtic race.

He it was who 'planted' a workman in Ballantyne's printing office in Edinburgh, or, more probably bribed one who was already there. Through this individual, either planted or bribed, Carey got advance galley proofs or sheets of the novels as they came off the press and easily outdid his competitors in the earlier stages. An extremely interesting article in *The Colophon*, an American 'quarterly for bookmen', appeared in the summer number of 1935. It is by David A. Randall and is entitled 'Waverley in America'.

Mr Randall quotes a letter from Constable, the publisher, to the Postmaster in Edinburgh in 1822. It runs as follows:

Having reason to believe that one or more of the workmen in Mr Ballantyne's Printing Office are in the Practice of Abstracting works in progress of Printing—more especially those of the Author of Waverley—and forwarding the said sheets by means of the Post Office to America, and particularly to Philadelphia, we beg to know if it is consistent with the rules of the Post Office to stop any such sheets so transmitted in order to effect the detection of the person found abstracting our property in this manner.

Constable's appeal to the Post Office had no effect. Advance galleys or sheets of everything Scott had printed in Edinburgh continued for the rest of his life to reach Carey in Philadelphia. Mr Randall even suggests that Ballantyne himself may have been the culprit. It is possible.

Carey worked with ferocious energy as soon as he had received the fruits of his bribery and of his outlay upon especially fast transatlantic schooners. Copy was immediately sent to every printing house in Philadelphia. Mr Randall says that 'it was necessary to keep relays of compositors working over the early sheets night and day'. By such means Carey would have the material ready for the binders in three days. When the binder had got enough done (possibly in one day) to despatch to Carey's outlying clients, he chartered a stage coach; and a young employee called William A. Blanchard (later to become a partner) would gallop off to New York. 'Mounted gallantly on a large pile of Waverley he would ride night and day, ferrying his precious cargo of romance across the North River to the waiting booksellers.'

Even with all this Celtic energy, bribery and extravagant outlay on shipping and special stage coaches, Carey was only able to cover the larger centres in the neighbourhood of Philadelphia, with New York in the lead. Other ships bearing the Edinburgh published novels *in their correct form* would soon be coming across the Atlantic in other fast ships. Carey made no attempt to compete with them, and still they came despite Carey's edge on them.

Men stood on Beacon Hill in Boston scanning the horizon for the sails of their ships bringing over the latest Waverley novel, and when they saw them they would run to the harbour.

It was the same in the South. Mr John Hay said when, as American Ambassador, he unveiled the bust of Sir Walter Scott in Westminster Abbey on 1st May 1897, 'I have heard from my father—a pioneer of Kentucky—that in the early days of this century men would saddle their horses and ride from all neighbouring counties to the principal post-town of the region when a new novel by the Author of Waverley was expected'.

There has never been before or since such a universal craze in America for the works of one novelist. It touched the illiterate as well as the literate. Those who could read did read each novel as it came, read it aloud to families with their servants gathered round them. Not even Dickens whose popularity, despite his attacks on American copyright piracy, was enormous, approached the universal impact of Scott upon *all* North America.

Such an impact by a novelist had never occurred in the United States before Scott, and has not occurred since. In these days of mass entertainment by the many means of mass communication, it is safe to say that it will never happen again. More copies of a popular novelist may be printed and sold in the larger America of today than the Author of Waverley achieved, but they do not strike the heart of a whole nation so that its force is felt for over half a century. This Sir Walter Scott achieved. But he did not get a penny for it. He didn't mind. At least he never complained.

This ferocious piracy of another man's works—a piracy standing merely on an unsatisfactory point of law which everyone knew would have to be changed sometime—was very characteristic of America in its earlier and pioneering days. Equally characteristic of the warm-hearted generosity of the American spirit was the country's reaction when it heard of Scott's later huge financial failure. *The New York American* published an editorial which was copied in every journal in the States. In this article it was suggested that Congress should pass a law granting Scott, and Scott alone, the privilege of American copyright until he was out of his difficulties. Congress was besieged by requests from all over the Republic to pass such a law. That nothing came of it was due to Scott's well-known and much-publicized determination to do the job for himself with his own right hand— and he did.

A point of interest to bibliophiles as well as to the more detailed Walter Scott scholars arises from Carey's practice of stealing advance proofs in galley form. A number of these proofs were radically changed or even entirely cancelled by Scott who, usually extremely anxious to get antiquarian details right was ruthless in the excision of faults arising from his first fine careless raptures. He was right, but those original raptures often concern matters which hold the attention of posterity. By comparing Carey's editions based

144

on uncorrected proofs, we have exact details. Mr Randall in his essay in *Colophon* makes these exact comparisons over a number of books. None need concern a study of Scott such as this is intended to be, but Mr Randall's contention that through Carey we now often know 'what Scott first meant to write' is justified.

It cannot be too strongly stressed that Scott's first impact on America through the Scottish Waverley Novels covered the whole country from North to South. When, however, he branched out into the novels of chivalry placed in England, France or elsewhere, his deepest and most long-lasting influence was upon the Southern States. From Virginia to Texas no less than thirty-five towns were named 'Waverley', others were called 'Kenilworth' and so on. Steamboats on the Mississippi bore the names of 'Rob Roy' and 'The Lady of the Lake'.

No one today can seriously doubt that Scott's mediaeval novels of chivalry had their influence on the 'Gentlemen of the South'. Their manner of fighting in the Civil War, their behaviour at home, kindly, paternal yet aristocratically absolute, leaves no doubt on that question. But how far did that influence go? It would be pointless to examine this question which has been debated at length in the books and literary journals of America for over a hundred years. One of the most famous and eminent writers who took part in this game was Mark Twain, who in his well-known *Life on the Mississippi* said that 'Sir Walter Scott had so large a hand in making Southern Character as it existed before the War that he is in a great measure responsible for the War'.

Mark Twain elaborated his point: 'But for the Sir Walter Scott disease the character of the Southerner—or Southron according to Sir Walter's starchier way of phrasing it would be wholly modern, in place of modern and medieval mixed, and the South would be further advanced than it really is'.

Scott may have been responsible for the sham 'gothick' architecture as seen in the Louisiana Capitol—and it should be remembered he may have been responsible for such bogus building in many other parts of the world outside America. He may have brought in the word 'chivalry' which was unknown in the regional vocabulary before his time. He did not, however, create cotton crops that made for a plantation system; and he did not invent the cotton gin that made slavery possible. It is just possible that, in defeat, the South may have taken some of its forms of expression from Scott's novels—the 'clansmen' of the Klu Klux Klan, and the Fiery Cross, but he did not create them.

Like took to like, and his (Scott's) popularity was as much an effect as the cause of the South's aristocratic and chivalric bias.

This is the truth of the matter; and it is really outside the scope of this study to examine in detail the pro and anti Mark Twain arguments that have gone on ever since he made his charges against Scott in his famous book. They concern domestic American politics rather than the life of Walter Scott.

This point, however, may be made by one who is a compatriot of Scott's.

Mark Twain's ignorant animus against Walter Scott is displayed in one small point already given, but having observed that one point one can read on and see the way his mind was going. In one of the sentences quoted above Mark Twain speaks of the Southerner 'or Southron according to Walter Scott's starchier way of phrasing it'—the implication being that Scott was deliberately using a pompous expression from the world of chivalry. This is completely wrong; the word was and is current in Lowland Scottish speech. In Sir Walter's day it was used by all Border peasants and by most country folk of any class. Walter Scott, whenever he could, and when it did not impede his meaning, loved to use Lowland Scottish words, not so much because they were old, but because the use of them was democratic; it put ordinary folk at their ease when speaking or writing to them.

A small verbal point maybe, but illuminating. Of course Walter Scott threw the highlight of some of his novels on knightly deeds of chivalry and good manners. This was his way of making a part of the past live. In contrast with this, in how many novels does he not make the true hero or heroine a person of the humblest birth? To maintain as Mark Twain did that Scott was deliberately encouraging snobbish anti-democratic feelings is nonsense. The 'Southern Gentlemen' may have used certain characters of his in his novels for models in their 'chivalrous' behaviour. But for this Scott is neither to be praised or blamed. We can safely leave this apparently endless dispute to the American writers and historians of the South. To them it is a dispute in which the word 'chivalry' is constantly being bandied about, and often with little meaning. The dispute will doubtless continue.

In the oddest manner, and while I was preparing this chapter and on American soil, I was confirmed in my opinion—but not in a very literary way. The walls of the subways both in Boston and New York, and other walls in the smaller New England towns, often bear the scribbled message: 'Chivalry is dead'.

These appear so frequently that it is clear that a group of young people have obviously organized themselves in this part of the U.S.A. to spread the message. Of course it is nothing to do with Walter Scott, Mark Twain or the Southern States. Probably a group of beatniks have organized these scribblings to announce their own freedom from what may seem to them the servile cult of good manners.

Whatever the cause, it is an odd experience while preparing for and writing this chapter to see these *graffiti* upon so many walls, announcing in this year so soon before Sir Walter Scott's bicentenary year that 'Chivalry is dead'.

And there is yet one more coincidence. The film of *Gone with the Wind* is enjoying yet one more revival before crowded houses on Broadway as these words are being written. It has now been also revived in England. An American friend of mine who comes from the Southern States, said to me: 'The book of the film could never have been conceived and begotten had it not been for Sir Walter Scott.'

Maybe he is right.

------◆◆◆◆◆------

14

Edinburgh and Abbotsford

By 1820 Walter Scott, though permanently bearing the marks of the broken years, had come over the hill. His *Ivanhoe*, a mediaeval romance now only used in schools, but at that time the most popular of his extra-territorial works, was, outside Scotland and England, 'the most popular of his works' and sold everywhere. Lockhart now became engaged to his daughter, Sophia, whom he married in April.

In March Scott went to London where his portrait was painted by Lawrence at the command of the late Regent now George IV for the Great Gallery at Windsor. His baronetcy was gazetted on March 30th and Oxford and Cambridge each offered him a Doctor's degree. By now Scott often used England and Europe for the scenes of his romances of the past; but he was continually returning to Scottish themes or Scottish characters.

He never truly left the background which had begun his novel writing, and he himself must have been conscious of how his dialogue sprang to life when he had a Scottish character speaking. *The Fortunes of Nigel*, though placed in London, is animated by James VI and I.

His week in Edinburgh was spent at his house in Castle Street, but at the end of the week he turned to his beloved Abbotsford. He would wear his country clothes under his lawyer's black gown, and by evening he was in his own Sheriffship, on his way to Abbotsford where he could stay until late on Monday. Monday is a *Dies Non* in the Edinburgh Courts. As his work at the Court of Session only occupied six months of the year, he was free to come down to Abbotsford to undertake his light Sheriff duties. In his absence in Edinburgh his place in the Sheriff Court was filled by his Sheriff Substitute.

Both in Edinburgh and at Abbotsford he took his main meal of the day at breakfast between nine and ten; but before that he had got up early and put in a full day's work at his writing beginning at five o'clock when the rest of the household still slept. Those who met him at Castle Street, Edinburgh, or those who enjoyed his increasing hospitality at Abbotsford had no idea they were speaking to a man whose private work for the day was behind him. He could then join in society and in his club life.

In Edinburgh, which by 1820 was still trailing clouds of glory from the late eighteenth century, there was much good conversation and many dining clubs for men only. Scott loved these clubs; and it was he who as far back as 1803 had founded 'The Friday Club', one without politics for it contained both Whigs and Tories.

Henry Cockburn, later Lord Cockburn, was an ardent Whig and author of *Memorials of his Time*, still read today. He was a member of one of these clubs. Lockhart quotes him: 'I can never forget the pregnant expression of one of the ablest of that school and body [The Whigs], Lord Cockburn who, when some glib youth chanced to echo in his hearing the consolatory level of local mediocrity, answered quietly: "I have the misfortune to think differently from you—in my humble opinion Walter's Scott's sense is a still more wonderful thing than his genius".'

There was one daily duty he attended to vigorously. Both at Edinburgh and at Abbotsford, Scott's daily post was enormous and increased. He made it a rule to answer all of these letters (with the exception of those which were impertinent or merely frivolous) and in his own handwriting every day. Some of these letters were of use to him. Antiquarians sent him curious bits of lore and there were ghost stories and fragments of Jacobite tradition; but most of them, apart from those from his friends, were soliciting help on literary matters; but he answered them all. He even had to cope with a novel sent to him by a female admirer in America. Yet he dealt with it.

His late breakfast his main meal, Scott would, however, join in late suppers, often moving round the table. The war with France being over he was able to serve French wines. He gave champagne when it was available and insisted on at least a pint of claret for guests young or old after the meal. He did not care for port and supported John Home's belief, expressed in the well-known quatrain:

> Firm and erect the Caledonian stood,
> Old was his mutton, and his claret good.
> You shall drink port, the Saxon cried;
> He took the poison and his spirit died.

This refers to England's treaty with Portugal by means of which she tried to enforce port on Scotland after 1770—but failed.

Scott liked claret well enough but in the evenings he preferred to take whisky and water. He gave large quaichs of whisky to his piper at Abbotsford, but was distressed by those who ruined themselves by indiscriminate drinking—what we would now call alcoholism. He looked upon wine and whisky as the gifts of God to be enjoyed, not misused.

All agree that his conversation, particularly at Abbotsford, was fascinating. He loved to quote stories, reminiscences and, using his prodigious memory, extracts from books. Lockhart says of him:

In the course of conversation he happened to quote a few lines from one of the old Border ballads, and, looking round I was quite astonished with the changes which seemed to have passed over every feature in his countenance. His eyes seemed no longer to glance quick and grey from beneath his impending brows, but were fixed in their expanded eyelids with a sober, solemn lustre. His mouth (about which are at all times lines wonderfully expressive) instead of the usual language of mirth or benevolence or shrewdness was filled with a sad and peculiar earnestness. The whole face was tinged with a glow which showed its lines in new energy and transparence, and the thin hair, parting backwards displayed in tenfold majesty his Shakespearean pile of forehead.

John Adolphus, who published criticisms of the Waverley novels and who often saw Scott at Abbotsford, says:

Never, perhaps, did a man go through the gradations of laughter with such complete enjoyment or countenance so radiant. The first dawn of a humorous thought could show itself sometimes as he sat silent by an involuntary lengthening of the upper lip, followed by a shy sidelong glance at his neighbours, indescribably whimsical and seeming to ask from their looks whether the spark of drollery should be allowed to blaze out. In the full tide of mirth he did indeed laugh 'the heart's laughter' . . . but it was not boisterous and overpowering, nor did it check the course of his words; he could go on telling or descanting while his lungs 'did crow like Chantecleer', his syllables, in the struggle growing more emphatic, his accent more strongly Scotch, and his voice plaintive with excess of merriment.

Adolphus was an English barrister and Scott's normal voice would seem to him 'Scotch'. He never attempted to speak Southern English and there is reason to believe that he had the East of Scotland 'burr' in his rs. He could, of course, speak with his tenantry and with those he met on the roads round Abbotsford in pure Border—of a kind you can still hear.

Scott had no musical ear and could not sing or whistle the simplest tune. As all know who have read Madge Wildfire's wild speech in *The Heart of Midlothian*, he had a strong lyrical gift in verse. When he quoted his or other poets' lyrics his whole face became illuminated.

At Abbotsford Scott was easily the most popular figure on the Borders. Hogg, the Ettrick shepherd, said: 'He was the only one I ever knew whom no man either poor or rich held at ill will.' And in illustration tells a simple story. Once when Scott was dining with the Hoggs at Mount Benger, he took up his hostess's little daughter, kissed her, and laying his hand on her head said: 'God Almighty bless you, my dear child.' Hogg found his wife in tears and asked why she was weeping. 'Oh,' she cried, 'I thought that if he had just done the same to them all, I do not know what in the world I should not have given.'

Maria Edgeworth made a pertinent remark about the Abbotsford régime: 'Dean Swift had written his books in order that people might treat him like a great lord. Sir Walter Scott writes his that he may be able to treat his people as a great lord ought to do.'

Walter Scott has sometimes been accused in his foundation and treatment of Abbotsford of trying to rise in the social scale by becoming a Border laird. There is nothing in this accusation. His father may have been an Edinburgh solicitor but he was cousin to the Scotts of Harden, an ancient family whose descent had not had to pass through the female line as had the Buccleuchs. Walter's mother was a Haliburton, a Border family of lineage who had the right of burial at Dryburgh Abbey. Scott's ambition at Abbotsford may have moved from his boyhood in George's Square and his pleading at Parliament House, but at Abbotsford he was socially doing no more than reverting to type.

No, if there is a criticism of Scott at Abbotsford it lies in his passion for buying more and more land about it—not for farming but merely to possess it and to plant it with trees. This was to be one of the sources of his eventual ruin. But such ruin in the early days at Abbotsford was something he never thought of. In the early hours of each morning he could go on writing novels which could safely go on bringing him in many thousands of pounds. He was by means of his Waverley novels earning more money than any author in Europe or America, at its best £10,000 a year. Why should this happy state of affairs stop?

Why indeed? But Scott had already had warning of the plight he could find himself in when the printing firm with which he had involved himself got into difficulties over the pernicious habit of the backing of bills which passed from hand to hand in the small country of Scotland where cash and even bank notes were scarce.

To quote a biography which appeared at the time of the centenary of his death in 1832: 'He drew bills on the Ballantyne firm which Constable backed; he drew bills on Constable for work not yet done; and always there were counter bills whereby accommodation granted to one party was set off by a like accommodation to another. The consequence was that the true meaning of each transaction was obscured. When cash was received the temptation was to apply it for some purpose for which cash was obligatory like the masons' accounts at Abbotsford instead of paying off the bills which could be easily renewed. So long as a man was able to work and in good repute there was no need to be a hitch, but ill health, death or the disaster of a colleague might bring down the whole edifice in ruins.'

This was to happen to Walter Scott in 1826. But he ought to have seen it coming and, above all, he should have curbed his apparently almost insatiable desire to buy land round Abbotsford, land which brought him not one penny.

It is easy for us at this date to blame Scott, but one has only to think of the effect of the publication of *The Fortunes of Nigel* in 1822 which stormed London at once. The London orders reached there on a Sunday by boat. On Monday 9,000 copies were in the publisher's hands. Men, going to work were seen reading copies of it in the street.

Why should all this stop? But it did, and it was Abbotsford that was largely the cause of it and of Scott's ruin.

There is a saying that 'whenever a Scotsman gets his head above water he turns it to land'. This certainly was true of Scott and Abbotsford—the planting of trees on the estate there became an obsession with him.

'Trees', he exclaimed, 'are like children, interesting to strangers when grown up, but to parents and planters from the nursery. Interesting! You can have no idea of the exquisite delight of a planter; he is like a painter laying on his colours: at every moment he sees his efforts coming out. There is no art or occupation comparable to this; it is full of past, present and future enjoyment. I look back to the time when there was not a tree here, only a bare heath. I look round and see thousands of trees growing up each and all of which, I may say almost each of which have received my personal attention.

'Unlike building or painting or indeed any other kind of pursuit this has no end and is never interrupted but goes on from day to day and from year to year with perpetual mounting interest.

'Farming I hate—what have I to do with fattening and killing beasts or raising corn only to cut it down and to wrangle with farmers about it, and be constantly at the mercy of the seasons? There can be no disappointments or annoyance in planting trees.

'I promise you my oaks will outlive my laurels [a reference to his books], and I pique myself more upon my compositions for manure than any other compositions to which I was ever accessory.'

This was going too far. If it had not been for his laurels he could not have planted his oaks. His literary compositions, his poems and, above all, his novels were far more fruitful to his native land of Scotland than horse-dung and thousands upon thousands of trees.

The laird of Abbotsford was the most famous landed proprietor in the Borders and, indeed, in all Scotland. Not only his friends and neighbours but people from England and all over the world flocked to see him at his Border home. He relished their arrival, and did his best to entertain them.

Those like Sir Humphrey Davy, who was a keen angler, would be sent off accompanied by Scott's servant to fish Tweed. Others mounted on Shetland ponies would ride, find their way through the green rides of the plantation, go on the magical Eildon Hills and drop down to Melrose. There was always something for everyone to do, and Scott's pleasure was to see that they were able to do it even if his body, broken by years of illness, would not allow him to accompany them. His own angling and coursing days were over. He could no longer wield a spear at the 'burning of the water' on Tweed, but he took the ship's helm and would hold a light.

His hospitality was endless, and about it there was not a touch of the Border laird's snobbishness. Famous people, including an occasional foreign prince, called on him to see the great man at home. There would be brother writers, Edinburgh lawyers and innumerable people who had enjoyed his books. Modestly Scott felt that to entertain them at his best was no more than he owed a public which had treated him so handsomely.

All this was excellent, and if I may be allowed to express one regret, it is that I was born too late to have enjoyed Walter Scott at Abbotsford.

The Abbotsford Hunt was the scene of splendiferous hospitality. Lockhart says, 'How they all got home in safety Heaven only knows—but I never heard of a serious accident except upon one occasion when James Hogg made a bet at starting that he would leap over the wall on his one-eyed pony as she stood and broke his nose in this experience of o'er vaulting ambition'. One goodwife, far off among the hills, told Scott that when her husband alighted at home he said, 'Oh, Ailie my woman, I'm ready for my bed—and oh lass I could sleep for a towmonth, for there's only as thing in this world worth living for and that's the Abbotsford Hunt.'

Scott's ambition as the laird of Abbotsford was worthy and generous. It is a pity that he did not take thought of the financial outcome of that boundless ambition and that generosity.

A pity maybe, but if he had never encountered that outcome in later years, we would never have known of what heroic stuff he was made.

------◆◆◆◆◆------

15

The Royal Visit to Edinburgh.
Royal Junketings

Walter Scott through his genius and because his books were universally read in his time, saved his native country of Scotland at a period when she was in danger of becoming, for foreigners, little more than the 'knuckle end' of the greater, more potent and increasingly famous England. This is beyond dispute.

Nevertheless the modern Scottish Nationalist, particularly those associated in that literary movement which, for fifty years has been known as 'the Scottish Renaissance' are apt to dismiss him as a compromiser, one who unduly allowed himself to be influenced by England and the glory of Great Britain, and at a time when Britain (usually known as England) was at the beginning of her greatest century. While not, for one moment agreeing with this, it is possible to see what they mean.

Scott had considerable reservations about the Prince Regent, later to become George IV. He had little use for George's vanity, or luxurious living and free sexual behaviour. Earlier on Scott had met and sympathized with his abandoned wife, Caroline of Brunswick. This did not prevent him from being mildly flattered by the Royal attention he had received from George both as Regent and as King.

As Regent, George gave a select dinner party at Carlton House to which he invited Scott. The jokes were uncensored and the conversation free. They discussed Jacobitism openly. Scott called Charles Edward Stuart the Prince; the Regent referred to him as 'the Pretender'. This led to the Regent asking Scott whether he would have followed the Jacobites.

Rather regrettably Scott replied: 'I should have, at least, wanted one motive in doing so, in not knowing your Royal Highness.'

In a later letter to a friend he said: 'I never used the word 'Pretender', which is a most unseemly word, in my life except when (God help me) I was obliged to take the oaths of Abjuration and Supremacy at election time and so forth, and even then I did it with a qualm of conscience. Seriously, I am very glad I did not live in 1745, for though as a lawyer I could not have pleaded Charles's right, and as a clergyman I could not have prayed for him, yet as a soldier I would, I am sure, against the conviction of my better reason, have fought for him even to the bottom of the gallows. But I am not in the least afraid nowadays of making my feelings walk hand in hand with my judgement, though the former are Jacobital, the latter inclined for public weal to the present succession.'

The Regent's amiability to Scott pleased him. He refused, however, to admit that his abilities were exceptional (he made something of a mistake here), and called him in private correspondence by Beau Brummel's name 'our fat friend'. The Regent gave Scott a golden, jewel-studded snuff-box with a medallion of the donor's head on it. Scott took this back to Abbotsford.

Edinburgh and Scotland in general were only too pleased that their most famous man of letters should have won Royal approval in this way. It is doubtful, however, if Whig Edinburgh and Whig London would have approved his openly expressed admiration amounting to veneration for the Duke of Wellington, whom he met after Waterloo.

In justice to Scott it should be remembered that he had passed all his youth until middle-age under the threat of a Napoleonic invasion. At the same time it should not be forgotten that a fair amount of Whig society, particularly in London, was not anti-Napoleon. Byron himself, when he heard of Waterloo, said, 'I'm damned sorry'. Politicians such as Charles James Fox felt that life after Napoleon's final defeat and exile to St Helena made the world a duller place.

Scott, the Scottish Tory, was quite untouched by this. He did not hear much of it, and Byron's difference from him on the point afforded the only flaw in their friendship.

The victory of Waterloo caused Scott's British patriotism to arise to fever-pitch. Accompanied by three friends he made a pilgrimage to the battlefield to write a book about it. In Paris he had the supreme gratification of sitting next to the great general at supper and at Wellington's request.

Scott was completely bowled over and later confessed that 'although he had conversed with all classes of society, princes, poets, peers and peasants, he had never felt awed or abashed except in the presence of the Duke, the greatest soldier and statesman in history'. Someone later suggested that the Duke might have been pleased at meeting a great poet and novelist. To which Walter Scott replied: 'What would the Duke of Wellington think of a few bits of novels which perhaps he had never read, and for which the probability is that he could not care sixpence if he had?'

As one of the best of his biographers points out: 'In this instance Scott's natural humility was a vice, however attractive on most occasions. To imply as he did that literary creation was inferior to martial action displayed a lamentable lack of values. *Macbeth* means more to humanity than the defeat of the Spanish Armada and *Old Mortality* gives pleasure to generations that have lost interest in the Battle of Waterloo. We could not even say that Scott's feeling of inferiority was because he wrote for money. He wrote because he could not help writing, delighted though he was that the money poured in. His awe in the Duke's presence was primarily caused by his shrunken leg which kept him from military life and gave him a permanent feeling of frustration, and secondly by his under-estimation of his own work due to the ease with which he wrote it. If anyone had told him that Shakespeare was abashed in the presence of Drake he would have laughed at the notion, but he would still have failed to see the absurdity of his own feeling in the presence of the Duke.' That has just about said it.

Scott wrote a poem, *The Field of Waterloo*, giving the profits of the first edition to the widows and children of the slain. It is not one of his happiest efforts and provoked the lines of a contemporary critic:

> On Waterloo's ensanguined plain
> Full many a gallant man was slain,
> But none by bullets or by shot
> Fell half as flat as Walter Scott.

Scott's reservations about the character of George IV and his sympathy for the abandoned wife, Queen Caroline, did not prevent him from going to London to attend the huge coronation of 1821. He offered to take James Hogg with him with the idea of getting some job or pension for him. The sturdy independence of the Ettrick Shepherd made him refuse on the ground that he did not wish to miss the annual fair at St Boswell's Green. Scott loved such pageantrys as coronations and sent a vivid account to James Ballantyne's paper in which he didn't mind paying tribute to his own fame:

Missing his carriage, he had to return home on foot after the banquet—that is to say between two or three o'clock in the morning—when he and a young gentleman, his companion, found themselves locked in a crowd somewhere near Whitehall, and the bustle and tumult were such that his friend was afraid that some accident might happen to the lame limb. A space for the dignataries was kept clear at that part by the Scots Greys. Sir Walter addressed a serjeant of this celebrated regiment, begging to be allowed to pass by him into the open ground in the middle of the street. The man answered sternly that his orders were strict—that the thing was impossible. While he was endeavouring to persuade the serjeant to relent his young companion exclaimed in a loud voice 'take care, Sir Walter, take care'. The stalwart dragoon, on hearing the name, said: 'What, Sir Walter Scott? He shall get through anyhow.' He then addressed the soldiers near him. 'Make room, men, for Sir Walter Scott, our illustrious countryman!' The men answered: 'Sir Walter Scott! God bless him!'—and he was in a moment over the guarded line of safety.

Queen Caroline caused a jarring note at the Coronation. She had been supported by the Tories when she had separated from the Whiggish Prince, and Scott had visited her at Blackheath. In all but name the King had forsaken his one-time friends and become a Tory, and the Whigs therefore leapt to the defence of what they called 'a much wronged woman'. She left England in 1814 for Italy from which odd rumours of her conduct reached the ears of her husband, who now assumed a moral position and arranged for a Bill of Divorcement in the House of Lords.

But the Regent (as he still was then) was unpopular with the mob; Caroline was ably defended by Brougham; and the Bill was withdrawn for fear of revolution. When they heard of this the populace went wild with excitement. They paraded the streets of London, and threw stones at windows that were not lighted up to celebrate the abandonment of the divorce proceedings.

They lit a huge fire on Hampstead Heath, and the figures of those Italians who had given evidence against the Queen's chastity were burnt in effigy. Bergami, with whom she was supposed to have committed adultery, became a national hero and might indeed have been feasted and drawn through the streets in an unhorsed carriage had he appeared in public. The newspapers went so far as to say that a mob had attacked Abbotsford and had broken the windows, for it was known that Scott was Royal George's friend. One of Scott's friends in England wrote to him about this. Scott answered: 'I can never conceive a Selkirk mob so numerous but I would have met them beard to beard and driven them backward home before they came within two miles of Abbotsford. I can only add that if a set of madmen had been so determined as to come within four miles of my peaceful home, I would have fired from window and battlement and kept my castle, while my castle kept me.'

Scott, because of his earlier support of Caroline, was not surprised that she wished to be avenged on her husband, but he was under no illusions about her or her supporters. 'If she had as many followers of high as of low degree (in proportion) and funds to equip them,' he said, 'I should not be surprised to see her fat bottom in a pair of buckskins, and at the head of our army in England—God mend all!' He added that the mob did not really want a happy reunion of George and Caroline, their real feeling being expressed by the gallery of an Irish theatre which yelled a compliment to a lady whose amours were notorious: 'Huzza for Lady C.! —and long may she live to cuckold the Chancellor!'

Scott brought his usual good sense to the scandal of the day. When the Regent became King, Caroline announced her intention of coming to live at Holyrood Palace in Edinburgh; the Privy Council asked him how this could be prevented. He replied that the Queen's entry could not possibly be opposed by force, but he recommended that fifty or sixty workmen should at once be put into the Palace to repair part of it, take up the floors of rooms, thus making the building uninhabitable. His advice was taken. The Queen gave up her intention of retiring to Scotland, but caused an uproar by attempting to force an entry to her husband's coronation at Westminster Abbey.

Some of the crowd cried 'Shame! Shame!' but there were others (possibly hired for the purpose) who encouraged her with shouts of 'That's it, Caroline! Go it, my girl!' A discreditable episode which made Scott dismiss her as 'the Bedlam bitch of a Queen'!

In 1822 George IV decided to visit Scotland—the first Hanoverian monarch to come to the Northern Kingdom. Scott not only persuaded the King to visit Edinburgh, but became entirely responsible for running the whole show. Such trivial questions were put to him by the Town Council as to whether the inscription on Waterloo Bridge, recording that Prince Leopold of Belgium had been present at its opening should be erased, since King George would pass over it and he was not on speaking terms with his son-in-law, the future ruler of Belgium. Scott's reply was characteristic. 'I would rather see Edinburgh on fire than attempt to spare the King's feelings by a sacrifice of our own dignity.'

There were countless committees to prepare for the Royal visit. But as soon as Scott reached Edinburgh he found everything in confusion, and, at the Town Council's request, was made a general adviser on every matter so that all were soon placed voluntarily into his hands. From early morning his house in Castle Street was 'like a fair' until midnight. At least sixty people a day came to him for advice, to settle quarrels, to smooth difficulties, soften prejudices and be in touch with all societies, creeds, professions and public bodies in Scotland. In the end everything was arranged in Walter Scott's way.

Some three hundred Highlanders were brought down from the North, well armed and bearing pipes. As the chiefs were jealous of each other this was all submitted to Scott's management, and he had scores of them parading in Castle Street each day with their pipes and banners; indeed some critics felt that these Celtic Highlanders stole the show by occupying too prominent a place in the various ceremonies. But Scott found them picturesque and romantic, as indeed they were.

For a month he worked hard at the job with unblemished good humour and zeal. He even found time to show the ruins of St Anthony's Chapel and Muschat's Cairn by Arthur's Seat (memorable for a scene from *The Heart of Midlothian*) to the English poet Crabbe who came up to stay in Castle Street about a week before the King's arrival.

'Crabbe is such a sly hound', said Scott, 'that I could never find out whether he was pleased or not. Crabbe was amazed when confronted with the Highland chieftains to whom he spoke French, supposing their lingo "was a sort of Gallic dialect".' Crabbe was the rural parson poet of England. His 'sly behaviour' may be accounted for by the not generally known fact referred to earlier, that to the end of his life he indulged in increasing doses of morphia. Scott, whose body and principles loathed the drug, certainly did not know this.

King George, accompanied by warships, came up in his own yacht and anchored off Leith in pouring rain. When the yacht touched the shore Scott's presence was announced to the Royal visitor, who exclaimed: 'What, Sir Walter Scott! The man in Scotland I most want to see. Let him come up.' Walter Scott made a speech of welcome on the quarterdeck. King George replied, called for whisky and drank to his baronet's health. Scott returned the compliment and begged for the glass from which the King had drunk. This he placed carefully in the skirt tail pocket of his coat.

When he got back to Castle Street he got so absorbed in telling the story to his visitor, Crabbe, that he sat on it, crushing the carefully salvaged glass to bits.

Now began the great tartan eruption which has caused much merriment to posterity. The King, in an effort to carry on the tradition of Prince Charles Edward Stuart when at Holyrood in 1745, draped his podgy legs in what was described as the Royal Stuart Tartan. He was accompanied by a large London alderman, Sir William Curtis, who made a bigger, fatter Highlandman than the King.

To follow the Royal example the fashionable set in Edinburgh and even some of the middle classes arrayed themselves in the 'garb of old Gaul'; and even Scott sported the tartan. All this was extremely bogus. In the eighteenth century Lowlanders, and particularly the upper class in the Edinburgh set, regarded the Highlanders as so many savages, and would never have dreamed of wearing the tartan, still less the kilt; but Scott's romantic novels combined with the Royal visit changed their minds and did the trick. The fashion still remains. You may find in the streets of Edinburgh plenty of middle-class Lowland Edinburgh people wearing the kilt and sporting a tartan to which they vaguely say they 'have a right' in some ill-defined way on their mother's side.

In the eighteenth century there was little, if any, tartan tradition attached to name and clans; in general the Macdonalds and their septs wore red and the Campbells green. But the result of the Royal visit in 1822 was that an enterprising tailor at Bannockburn invented (there is no other name for it) tartan for every Highland name and even for some Lowland ones. The purists smile at this, but it is worth pointing out that a tradition that began in 1822 has now some weight behind it.

All this was the direct result of the Waverley novels and of the Hanoverian Royal visit. The modern Scottish Nationalists and the supporters of the nineteenth-century 'Scottish Renaissance' blame Walter Scott for this. But why should they? His epic poem *The Lady of the Lake* had sent tourists flocking into Scotland to visit Loch Katrine. He was only doing the same for the capital of Scotland in 1822.

The King stayed at Dalkeith Palace, but came into Edinburgh every day. Scott accompanied him everywhere. When he was walking in the High Street with his monarch, Sir Robert Peel noticed that the people received him with 'hardly less veneration' than the King.

After his success over the Scottish regalia Scott took advantage of the King's presence in Scotland to press national points on which he was anxious. He obtained a promise that the famous Scottish cannon 'Mons Meg' should return to Edinburgh Castle. This was a massive piece of ordnance made in France or Flanders which had burst whilst firing a salute in 1689 and it had been much treasured by the Scottish nation, but had been removed to London after the failure of the Rising of 1745. Nearer to Scott's heart was a petition which he successfully pressed upon the King; that was that the peerages forfeited after the Jacobite risings of 1715 and 1745 should be restored.

It is easy at this date to smile at Scott's tartan junketings in the Edinburgh of 1822, but he at least was assiduous in pressing Scotland's claims, and, more practically than in his novels, doing something about it.

The King's visit to Edinburgh lasted a fortnight, and George was deeply aware of how much Scott had done to make it a success; he was very grateful. It was just as well that he never learned of Scott's refusal to write the words for a new National Anthem; and he would not have been very pleased if he could have seen a letter from Morrit, Scott's English friend, who said of the King's favourite buildings at Brighton: 'Will you do me a favour? Set fire to the Chinese stables, and if it embraces the whole of the Pavilion [put up at the King's behest] it will rid us of a great eyesore.'

Today all that remains of an outward and visible sign of the great tartan fortnight of the Edinburgh Royal visit is a handsome and rather flattering statue of George IV in George Street at the corner of Hanover Street. The King stands there gazing up at the High Street on the Castle Rock.

The tartan fortnight in Edinburgh being over, Scott retired quietly to Abbotsford where he got on with his real job in projecting his country to a larger world in his Waverley novels.

16

Waverley and Wealth

Scott, like other prolific authors, could write very limpingly as well as on the top of his form. His style has often and with justification been criticized as clumsy, but sometimes the tales themselves lack fire and interest only to be followed by brilliant inventions. He had the true itch to write and write at all costs, but alas! the desire to write was sometimes stronger than the power to create. Then hot on the heels of such a failure might well follow a splendid unforgettable tale.

Examples may be found in two Waverley novels which followed soon after the Royal visit. *The Pirate* was the result of a visit he had made to the islands of Orkney and Shetland in 1814 and which made him long to write of their unique landscape. He did so, attempting to bring the Northern Isles into contrast with the modern world of Scotland's mainland. It was a good idea but failed in that the inspiration was as 'shadowy as the Shetland sky'. His descriptions of island scenery are excellent, but it is difficult to believe in the characters which he made himself believe inhabited it. They are buckram. Once again, as in *Guy Mannering*, he tries to introduce a spae-wife like Meg Merrilies, but he fails. Scott's knowledge of the northern part of Scotland (true knowledge) does not go much beyond Perthshire, and when he tries to write about the far Highlands or anything so remote as the Northern Isles his inspiration for writing on the people who live there does not rise to a point that can convince us.

Despite the tartan fever of picturesqueness which he was able to provoke in Edinburgh at the Royal visit, Scott was essentially a Lowlander of the Lowlanders and in essence a

Border man at that. He had in his ancestry certain remote Highland and Celtic strains which, incidentally, enabled him to wear the Campbell tartan during the Royal visit. But oddly enough his very name proclaimed his true original Highland origin. 'Scott' means or meant an Irish incomer to Scotland of the immigration that centuries before passed into the Highlands. Neither in Walter Scott's day were there, nor in our day are there, any indigenous Scotts in the Highlands. They all marched south across the Firth of Forth, particularly into the Borders long before.

After *The Pirate* and the not very successful *The Abbot*, Scott achieved one of the most memorable of his novels, *The Fortunes of Nigel*, published in 1822 which at once deals with Scottish affairs and with London. It concerns the 'flitting', as the Scots say, of James VI of Scotland to become James I of England. He is accompanied by his purse-bearer, the wealthy George Heriot, or Jingling Geordie. This Waverley novel has also the distinction of an introductory letter in which Scott for the first time sets forth his own view of the novelist's craft. He frankly decides to give the public what it wanted: 'No man shall find me rowing against the stream', nor did he usually think much of the form of his novels: 'I should be chin deep in the grave, man,' he wrote to Constable, 'before I had done with my tasks, and in the meanwhile all the "quirks and quiddities" which I have devised for my readers' amusement would lie rotting in my gizzard.' He also speaks in favour of rapid and frequent production: 'A man should strike while the iron is hot, and hoist sail while the wind is fair. If a successful writer keeps not on the stage, another instantly takes his ground.' Shakespeare would have approved of this.

Having given us this interesting introduction, Scott launches as vividly into the world of London after 1603 when the Scots King came down to succeed to Queen Elizabeth's throne.

James VI and I, the 'wisest fool in Christendom', is one of the oddities of Scottish and English history. He was the only Stuart monarch in the long line of that succession to be totally lacking in charm or glamour. Yet he was at once ridiculous and impressive. Speaking his native broad Scots in London, without any attempt to anglify it, he must have puzzled his English courtiers. For all this speech, which must have seemed to the Londoners half foreign, half provincial, he impressed them by his scholarship and learning.

Much of the success of his talk in Scott's novel about him in London rests in Latinized jargon followed quickly by exact Scots translation—as example, his knighting of Richard Monoplies:

> He took the drawn sword, and with averted eyes, for it was a sight he loved not to look on, endeavoured to lay it on Richies' shoulder, but nearly stuck it in his eye. Richie, starting back, attempted to rise, but was held down by Lowestoffe while Sir Mungo, guiding the royal weapon, the honour-bestowing blow was given and received; 'Surge carnifex—rise up, Sir Richard Monoplies of Castle-Callop!—and, my lords and lieges let us all to our dinner for the cock-a-leekie is cooling.'

Lockhart quotes Constable, who was in London the day of publication. He wrote thus to Scott: 'I was in town yesterday, and so keenly were the people devouring my friend *Jingling Geordie* that I actually saw them reading it in the streets as they passed along. I assure you there is no exaggeration in this. A new novel from the Author of Waverley puts aside—in other words puts down for the time, every other literary performance. The smack *Ocean*, by which the new work was shipped, arrived at the wharf on Sunday; the bales were got out one by one on Monday morning and before half past they had dispersed. . . . I wish I had the power of prevailing with you to give us a similar production every three months; and that our ancient enemies on this side the Border might not have it too much their own way, perhaps your next venture might be Bannockburn.'

As Scott extended the field of what he was writing about in the Waverley novels he continually, as it were, kept glancing over his shoulder home to Scotland. He did this in the novel which was to make his fame in France and to influence so many French novelists, *Quentin Durward*. This novel was largely responsible for much of Dumas' output and for much historical novel-writing in France.

Situated in France at the time of the strange, superstitious Louis XI, the hero of the tale is a young member of the Royal Scots Guard which, since the Franco-Scottish Alliance had been drawn from the Scottish aristocracy to protect the person of the French Kings. Quentin Durward, and his adventures, coming so recently from Scotland, in France and in particular with the preposterous, crafty, scheming Louis XI make excellent reading. It is a study of the 'auld alliance' between Scotland and France.

The Waverley novels were coming out so quickly now that people in England had not time to digest *Quentin Durward* before they heard of its overwhelming success in France.

It created a furore there. Fashionable ladies began to wear gowns of the Stuart tartan 'à la Walter Scott' and there were strings of carriages outside the shops where the novel was on sale. This had its effect on the home market, and despite the proliferation of the Waverley novels, it too became a success here. All seemed set fair for the laird of Abbotsford. If he could have been able to produce his extraordinary five books during the years of illness, what could he not do when his strength was restored?

17

The Strange Case of Redgauntlet

Redgauntlet was the only novel Scott published in 1824. It is in many ways and at once the most remarkable product of Walter Scott's imagination and the most personal.

It is personal in that the two young men through whose eyes and pens and mouths the novel is begun and carried forward are based on himself and his friend Will Clerk; there is also a sympathetic and likeable portrait of Scott's own father.

It is more deeply personal in that through a purely imaginary Jacobite adventure in the latter half of the eighteenth century and well after the last real failure of Jacobitism in Prince Charles Edward Stuart's gallant affair of 1745–46 Scott lets us see his true feelings about the decline of Scotland into England.

Whether he intended to do this or not does not matter; he may well have been impelled by his subconscious dreams; but Scott's subconscious feelings about Scotland often represent the true Walter Scott.

It is perhaps not too much to say that large parts of the novel spring from Walter Scott's personal feelings about the dying old Scottish tongue. Nowhere else does he write dialogue and, indeed, long passages in the Scots tongue more effectively, more truly, than here.

In *Redgauntlet* Scott presents us with a supposed Jacobite attempt, this time on the Lowlands near the Solway Firth. He does not give an exact date for it; but as the middle-aged Prince Charles Edward comes into the tale and is addressed by his followers as 'King', it must have been soon after the death of his exiled father (the Old Pretender or, more properly, James VIII and III) in 1766.

The novel begins in that now outmoded, but at that time still effective device of an exchange of letters between Alan Fairford (the youthful Scott) and Darsie Latimer (Will Clerk). Later when Fairford joins his friend in the South West of Scotland the tale takes the now more usual narrative form.

At the beginning Latimer bombards his friend with long letters describing his adventures in Dumfriesshire and on the way to the South West. In the course of this he transcribes a blind beggar's tale (Wandering Willie's Tale) which a well-known critic has described as 'one of the greatest of the world's short stories'; certainly Walter Scott never surpassed anything in this vein. What it is about and extracts from it come later.

Alan Fairford (Scott, be it remembered) learns that his friend Darsie Latimer is in some mysterious way caught up in plots and counter plots in the South West of Scotland, and that Darsie's birth and blood have involved him in these. He then sets off to join his friend and to find out what it is all about, and leaves a letter for his father to say so. Alexander Fairford (Scott's father) is much distressed by this, for he knows something of the mystery which his son is pursuing but he fails to prevent his son's flight to his friend.

The two young men find themselves involved in strange happenings in the South West of Scotland, where the Firth of Solway moves in tides and storms between the Kingdom of Scotland and the Kingdom of England. This leads us to the crux of the tale, the imaginary Jacobite rising amidst this wild scenery in about 1766. This we shall return to later, for it is, apart from being a high piece of drama, most significant as showing Walter Scott's feelings.

That Walter Scott's prose leaps to life the moment he writes dialogue in the Scottish language is generally agreed; indeed it is self-evident. It makes his English prose, and certainly his English dialogue, stilted. When Scott wrote letters to his friends you can hear the Scotch accent which Adolphus remarked at Abbotsford, but when he wrote his fiction in English that accent disappears.

In *Redgauntlet* the letters between the two young men are not stilted because they are personal reminiscences drawn from his own youth and from the youth of a close friend of his. In the occasional dialogue in the Borders the Scots is authentic, but it is not enough to suit the author's half-secret longing for a something more than a dialogue. This he satisfied in 'Wandering Willie's Tale', told by a blind man to David Latimer and recalled in a letter to his friend. It is worth quoting two extracts from it, the opening of the blind beggar's tale, and secondly a scene from Hell. The opening is in Scots. The scene in Hell has a strong Scots flavouring.

'It is very true,' said the blind man, 'that when I am tired of scraping thairm or singing ballants, I whiles mak a tale serve the turn among the country bodies, and I have some fearsome anes, that make the auld carlines shake on the settle, and the bits o' bairns skirl on their minnies out frae their beds. But this that I am going to tell you was a thing that befell in our ain house in my father's time—that is, my father was then a hafflins callant; and I tell it to you, that it may be a lesson to you that are but a young thoughtless chap, wha ye draw up wi' on a lonely road; for muckle was the dool and care that came o't to my gudesire.

'Ye maun have heard of Sir Robert Redgauntlet of that Ilk, who lived in these parts before the dear years. The country will lang mind him; and our fathers used to draw breath thick if ever they heard him named. He was out wi' the Hielandmen in Montrose's time; and again he was in the hills wi' Glencairn in the saxteen hundred and fifty-twa; and sae when King Charles the Second came in, wha was in sic favour as the Laird of Redgauntlet? He was knighted at Lonon court, wi' the King's ain sword; and being a redhot prelatist, he came down here, rampauging like a lion, with commissions of lieutenancy (and of lunancy, for what I ken) to put down a' the Whigs and Covenanters in the country. Wild wark they made of it; for the Whigs were as dour as the Cavaliers were fierce, and it was which should first tire the other. Redgauntlet was aye for the strong hand; and his name is kend as wide in the country as Claverhouse's or Tam Dalyell's. Glen, nor dargle, nor mountain, nor cave, could hide the puir hill-folk when Redgauntlet was out with bugle and bloodhound after them, as if they had been sae mony deer. And troth when they fand them, they didna mak muckle mair ceremony than a Hielandman wi' a roebuck—It was just "Will ye tak the test?"—if not—"Make ready—present—fire!" and there lay the recusant.

'But, Lord, take us in keeping, what a set of ghastly revellers they were that sat round that table!—My gudesire kend mony that had long before gane to their place, for often he had piped to the most part in the hall of Redgauntlet. There was the fierce Middleton, and the dissolute Rothes, and the crafty Lauderdale;

and Dalyell, with his bald head and a beard to his girdle; and
Earlshall, with Cameron's blude on his hands; and wild Bonshaw,
that tied blessed Mr Cargill's limbs till the blude sprang; and
Dunbarton Douglas, the twice-turned traitor baith to country and
king. There was the Bluidy Advocate Mackenyie, who, for his
wordly wit and wisdom had been to the rest as a god. And there
was Claverhouse, as beautiful as when he lived, with his long,
dark, curled locks, streaming down over his laced buff-coat, and
his left hand always on his left spule-blade, to hide the wound that
the silver bullet had made. He sat apart from them all, and looked
at them with a melancholy, haughty countenance; while the rest
hallooed, and sung, and laughed, that the room rang. But their
smiles were fearfully contorted from time to time; and their laugh
passed into such wild sounds, as made my gudesire's very nails
grown blue, and chilled the marrow in his banes.

'They that waited at the table were just the wicked servingmen
and troopers, that had done their work and cruel bidding on earth.
There was the Lang Lad of the Nethertoun, that helped to take
Argyle; and the Bishop's summoner, that they called the Deil's
Rattle-bag; and the wicked guardsmen in their laced coats; and
the savage Highland Amorites, that shed blood like water; and
mony a proud serving-man, haughty of heart and bloody of hand,
cringing to the rich, and making them wickeder than they would
be; grinding the poor to powder, when the rich had broken them
to fragments. And mon, mony mair were coming and ganging, a'
as busy in their vocation as if they had been alive.'

Alan Fairford pursues his friend as far as Dumfries where
he gets the first news of what is happening to Darsie Latimer
whom he now learns is caught up with the mysterious
Redgauntlet, to whom Darsie is 'related'. He is asked to
dinner by the Provost of Dumfries where he meets an old-
fashioned Scottish laird, who laments the passing of the old
Scottish fashions and customs.

'Come away, Mr Fairford—The Edinburgh time is later than
ours,' said the Provost.

And, 'Come away, young gentleman,' said the Laird; 'I remember your father weel at the Cross, thirty years ago—I reckon you
are as late in Edinburgh as at London, four o'clock hours—eh?'

'Not quite so degenerate,' replied Fairford; 'but certainly many
Edinburgh people are so ill-advised as to postpone their dinner
until three, that they may have full time to answer their London
correspondents.'

'London correspondents!' said Mr Maxwell; 'and pray, what
the devil have the people of Auld Reekie to do with London
correspondents?'

'The tradesmen must have their goods,' said Fairford.

'Can they not buy our own Scottish manufactures, and pick their customers' pockets in a more patriotic manner?'

'Then the ladies must have fashions,' said Fairford.

'Can they not busk the plaid over their heads, as their mothers did? A tartan screen, and once a year a new cockermoney from Paris, should serve a countess. But ye have not many of them left, I think—Mareschal, Airley, Winton, Wemyss, Balmerino, all passed and gone—ay, ay, the countesses and ladies of quality will scarce take up too much of your ball-room floor with their quality hoops now-a-days.'

'There is no want of crowding, however, sir,' said Fairford; 'they begin to talk of a new Assembly Room.'

'A new Assembly Room!' said the old Jacobite Laird—'Umph—I mind quartering three hundred men in the old Assembly Room—but come, come—I'll ask no more questions—the answers all smell of new lords, new lands, and do not spoil my appetite, which were a pity, since here comes Mrs Crosbie to say our mutton's ready.'

Fairford tells of his anxiety about his friend. The laird gives him a letter to help to discover him. He does so, and the two young men find themselves in the thick of a revived Jacobite attempt in 1766. The middle-aged Prince (now *de jure* King) is once more in Scotland in an attempt to regain the throne of his ancestors.

Extravagant and all but impossible though such a scheme would have been in 1766 a fresh and characteristic obstacle is introduced. Charles Edward has brought with him his mistress who, it is believed, is in the pay of the Hanoverian Court, this despite the fact that those who had invited him to Scotland had made an express condition that he should come alone. It is through the Royal mistress that the Government is made aware of what is happening on the Solway Firth. His supporters, in distress, raise the broken condition. The reader's pardon is asked for introducing the whole of this last scene. But it is indeed significant.

Sir Richard Glendale seemed personally known to Charles Edward, who received him with a mixture of dignity and affection and seemed to sympathize with the tears which rushed into that gentleman's eyes, as he bade his Majesty welcome to his native kingdom.

'Yes, my good Sir Richard,' said the unfortunate Prince, in a tone melancholy, yet resolved, 'Charles Edward is with his faithful friends once more—not, perhaps, with his former gay hopes which undervalued danger, but with the same determined contempt of the worst which can befall him, in claiming his own rights, and those of his country.'

'I rejoice, sire—and yet, alas! I must also grieve to see you once more on the British shores,' said Sir Richard Glendale, and stopped short—a tumult of contradictory feelings preventing his further utterance.

'It is the call of my faithful and suffering people which alone could have induced me to take once more the sword in my hand. For my own part, Sir Richard, when I have reflected how many of my loyal and devoted friends perished by the sword and by proscription, or died indigent and neglected in a foreign land, I have often sworn that no view to my personal aggrandisement should again induce me to agitate a title which has cost my followers so dear. But since so many men of worth and honour conceive the cause of England and Scotland to be linked with that of Charles Stuart, I must follow their brave example and, laying aside all other considerations, once more stand forward as their deliverer. I am, however, come hither upon your invitation; and as you are so completely acquainted with circumstances to which my absence must necessarily have rendered me a stranger, I must be a mere tool in the hands of my friends. I know well I never can refer myself implicitly to more loyal hearts or wiser heads than Herries Redgauntlet and Sir Richard Glendale. Give me your advice, then, how we are to proceed, and decide upon the fate of Charles Edward.'

Redgauntlet looked at Sir Richard, as if to say, 'Can you press any additional or unpleasant condition at a moment like this?' And the other shook his head and looked down, as if his resolution was unaltered, and yet as feeling all the delicacy of the situation.

There was a silence, which was broken by the unfortunate representative of the unhappy dynasty, with some appearance of irritation. 'This is strange, gentlemen,' he said; 'you have sent for me from the bosom of my family, to head an adventure of doubt and danger; and when I come, your own minds seem to be still irresolute. I had not expected this on the part of two such men.'

'For me, sire,' said Redgauntlet, 'the steel of my sword is not truer than the temper of my mind.'

'My Lord's and mine are equally so,' said Sir Richard; 'but you had in charge, Mr Redgauntlet, to convey our request to His Majesty, coupled with certain conditions.'

'And I discharged my duty to His Majesty and to you,' said Redgauntlet.

'I looked at no condition, gentlemen,' said their King, with dignity, 'save that which called me here to assert my rights in person. *That* I have fulfilled at no common risk. Here I stand to keep my word, and I expect of you to be true to yours.'

'There was, or should have been, something more than that in our proposal, please your Majesty,' said Sir Richard. 'There was a condition annexed to it.'

'I saw it not,' said Charles, interrupting him. 'Out of tenderness to the noble hearts of whom I think so highly, I would neither see nor read anything which would lessen them in my love and my esteem. Conditions can have no part twixt Prince and subject.'

'Sire,' said Redgauntlet, kneeling on one knee, 'I see from Sir Richard's countenance that he deems it my fault if your Majesty seems ignorant of what your subjects desired that I should communicate to your Majesty. For Heaven's sake! for the sake of all my past services and sufferings, leave not such a stain upon my honour! The note, Number D, of which this is a copy, referred to the painful subject to which Sir Richard again directs your attention.'

'You press upon me, gentlemen,' said the Prince, colouring highly, 'recollections, which, as I hold them most alien to your character, I would willingly have banished from my memory. I did not suppose that my loyal subjects would think so poorly of me, as to use my depressed circumstances as a reason for forcing themselves into my domestic privacies, and stipulating arrangements with their king regarding matters, in which the meanest hinds claim the privilege of thinking for themselves. In affairs of state and public policy, I will ever be guided, as becomes a prince, by the advice of my wisest counsellors; in those which regard my private affections, and my domestic arrangements, I claim the same freedom of will which I allow to all my subjects, and without which a crown were less worth wearing than a beggar's bonnet.'

'May it please your Majesty,' said Sir Richard Glendale, 'I see it must be my lot to speak unwilling truths, but believe me, I do so with as much profound respect as deep regret. It is true, we have called you to head a mighty undertaking, and that your Majesty, preferring honour to safety, and the love of your country to your own ease, has condescended to become our leader. But we also pointed out as a necessary and indispensable preparatory step to the achievement of our purpose—and, I must say, as a positive condition of our engaging in it—that an individual, supposed, —I presume not to guess how truly—to have your Majesty's most intimate confidence, and believed, I will not say on absolute proof, but upon the most pregnant suspicion, to be capable of betraying that confidence to the Elector of Hanover, should be removed from your royal household and society.'

'This is too insolent, Sir Richard!' said Charles Edward. 'Have you inveigled me into your power to bait me in this unseemly manner? And you, Redgauntlet, why did you suffer matters to come to such a point as this, without making me more distinctly aware what insults were to be practised on me?'

'My gracious Prince,' said Redgauntlet, 'I am so far to blame in this, that I did not think so slight an impediment as that of a woman's society could have really interrupted an undertaking of this magnitude. I am a plain man, sire, and speak but bluntly; I could not have dreamt but what, within the first five minutes of this interview, either Sir Richard and his friends would have ceased to insist upon a condition so ungrateful to your Majesty, or that your Majesty would have sacrificed this unhappy attachment to the sound advice, or even to the over-anxious suspicions, of so many faithful subjects. I saw no entanglement in such a difficulty, which on either side might not have been broken through like a cobweb.'

'You were mistaken, sir,' said Charles Edward, 'entirely mistaken—as much so you are at this moment, when you think in your heart my refusal to comply with this insolent proposition is dictated by a childish and romantic passion for an individual. I tell you, sir, I could part with that person tomorrow, without an instant's regret—That I have had thoughts of dismissing her from my court, for reasons known to myself; but I will never betray my rights as a sovereign and a man, by taking this step to secure the favour of anyone, or to purchase that allegiance which, if you owe it to me at all, is due to me as my birthright.'

'I am sorry for this,' said Redgauntlet; 'I hope both your Majesty and Sir Richard will reconsider your resolutions, or for bear this discussion, in a conjecture so pressing. I trust your Majesty will recollect that you are on hostile ground; that our preparations cannot have so far escaped notice as to permit us now with safety to retreat from our purpose; insomuch that it is with the deepest anxiety of heart I foresee even danger to your own royal person, unless you can generously give your subjects the satisfaction which Sir Richard seems to think they are obstinate in demanding.'

'And deep your anxiety ought to be,' said the Prince. 'Is it in these circumstances of personal danger in which you expect to overcome a resolution, which is founded on a sense of what is due to me as a man or a prince? If the axe and scaffold were ready before the windows of Whitehall, I would rather tread the same path with my great-grandfather, than concede the slightest point in which my honour is concerned.'

He spoke these words with a determined accent, and looked round him at the company, all of whom (excepting Darsie, who saw, he thought, a fair period to a most perilous enterprise) seemed in deep anxiety and confusion. At length, Sir Richard spoke in a solemn and melancholy tone.

'If the safety,' he said, 'of poor Richard Glendale were alone concerned in this matter, I have never valued my life enough to weigh it against the slightest point of your Majesty's service. But

I am only a messenger—a commissioner, who must execute my trust, and upon whom a thousand voices will cry, Curse and woe, if I do not it with fidelity. All of your adherents, even Redgauntlet himself, see certain ruin in this enterprise—the greatest danger to your Majesty's person—the utter destruction of all your party and friends, if they insist not on the point, which unfortunately, your Majesty is so unwilling to concede. I speak it with a heart full of anguish—with a tongue unable to utter my emotions—but it must be spoken—the fatal truth—that if your royal goodness cannot yield to us a boon which we hold necessary to our security and your own, your Majesty with one sword disarms ten thousand men, ready to draw their swords in your behalf; or, to speak more plainly, you annihilate even the semblance of a royal party in Great Britain.'

'And why do you not add,' said the Prince scornfully, 'that the men who have been so ready to assume arms in my behalf, will atone for their treason to the Elector by delivering me up to the fate for which so many proclamations have destined me? Carry my head to St James's, gentlemen; you will do a more acceptable and a more honourable action, than, having inveigled me into a situation which places me so completely in your power, to dishonour yourselves by propositions which dishonour me.'

'My God, sire!' exclaimed Sir Richard, clasping his hands together, in impatience, 'of what great and inexpiable crime can your Majesty's ancestors have been guilty, that they have been punished by the infliction of judicial blindness on their whole generation!—Come, my Lord—, we must to our friends.'

'By your leave, Sir Richard,' said the young nobleman, 'not till we have learned what measures can be taken for his Majesty's personal safety.'

'Care not for me, young man,' said Charles Edward, 'When I was in the society of Highland robbers and cattle-drovers, I was safer than I now hold myself among the representatives of the best blood in England. Farewell, gentlemen—I will shift for myself.'

'This must never be,' said Redgauntlet. 'Let me that brought you to the point of danger, at least provide for your safe retreat.'

So saying, he hastily left the apartment, followed by his nephew. The Wanderer, averting his eyes from Lord —— and Sir Richard Glendale, threw himself into a seat at the upper end of the apartment, while they, in much anxiety, stood together at a distance from him, and conversed in whispers.

Meanwhile the smugglers' vessels appear on the Solway Firth. The plotters hope to use these to make a safe retreat. But their plotting is now known by the Government and ends on one of the most moving passages Scott ever wrote. The emissary of the Government is a General Campbell.

'Do not concern yourself about me,' said the unfortunate Prince; 'this is not the worst emergency in which it has been my lot to stand; and if it were, I fear it not. Shift for yourselves, my lords and gentlemen.'

'No, never!' said the young Lord ——. 'Our only hope now is in an honourable resistance.'

'Most true,' said Redgauntlet; 'let despair renew the union amongst us which accident disturbed. I give my voice for displaying the royal banner instantly, and—How now?' he concluded sternly, as Lilias, first soliciting his attention by pulling his cloak, put into his hand the scroll, and added, it was designed for that of Nixon.

Redgauntlet read—and, dropping it to the ground, continued to stare upon the spot where it fell, with raised hands and fixed eyes, Sir Richard Glendale lifted the fatal paper, read it, and saying. 'Now all is indeed over,' handed it to Maxwell, who said aloud, 'Black Colin Campbell, by God! I heard he had come post from London last night.'

As if to echo his thoughts, the violin of the blind man was heard, playing with spirit, 'The Campbells are coming', a celebrated clan-march.

'The Campbells are coming in earnest,' said MacKellar; 'they are upon us with the whole battalion from Carlisle.'

There was a silence of dismay, and two or three of the company began to drop out of the room.

Lord —— spoke with the generous spirits of a young English nobleman. 'If we have been fools, do not let us be cowards. We have one here more precious than us all, and come hither with our warranty—let us save him at least.'

'True, most true,' answered Sir Richard Glendale, 'Let the King be first cared for.'

'That shall be my business,' said Redgauntlet; 'if we have but time to bring back the brig, all will be well—I will instantly despatch a party in a fishing skiff to bring her to.' He gave his commands to two or three of the most active amongst his followers.—'Let him be once on board,' he said, 'and there are enough of us to stand to arms and cover his retreat.'

'Right, right,' said Sir Richard, 'and I will look to points which can be made defensible; and the old powder-plot boys could not have made a more desperate resistance than we shall.—Redgauntlet,' continued he, 'I see some of our friends are looking pale; but methinks your nephew has more mettle in his eye now than when we were in cold deliberation, with danger at a distance.'

'It is the way of our house,' said Redgauntlet; 'our courage ever kindles highest on the losing side. I, too, feel that the catastrophe I have brought on must not be survived by its author. Let me first,' he said, addressing Charles, 'see your Majesty's sacred person in such safety as can now be provided for it, and then——'

'You may spare all considerations concerning me, gentlemen,' again repeated Charles, 'yon mountain of Criffel shall fly as soon as I will.'

Most threw themselves at his feet with weeping and entreaty; some one or two slunk in confusion from the apartment, and were heard riding off. Unnoticed in such a scene, Darsie, his sister, and Fairford, drew together, and held each other by the hands, as those who, when a vessel is about to founder in the storm, determine to take their chance of life and death together.

Amid this scene of confusion, a gentleman, plainly dressed in a riding-habit, with a black cockade in his hat, but without any arms except a *couteau-de-chasse*, walked into the apartment without ceremony. He was a tall, thin, gentlemanly man, with a look and bearing decidedly military. He had passed through their guards, if in the confusion they now maintained any, without stop or question, and now stood, almost unarmed, amongst armed men, who, nevertheless, gazed on him as on the angel of destruction.

This was General Campbell, a representative of the Hanoverian Court in London.

'You look coldly on me, gentlemen,' he said, 'Sir Richard Glendale—My Lord——. We were not always such strangers. Ha, Pate-in-Peril, how is it with you? and you too, Ingeldsby?—I must not call you by any other name—why do you receive an old friend so coldly? But you guess my errand.'

'And are prepared for it, General,' said Redgauntlet; 'we are not men to be penned up like sheep for the slaughter.'

'Pshaw! you take it too seriously—let me speak but one word with you.'

'No words can shake our purpose,' said Redgauntlet, 'were your whole command, as I suppose is the case, drawn round the house.'

'I am certainly not unsupported,' said the General; 'but if you would hear me——'

'Hear *me*, sir,' said the Wanderer, stepping forward; 'I suppose I am the mark you aim at—I surrender myself willingly, to save these gentlemen's danger—let this at least avail in their favour.'

An exclamation of 'Never, never!' broke from the little body of partisans, who threw themselves round the unfortunate Prince, and would have seized or struck down Campbell, had it not been that he remained with his arms folded, and a look, rather indicating impatience because they would not hear him, than the least apprehension of violence at their hand.

At length he obtained a moment's silence. 'I do not,' he said, 'know this gentleman'—(making a profound bow to the unfortunate Prince)—'I do not wish to know him; it is a knowledge which would suit neither of us.'

'Our ancestors, nevertheless, have been well acquainted,' said Charles, unable to suppress, even at that hour of dread and danger, the painful recollections of fallen royalty.

'In one word, General Campbell,' said Redgauntlet, 'is it to be peace or war?—You are a man of honour, and we can trust you.'

'I thank you, sir,' said the General; 'and I reply that the answer to your question lies with yourself. Come, do not be fools, gentlemen; there was perhaps no great harm meant or intended by your gathering together in this obscure corner, for a bear-bait or a cock-fight, or whatever other amusement you may have intended, but it is a little imprudent, considering how you stand with government, and it has occasioned some anxiety. Exaggerated accounts of your purpose have been laid before government by the information of a traitor in your own councils; and I was sent down post to take the command of a sufficient number of troops, in case these calumnies should be found to have any real foundation. I have come here, of course, sufficiently supported both with cavalry and infantry, to do whatever might be necessary; but my commands are—and I am sure they agree with my inclination—to make no arrests, nay, to make no further enquiries of any kind, if this good assembly will consider their own interest so far as to give up their immediate purpose, and return quietly home to their own houses.'

'What!—all?' exclaimed Sir Richard Glendale—'all, without exception?'

'ALL, without one single exception,' said the General; 'such are my orders. If you accept my terms, say so, and make haste; for things may happen to interfere with His Majesty's kind purposes towards you all.'

'His Majesty's kind purposes!' said the Wanderer. 'Do I hear you speak aright, sir?'

'I speak the King's very words from his very lips,' replied the General. ' "I will" said his Majesty, "deserve the confidence of my subjects by reposing my security in the fidelity of the millions who acknowledge my titles—in the good sense and prudence of the few who continue, from the errors of education, to disown it."—His Majesty will not even believe that the most zealous Jacobites who yet remain can nourish a thought of exciting a civil war, which may be fatal to their families and themselves, besides spreading ruin and bloodshed through a peaceful land. He cannot even believe of his kinsman, that he would engage brave and generous, though mistaken men, in an attempt which must ruin all who have escaped former calamities; and he is convinced, that, did curiosity or any other motive lead that person to visit this country, he would soon see that it was his wisest course to return to the Continent; and his Majesty compassionates his situation too much to offer any obstacle to his doing so.'

'Is this real?' said Redgauntlet. 'Can you mean this?—Am I— are all, are any of these gentlemen at liberty, without interruption, to embark in yonder brig, which, I see, is now again approaching the shore?'

'You, sir—all—any of the gentlemen present,' said the General— 'all whom the vessel can contain, are at liberty to embark uninterrupted by me; but I advise none to go off who have not powerful reasons unconnected with the present meeting, for this will be remembered against no one.'

'Then, gentlemen,' said Redgauntlet, clasping his hands together as the words burst from him, 'THE CAUSE IS LOST FOR EVER.'

General Campbell turned away to the window, as if to avoid hearing what they said. Their consultation was but momentary; for the door of escape which thus opened was as unexpected as the exigence was threatening.

'We have your word of honour for our protection,' said Sir Richard Glendale, 'if we dissolve our meeting in obedience to your summons?'

'You have, Sir Richard,' answered the General.

'And I also have your promise,' said Redgauntlet, 'that I may go on board yonder vessel, with any friend whom I may choose to accompany me?'

'Not only that, Mr Ingoldsby—or I *will* call you Mr Redgauntlet once more—you may stay in the offing for a tide, until you are joined by any person who may remain at Fairladies. After that there will be a sloop of war on the station, and I need not say your condition will then become perilous.'

'Perilous it should not be, General Campbell,' said Redgauntlet, 'or more perilous to others than to us, if others thought as I do in this extremity.'

'You forget yourself, my friend,' said the unhappy Adventurer, 'you forget that the arrival of this gentleman only puts the copestone on our already adopted resolution to abandon our bull-fight, or by whatever wild name this headlong enterprise may be termed. I bid you farewell, unfriendly friends—I bid *you* farewell' (bowing to the General), my friendly foe—I leave this strand as I landed upon it, alone and to return no more!'

'Not alone,' said Redgauntlet, 'while there is blood in the veins of my father's son.'

'Not alone,' said the other gentlemen present, stung with feelings which almost overpowered the better reasons under which they had acted. 'We will not disown our principles, or see your person endangered.'

'If it be only your purpose to see the gentleman to the beach,' said General Campbell, 'I will myself go with you. My presence among you, unarmed, and in your power, will be a pledge of my friendly intentions, and will overawe, should such be offered, any interruption on the part of officious persons.'

'Be it so,' said the Adventurer, with the air of a Prince to a subject; not of one who complied with the request of an enemy too powerful to be resisted.

They left the apartment—they left the house—an unauthenticated and dubious, but appalling sensation of terror had already spread itself among the inferior retainers, who had so short a time before strutted, and bustled, and thronged the doorway and the passages. A report had arisen, of which the origin could not be traced, of troops advancing towards the spot in considerable numbers; and men who, for one reason or other, were most of them amenable to the arm of power, had either shrunk into stables or corners, or fled the place entirely. There was solitude on the landscape excepting the small party which now moved towards the rude pier, where a boat lay manned, agreeably to Redgauntlet's orders previously given.

The last heir of the Stuarts leant on Redgauntlet's arm as they walked towards the beach; for the ground was rough, and he no longer possessed the elasticity of limb and of spirit which had, twenty years before, carried him over many a Highland hill, as light as one of their native deer. His adherents followed, looking on the ground, their feelings struggling with the dictates of their reason.

General Campbell accompanied them with an air of apparent ease and indifference, but watching, at the same time, and no doubt with some anxiety, the changing features of those who acted in this extraordinary scene.

Darsie and his sister naturally followed their uncle, whose violence they no longer feared, while his character attracted their respect, and Alan Fairford attended them from interest in their fate, unnoticed in a party where all were too much occupied with their own thoughts and feelings, as well as with the impending crisis, to attend his presence.

Half-way between the house and the beach, they saw the bodies of Nanty Ewart and Cristal Nixon blackening in the sun.

'That was your informer?' said Redgauntlet, looking back to General Campbell, who only nodded his assent.

'Caitiff wretch!' exclaimed Redgauntlet;—'and yet the name were better bestowed on the fool who could be misled by thee.'

'That sound broadsword cut,' said the General, 'has saved us the shame of rewarding a traitor.'

They arrived at the place of embarkation. The Prince stood a moment with folded arms, and looked round him in deep silence.

A paper was then slipped into his hands—he looked at it, and said, 'I find the two friends I have left at Fairladies are apprised of my destination, and proposed to embark from Bowness. I presume this will not be an infringement of the conditions under which you have acted?'

'Certainly not,' answered General Campbell, 'they shall have all facility to join you.'

'I wish, then,' said Charles, 'only another companion. Redgauntlet, the air of this country is as hostile to you as it is to me. These gentlemen have made their peace, or rather they have done nothing to break it. But you—come you and share my home where chance shall cast it. We shall never see these shores again; but we will talk of them, and of our disconcerted bull-fight.'

'I follow you, sire, through life,' said Redgauntlet, 'as I would have followed you to death. Permit me one moment.'

'The Prince looked round, and seeing the abashed countenances of his other adherents, bent upon the ground, he hastened to say, 'Do not think that you, gentlemen, have obliged me less, because your zeal was mingled with prudence, entertained, I am sure, more on my own account, and on that of your country, than from selfish apprehension.'

He stepped from one to the other, and, amid sobs and bursting tears, received the adieus of the last remnant which had hitherto supported his lofty pretensions, and addressed them individually with accents of tenderness and affection.

The General drew a little aloof, and signed to Redgauntlet to speak with him while this scene proceeded. 'It is now all over,' he said, 'and Jacobite will henceforward be no longer a party name. When you tire of foreign parts, and wish to make your peace, let me know. Your restless zeal alone has impeded your pardon hitherto.'

'And now I shall not need it,' said Redgauntlet. 'I leave England for ever; but I am not displeased that you should hear my family adieus. Nephew, come hither. In presence of General Campbell, I tell you, that though to breed you up in my own political opinions has been for many years my anxious wish, I am now glad that it could not be accomplished. You pass under the service of the reigning Monarch, without the necessity of changing your allegiance—a change, however,' he added, looking around him, 'which sits more easy on honourable men than I could have anticipated; but some wear the badge of their loyalty on their sleeve, and others in the heart. You will from henceforth be uncontrolled master of all the property of which forfeiture could not deprive your father—of all that belonged to him—excepting this, his good sword' (laying his hand on the weapon he wore), 'which shall never fight for the House of Hanover; and as my hand will never draw weapon more, I shall sink it forty fathoms deep in the wide ocean.

Bless you, young man! If I have dealt harshly with you, forgive me. I had set my whole desires on one point—God knows, with no selfish purpose; and I am justly punished by this final termination of my views, for having been too little scrupulous in the means by which I have pursued them. Niece, farewell, and may God bless you also!'

'No, sir,' said Lilias, seizing his hand eagerly. 'You have been hitherto my protector—you are now in sorrow, let me be your attendant, and your comforter in exile.'

'I thank you, my girl, for your unmerited affection; but it cannot and must not be. The curtain here falls between us. I go to the house of another—If I leave it before I quit the earth, it shall only be for the House of God. Once more, farewell both! The fatal doom,' he added, with a melancholy smile, 'will, I trust, now depart from the House of Redgauntlet, since its present representative has adhered to the winning side. I am convinced he will not change it, should it in turn become the losing one.'

The unfortunate Charles Edward had now given his last adieus to his downcast adherents. He made a sign with his hand to Redgauntlet, who came to assist him into the skiff. General Campbell also offered his assistance, the rest appearing too much affected by the scene which had taken place to prevent him.

'You are not sorry, General, to do me this last act of courtesy,' said the Chevalier; 'and on my part I thank you for it. You have taught me the principle on which men on the scaffold feel forgiveness and kindness even for their executioner.—Farewell!'

They were seated in the boat, which presently pulled off from the land. The Oxford divine broke out in a loud benediction, in terms which General Campbell was too generous to criticize at the time, or to remember afterwards;—nay, it is said, that, Whig and Campbell as he was, he could not help joining in the universal Amen! which sounded from the shore.

The poignant cry of Redgauntlet's 'The Cause is lost for ever!' comes straight from Scott's heart. As I said earlier, whether it comes from his subconscious or not matters little.

As I write these words and reflect on the impending doom which hangs over *Redgauntlet* as in *The Bride of Lammermoor*, a sentence of Redgauntlet springs to mind: 'The privilege of free action belongs to no mortal—we are too tied down by the fetters of duty—our mortal path is regulated by the regulations of honour—our most indifferent actions are but the web of destiny by which we are all surrounded.'

However attracted Scott was by the romance of Jacobitism, none knew better than he that the Cause was forever lost in 1746 on the bloody field of Culloden when Butcher

Cumberland defeated the Highland troops under Prince Charles.

None knew better than he that a revival of Jacobitism on the shores of Solway Firth as late as 1766 was wholly preposterous. Why then was he impelled to write the great novel of *Redgauntlet*, the most serious and heartfelt of all the Waverley novels?

I think the answer is simple. He was not speaking of Jacobitism but of the cause of Scotland, the once proud and independent Kingdom then sinking into the concept of Britain, or more properly England. It was her cause which he feared, in this Waverley novel published in 1824, was 'lost for ever'.

Looking back from today perhaps Walter Scott's gloomy prognostications were wrong. But then Scott could not see into the future of the latter half of the twentieth century.

------◆------

18

Ruin

In early January 1826 Scott at Abbotsford put his horse at Catrail, an early British earthwork consisting of a huge ditch and rampart. He had a bad fall, thought the accident a bad omen; and it was.

On 17th January 1826, Scott's old friend, Skene, called on him in Castle Street. Scott rose from his desk, and holding out a hand in greeting said: 'Skene, this is the hand of a beggar. Constable has failed, and I am ruined *au fond du comble*. It's a hard blow, but I must just bear up. The only thing which wrings me is poor Charlotte and the bairns.'

Even now it is extraordinary to look back on this admission of Scott's and on the facts which lay behind it. Since the publication of *Waverley* in 1814 he had, as we have seen, been earning up to £10,000 a year, and sometimes even more. No author in Great Britain, nor even in Europe or America, was earning money by his pen on this scale. How did his ruin come about?

Paradoxically Scott's financial affairs constitute one of the simplest and one of the most complicated problems of his life. We have already spoken of the pernicious system in Edinburgh of the exchange of bills as if they were real money, and particularly in Scott's affairs in relation with the Ballantynes and with Constable. This crazy system had extended itself to the important firm of Hurst and Robinson in London. When Hurst and Robinson were unable to meet their creditors, they turned to Constable and Constable to Ballantyne. The consequent fall brought down the whole connection.

The Ballantynes' firm had increased their floating debt to about £46,000, largely owing to the fact that their accounts were carelessly and incompletely kept, and partly to 'accommodation to Scott'.

To make matters worse, much of this sum had doubled because of the granting to Constable of counter bills. Constable owed Scott a considerable amount for recently purchased copyright, and Scott owed Constable for advances on future books.

The complications at this date seem endless as well as crazy; there is little point in trying to weave our way in and out of them. Let it be said that the Ballantyne final liability (which was, of course, Scott's) came to nearly £130,000. In the long run this was eventually paid off, though the other debtors, including Constable, were reduced to paying only so much in the pound.

The Edinburgh ruinous state of affairs was primarily due to Ballantyne's feckless incompetence and to the fact that he had never dared to admit to Scott the impending ruin. At the same time one should add that at this time not only the Edinburgh but the London banks were in something of a financial crisis. Money all over the United Kingdom was, to use a vulgar word, 'tight'.

Constable, crazed with anxiety, made a desperate fight. But Scott's illusions were gone. He made a trust of his property and resolved 'with my own right hand' to pay off every penny of debt. It seemed to him at the time that there was no hope of saving Abbotsford or anything from the wreck. In his Journal he wrote:

Naked we entered the world, and naked we leave it—blessed be the name of the Lord.

But the very size of the disaster tightened his courage. Six days after he knew the worst he wrote:

I feel neither dishonoured or broken . . . I have walked my last on the domains I have planted—sate my last in the halls I have built. But death would have taken them from me if misfortune had spared them. My poor people whom I loved so well! There is just another die to turn up against me in this run of ill-luck; i.e. if I should break my magic wand in the fall from this elephant, and lose my popularity with my fortune. Then *Woodstock* and *Bony* [he had begun a life of Bonaparte] may both go to the paper-maker, and I may take to smoking cigars and drinking grog, or turn devotee, and intoxicate the brains another way. In prospect of

186

absolute ruin, I wonder if they would let me leave the Court of Session. I would like, methinks, to go abroad

And lay my bones far from the Tweed.

But I find my eyes moistening, and that will not do. I will not yield without a fight for it. It is odd, when I set myself to write *doggedly*, as Dr Johnson would say, I am exactly the same man as ever I was, neither low-spirited nor *distrait*. In prosperous times I have sometimes felt my fancy and power of language flag, but adversity is to me at least a tonic and a bracer; the fountain is awakened from its inward recesses, as if the spirit of affliction had troubled it in his passage.

When he went back to the Court the first day after the tragedy was made public he felt 'like a man with a large nose', and that everyone was talking about him. An added source of embarrassment and distress was that his private dealings with the printing firm of Ballantyne were now made public.

Offers of help came in from everywhere. One unknown admirer said that he would put up £30,000. His servants wished to work without wages. The general feeling expressed by Lord Dudley to Morritt was: 'Good God, let every man to whom he has given months of delight give him sixpence and he will rise tomorrow richer than Rothschild.' As we have already seen, there was a strong movement in America to give Scott, and Scott alone, copyright for his work until he became free of his troubles. There were other shifts proposed to him to ease his burden, but Scott would have none of it.

In his Journal he wrote: 'No, if they [his creditors and the banks] permit me, I will be their vassal for life, and dig in the mine of my imagination to find diamonds (or what they sell for such) to make good my engagements, not to enrich myself. And this from no reluctance to allow myself to be called the Insolvent, which I probably am, but because I will not put out of the power of my creditors the resources, mental or literary, which yet remain to me.'

He recovered a kind of serenity. On 26th January he wrote to Laidlaw: 'For myself I feel like the Eildon hills—quite firm, though a little cloudy. I do not dislike the path that lies before me. I have seen all that society can show, and enjoyed all that wealth can give me, and I am satisfied much is vanity, if not vexation of spirit.'

187

He wrote to Miss Edgeworth: 'It is not in nature to look upon what can't be helped with any anxious or bitter remembrances. . . . The fact is that I belong to a set of philosophers who ought to be called Nymmites after their good founder Corporal Nym, and the fundamental maxim of whose school is "Things must be as they may".'

There were critics of the course he took. Thomas Carlyle has an odd passage: 'It was a hard trial. He met it proudly, bravely—like a brave, proud man of the world. Perhaps there had been a prouder way still: to have owned honestly that he was unsuccessful, then, all bankrupt, broken, in the world's goods and repute; and to have turned elsewhere for some refuge. Refuge did lie elsewhere; but it was not Scott's course, or fashion of mind, to seek it there. To say, Hitherto, I have been all in the wrong, and this my fame and pride, now broken was an empty delusion and spell of accursed witchcraft! It was difficult for flesh and blood! He said, I will retrieve myself, and make my point good yet, or die for it.'

This is merely loose rhetoric. It advocates some kind of theatrical renunciation and retirement, whereby his creditors would not have been paid anything and innocent people made to suffer from his folly.

Lockhart's great biography is not much to be trusted on this period of his subject's life; but there is an element of truth in his claim that the gambling element in Scott's temperament, his reluctance to set his affairs in order, sprang from the quality of his genius. This is what he had to say:

> Had not that adversity been preceded by the perpetual spur of pecuniary demands, he, who began life with such quick appetites for all its ordinary enjoyments, would never have devoted himself to the rearing of that gigantic monument of genius, labour and power, which his works now constitute. The imagination, which has bequeathed so much to delight and humanize mankind, would have developed few of its miraculous resources except in the embellishment of his personal existence. The enchanted spring would have sunk into earth with the rod that bade it gush, and left us no living waters. We cannot understand, but we may nevertheless respect even the strangest caprices of the marvellous combination of faculties to which our debt is so weighty. We should try to picture to ourselves what the actual intellectual life must have been of the author of such a series of romances. We

should ask ourselves whether, filling and discharging so soberly and gracefully as he did the common functions of social man, it was not, nevertheless, impossible but that he must have passed most of his life in other worlds than ours; and we ought hardly to think it a grievous circumstance that their bright visitors should have left a dazzle sometimes in the eyes which he so gently reopened on our prosaic realities. He had, on the whole, a command over the powers of his mind—I mean that he could control and divert his thoughts and reflections with a readiness, firmness and easy security of sway—beyond what I find it possible to trace in any other artist's recorded character and history; but he could not habitually fling them into the region of dreams throughout a long series of years, and yet be expected to find a corresponding satisfaction in bending them to the less agreeable considerations which the circumstances of any human being's practical lot in this world must present in abundance. The training to which he accustomed himself could not leave him as he was when he began. He must pay the penalty, as well as reap the glory, of this lifelong abstraction of reverie, this self-abandonment of Fairyland.

Scott has been blamed for his giving way to a fever for purchasing land all round Abbotsford. It is easy to make this criticism now. But Abbotsford was his most loved possession, and when he was earning ten or more thousand pounds a year with ease, it is hard to accuse him of reckless land hunger.

On the 20th of January there was a meeting of his creditors of which his old friend Sir William Forbes was chairman. Scott's lawyer sponsored a scheme for a trust deed announcing that it was his client's 'earnest desire to use every exertion in his power on behalf of his creditors, and by diligent employment of his talents, and the adoption of a strictly economical mode of life, to secure as speedily as possible full payment to all concerned'. Liabilities were at that time £104,081; the estate available for realization £48,494. Assets were his Edinburgh house, his library and furniture, and the value of the life-rent on Abbotsford.

There was a slight hitch with the banks who claimed not only the proceeds of a novel on which he was engaged, but the great life of Napoleon Buonaparte which Constable had engaged him to undertake, and more seriously to reduce the settlement on Abbotsford. But the hitch was settled.

The Scottish banks on the whole had behaved handsomely, and Scott, incapable of remaining idle, felt he ought to use his pen directly on their behalf.

The Government in London had recently proposed to limit the Bank of England to the issue of notes to the value of £5 and upwards, and, consequently to take away from the private banks—of which there were many in Scotland—the privilege of private note circulation. This gave Walter Scott's eager pen the chance he needed.

He published in the form of pamphlets issued by Blackwoods and under the name of Malachi Macgrowther. They were devoted as much to the plea of preserving Scotland's individuality as the so-called practical issue of the bank notes—'if you unscotch us' he had told Crocker, 'you will find us damned mischevious Englishmen'.

To some extent the pamphlet is modelled on Swift's *Drapier Letters* and shares the Irish Dean's great gusto. Malachi Macgrowther created a great stir and many of the politicians in England and even the Scottish Government politicians were angry with their author.

The irony of the situation was not lost on Scott, and he wrote in his Journal: 'Whimsical enough that when I was trying to animate Scotland against the currency bill, John Gibson [his lawyer] brought me the Deed of Trust assigning my whole estate to be subscribed by me; so that I am turning patriot, and taking charge of the affairs of the country, on the very day I was proclaiming myself incapable of managing my own.'

Walter Scott in the person of Malachi was angrily attacked in Parliament, but he cared nothing for the criticism of friends or opponents. In his Journal he wrote: 'I have, in my odd *sans souciance* character, a good handful of meal from the grist of the Jolly Miller.' And 'On the whole, I am glad of this brulzie, as far as I am concerned; people will not dare talk of me as an object of pity—no more "poor manning". Who asks how many punds Scots the old champion has in his pocket when

> He set a bugle to his mouth,
> And blew sae loud and shrill,
> The trees in greenwood shook thereat,
> Sae loud rang ilka hill.

With the Gaelic words 'Cha til mi tulidh'—Macrimmon's lament 'I shall return no more'—Walter Scott left his Castle Street house which he had inhabited for twenty-eight years and limped back to Abbotsford. He had attained peace of mind and did not object to solitude. It was a solitude which was to increase when he was forced to live in lodgings in Edinburgh. Again he confided in his Journal:

The love of solitude was with me a passion of early youth; when in my teens I used to fly from company to indulge in visions and airy castles of my own, the disposal of ideal wealth and the exercise of imaginary power. The feeling prevailed even till I was eighteen, when love and ambition awakening with other passions threw me more into society, from which I have, however, at times withdrawn myself, and have always been glad to do so. I have risen from the feast satisfied. . . . This is a feeling without the least tinge of misanthropy which I always consider as a kind of blasphemy of a shocking description. If God bears with the very worst of us we may surely endure each other. If thrown into society I always have, and always will endeavour to bring pleasure with me, at least to show willingness to please. But for all this I had rather live alone, and I wish my appointment so convenient otherwise, did not require my going to Edinburgh. But this must be, and in my little lodging I will be lonely enough.

———◆◆◆◆———

19

The Journal

Walter Scott was the nearest approach to what we might call a compulsive writer in the history of our literature. Of course he had his other pleasures—talk, hospitality, at Castle Street in Edinburgh and at Abbotsford—in his younger days long walks, the coursing of hares, angling for salmon, or more properly 'burning the water' on Tweed, the theatre and the company of his fellow men. But from his early youth until his death, he had the itch to write and not only for money—he could not bear to let his pen lie idle.

Having done his three or four hours on a novel before breakfast he would settle down afterwards to a large correspondence. Not all of these were replies to letters received but many were unsolicited letters to friends. Such as have not been lost have been collected into eleven thick volumes edited by the late Professor Sir Herbert Grierson. We have already told of the pathetic incident, how, when he was dying, the only thing that reduced him to tears was when he tried to write and found his strength unequal to holding a pen.

This passion for pen and paper induced him in 1825, and when he was still active as an author and still laird of Abbotsford, well before his ruin, to begin a Journal. He never intended that contemporary eyes should see it, but he must have thought of its ultimate publication after death for he was a stout believer in keeping records. One cannot do better than to quote John Buchan on the value of this Journal: 'It is fortunate that we possess such a document for the most difficult years of Scott's life. Its biographical worth is inestimable, and not less high is its quality as literature. For one thing it is one of the most complete expressions of a human soul that we possess, as complete as Swift's *Journal to Stella*, but without its self-consciousness. There is no reticence and no posturing because he is speaking to his own soul; he gives us that very thing in which Hazlitt declared him lacking, "what the heart whispers to itself in secret". The greatest figure he ever drew is in the *Journal*, and it is the man Walter Scott. His style, too, is purged of all dross. It is English, of no school and of no period, a speech as universal as that of St John's Gospel. "Whatever else of Scott may lose its colour with time", Professor Elton has written, "the *Journal* cannot do so, with its accurate, unexaggerated language of pain." Here are qualities which are found only at long intervals in the romances; a tenderness which keeps watch over man's mortality; and neither quails nor complains, a strange wistfulness, as if a strong and self-contained soul had at last found utterance.'

He began his *Journal* on 20th November 1825.

> I have all my life regretted that I did not keep a regular Journal. I have myself lost recollection of much that was interesting, and I have deprived my family and the public of some curious information by not carrying this resolution into effect.

> I have bethought me on seeing lately some volumes of Byron's notes that he had probably hit on the right way of keeping such a memorandum-book by throwing aside all pretence to regularity and order and marking down events just as they occurred to recollection. I will try this plan—and behold I have a handsome locked volume such as might serve for a Lady's Album. *Nota Bene*, John Lockhart and Anne and I are to raise a society for the suppression of Albums. It is a most troublesome shape of mendacity—Sir, your autograph—a line of poetry—or a prose sentence —Among all the sprawling sonnets and blotted trumpery that dishonours these miscellanies a man must have a good stomach that can swallow this botheration as a compliment.

It was not until January 1825 that the blow fell which precipitated Scott's ruin. We therefore have two months of the *Journal* reflecting the normal and generous Walter Scott we know. Of this kindly man there is plenty of evidence in the *Journal*. It is worth quoting some of the entries which show his normal generosity.

> *November 26.*—The court met late, and sat till *one*. Detained from that hour till four o'clock being engaged in the perplexed affairs of Mr James Stewart of Brugh. This young gentleman is

heir to a property of better than £1000 a year in Orkney. His mother married very young and was wife, mother and widow in the course of the first year. Being unfortunately under the direction of a careless perhaps an unfaithful agent she was unlucky enough to embarrass her own affairs by money transactions with this person. I was asked to accept the situation of one of his curators and trust to clear out his affairs and hers—at least I will not fail for want of application. I have lent her £300 on a second (and therefore doubtful) security over her house at Newington bought for £1000 and on which £600 is already secured. I have no connection with the family except by way of compassion and [may] not be rewarded even by thanks when the young man comes of age. I have known my father often so treated by those whom he had laboured to serve. But if we do not run some hazard in our attempts to do good, where is the merit of them? So I will bring through my Orkney Laird if I can.

Scott was constantly putting his hand in his pocket in this manner, even when not asked to do so. This is but one example. Many of the poor folk round Abbotsford had reason to benefit from this. He would often write from Edinburgh to his *major domo* at Abbotsford telling him to relieve the peasantry in periods of cold and bad weather, or poor crops. But he usually gave instructions that his name as benefactor should not be mentioned.

Apart from his generosity in money matters there are a number of other entries in the *Journal* for those two months which give us a picture of the good-natured humorous man Scott was before the blow had struck him—not that he was to lose these qualities after the blow. He had recently been in Ireland for the first time:

Wit.—I gave a fellow a shilling on some occasion when sixpence was the fee. 'Remember you owe me sixpence, Pat.' 'May your honour live till I pay you!' There was courtesy as well as wit in this, and all the clothes on Pat's back would have been dearly bought by the sum in question.

Good humour.—There is perpetual kindness in the Irish cabbin— butter-milk—potatoes—a stool is offered, or a stone is rolld that your honour may sit down and be out of their smoke, and those who beg everywhere else seem desirous to exercise free hospitality in their own houses. Their natural disposition is turned to gaiety and happiness. While a Scotchman is thinking about the term-day, or, if easy on that subject, about hell in the next world—while an Englishman is making a hell of his own in the present, because his muffin is not well roasted—Pat's mind is always turnd to fun and ridicule. They are terribly excitable to be sure and will murther you on slight suspicion and find out next day that it was all a mistake, and that it was not yourself they meant to kill at all at all.

This one is very good-tempered:

I had a bad fall last night coming home. There were unfinished houses at the east end of Atholl Place, and as I was on foot, I crossed the street to avoid the material which lay about; but, deceived by the moonlight, I slipped ancle-deep into a sea of mud (honest earth and water, thank God), and fell on my hands. Never was there such a representative of *Wall* in Pyramus and Thisbe. I was absolutely rough-cast. Luckily Lady S. had retired when I came home; so I enjoyed my tub of water without either remonstrances or condoleances. Cockburn's hospitality will get the benefit and renown of my downfall, and yet has no claim to it. In future though, I must take a coach at night—a controul on one's freedom, but it must be submitted to.

Here is Walter Scott in his *Journal* amusingly giving his consent to the marriage of other people:

Mrs Coutts, with the Duke of St Albans and Lady Charlotte Beauclerk, called to take leave of us. When at Abbotsford his suit throve but coldly. She made me, I believe, her confident in sincerity. She had refused him twice, and decidedly. He was merely on the footing of friendship. I urged it was akin to love. She allowed she might marry the Duke, only she had at present [not] the least intention that way. Is this frank admission more favourable for the Duke than an absolute protestation against the possibility of such a marriage? I think not.

It is the fashion to attend Mrs Coutts' parties and to abuse her. I have always found her a kind, friendly woman, without either affectation or insolence in the display of her wealth, and most willing to do good if the means be shewn to her. She can be very entertaining too, as she speaks without scruple of her stage life. So much wealth can hardly be enjoyed without some ostentation. But what then? If the Duke marries her, he ensures an immense fortune; if he marries a woman older than himelf by twenty years, she marries a man younger in wit by twenty degrees. I do not think he will dilapidate her fortune—he seems quiet and gentle. I do not think she will abuse his softness—of disposition, shall I say, or of heart? The disparity of ages concerns no one but themselves; so they have my consent to marry . . .

But he doesn't always respond to sponging letters:

People make me the oddest requests. It is not unusual for an Oxonian or Cantab. who had outrun his allowance and of whom I know nothing to apply to me for the loan of £20, £50, or £100. A captain of the Danish naval service wrote to me, that being in distress for a sum of money by which he might transport himself to Columbia to offer his services in assisting to free that province, he had dreamd I generously made him a present of it. I can tell him his dream by contraries. I begin to find like Joseph Surface that too good a character is inconvenient. I don't know what I have done to gain so much credit for generosity, but I suspect I owe it to being supposed as Puff says one of those 'whom Heaven has blessed with affluence'. Not too much of that neither, my dear petitioners, though I may thank myself your ideas are not correct.

And here is an often-quoted passage on which many writers have had their say:

What a life mine has been!—half educated, almost wholly neglected or left to myself, stuffing my head with most nonsensical trash, and undervalued in society for a time by most of my companions—getting forward and held a bold and clever fellow contrary to the opinion of all who thought me a mere dreamer—Broken-hearted for two years—my heart handsomely pieced again—but the crack will remain till my dying day. Rich and poor four or five times, once on the verge of ruin, yet opend new sources of wealth almost overflowing—now taken in my pitch of pride, and nearly winged (unless the good news hold), because London chuses to be in an uproar, and in the tumult of bulls and bears, a poor inoffensive lion like myself is pushd to the wall. And what is to be the end of it? God knows. And so ends the catechism.

Walter Scott has often been described as a mysterious character. He had his points of reserve, but if you had met him you would have found that he was on the surface a very easy man to know and talk with.

These two months of this invaluable *Journal* confirm this.

We shall deal with the shadows as reflected in the *Journal* later on.

------◆◆◆◆▶------

20

Recovery from Ruin

Having left his house in Castle Street for ever Scott during his work as Clerk of Session had to stay on in Edinburgh, and go to a much-reduced Abbotsford when the Courts were not sitting. He was so impoverished that he had to take refuge in what he called a 'bug-infested top lodgings' in North St David Street, one of the lesser avenues in the New Town of the East End of Princes Street.

He slept badly in the heat (Edinburgh in its rare heat spells can be muggy and lowering), and such rest as he achieved was disturbed by the quarrelling of the drunken Highland sedan chairmen all night outside his windows. All he remarked on this was: 'When I was at Home I was in a better place'.

On reading accounts of his exile in what was nearly a New Town slum, and particularly looking at his comments in his *Journal* one vacillates between being saddened at his fate and exhilarated by one's admiration of the way in which he took it all. He surveyed his poverty without complaint, and, though he must have felt it, was unperturbed by the disgrace of his secret compact with the Ballantynes now known to all Edinburgh and Scotland. People did not openly speak of this secret compact to have all his work printed by the Ballantynes, but he must have known it would have been commented on generally and unfavourably.

He had left Abbotsford on 11th May when his wife was too ill to say good-bye to him. Four days later news reached him in the bug-infested house that Lady Scott had died.

Impossible as it was not to suffer dejection at this melancholy event, in his *Journal* he was later to show recuperation.

I have seen her. The figure I beheld is, and is not, my Charlotte —my thirty years' companion. There is the same symmetry of form, though those limbs were rigid which were once so gracefully elastic—but that yellow masque, with pinched features, which seems to mock life rather than emulate it, can it be the face that was once so full of lively expression? I will not look on it again . . . If I write long this way, I shall write down my resolution, which I should rather write up, if I could. I wonder how I shall do with the larger portion of thoughts which were here for thirty years. I expect they will be here for a long time at least . . .

Another day, and a bright one to the external world, again opens on us, the air soft, and the flowers smiling, and the leaves glittering. They cannot refresh her to whom mild weather was a natural enjoyment; cerements of lead and of wood already hold her; cold earth must have her soon. But it is not my Charlotte, it is not the bride of my youth, the mother of my children, that will be laid away among the ruins of Dryburgh, which we have so often visited in gaiety and pastime. No, no. She is sentient and conscious of my emotions somewhere—somehow; yet would I not this moment renounce the mysterious yet certain hope that I shall see her in a better world for all that this world can give me . . .

I have been to her room; there was no voice in it, no stirring; the pressure of the coffin was visible on the bed, but it had been removed elsewhere; all was neat as she loved it, but all was calm, calm as death. I remembered the last sight of her; she raised herself in bed and tried to turn her eyes after me, and said, with a sort of smile, 'You all have such melancholy faces'. They were the last words I ever heard her utter, and I hurried away, for she did not seem quite conscious of what she said. When I returned, immediately before departure, she was in a deep sleep. It is deeper now. This was but seven days since.

They are arranging the chamber of death; that which was long the apartment of connubial happiness, and of whose arrangements (better than in richer houses) she was so proud. They are treading thick and fast. For weeks you could have heard a footfall Oh, my God!

In the heat and dirt of his lodgings he struggled away at his writing in the long uphill course. He finished *Woodstock* and then plunged into his life of Napoleon which Constable had commissioned from him, and which was to prove one of his best-selling works and one which more than any other was to reduce his debts to the bank.

Incredible though it may seem, he finished his nine-volumed *Life of Napoleon Bonaparte* by the Author of Waverley in June 1827. It sold extremely well, proving that recent history can be as attractive to the public as fiction. *Napoleon* enabled him to pay his creditors at the bank no less than £18,000.

So much has been written on and about the great son of the French Revolution between 1827 and now that Scott's work is little more than a curiosity.

Curiosity it may be, but one cannot but admire the prodigious feat of fast work which went into the making of it. It is admittedly history for the ordinary reader, rather than for the scholar. It is a well-proportioned work, with much vigour in the telling. It might have been written after the passing of centuries rather than almost under the shadow of the terror which had hung over Europe for twenty years. Scott is dispassionate about Napoleon. He thought him a bad man, but a very great one. Nevertheless he was able to hold the attention of the public with it.

The pure architecture of this large work completed so soon astonishes one, especially as Scott took a good deal of trouble to get his facts and background accurate.

I know the island of Corsica, Napoleon's birthplace, well, and I can testify to the fact that in his writing about this enchanting island, Walter Scott did not put a foot wrong. He might have been there, and he knew its history well under the great and good General Paoli.

Hesketh Pearson in his 'Study' of Sir Walter wrote:

'Naturally his life of the French Emperor aroused much hostile criticism in France, and one of Napoleon's generals was incensed. In going through the documents at the Colonial Office, Scott discovered that General Gourgaud, a member of Napoleon's staff at St Helena, had privately informed the British Government that the Emperor's complaints were groundless, that his health was good, his finances were ample, his means of escape both easy and frequent; such information inevitably resulting in a disregard of Napoleon's own remonstrances by the British authorities, and the taking of more vigorous measures to ensure his captivity. At the same time, and afterwards, Gourgaud's story to his fellow-countrymen was that Napoleon's treatment by his captors was unnecessarily harsh. In fairness to the British officials in charge of the Emperor, Scott had to use Gourgaud's evidence, while feeling that 'he will be in a rare passion, and may be addicted to vengeance, like the long-moustachoed son of a French bitch as he is'. Since the book was the talk of Paris, the General had to vindicate himself somehow, his first step being to call Scott a liar, his next to threaten him with a duel.

Scott was quite willing to fight, and asked his friend Will Clerk to act as his second. Having found that he had not a leg to stand on, Gourgaud issued a statement accusing Scott of conspiring with the British Government to slander him. 'I wonder he did not come over to try his manhood otherwise' thought Scott. 'I would not have shunned him, nor any Frenchman who ever kissed Bonaparte's breech.'

A long letter by Scott to the *Edinburgh Weekly Journal* exposed the facts of the case, from which it appeared that he had carefully abstained from using anything in the documents that would further have discredited Gourgaud, who had privately libelled several members of Napoleon's staff. The letter was copied by many English journals; and the General replied with a pamphlet abusing Scott, the British Government under Lord Castlereagh, and everyone else who dared to think that a French soldier of the Empire could be guilty of such dishonourable conduct. Scott let it go at that. The evidence was clear and substantiated by a number of men whose truth was less shaky than the General's honour. The French papers refused to publish Scott's explanation, for the liberty of the press includes the liberty to suppress; and as he had no leisure for a war of words, he dismissed the matter from his mind.

While he was living in straitened circumstances in Edinburgh, Scott still lent his presence to charitable gatherings. On 23rd February 1827 he attended and took the chair at a banquet in aid of the Theatrical Fund for out-of-work actors. It was at this banquet that at long last he formally acknowledged that he was 'the great unknown', the Author of Waverley.

Lord Meadowbank had proposed the chairman's health and in glowing terms referred to the mighty output of novels. Walter Scott rose to his feet and admitted the truth, which, of course, everyone had known for so long. Three hundred diners rose and applauded him to the echo.

The *Edinburgh Evening Courant* gave a detailed account of this banquet and of Walter Scott's long-waited open admission as to his being 'the Author of Waverley'. Through the ensuing weeks and months, on both sides of the Atlantic the world's Press repeated the *Courant*'s account and head-lined Scott's admission. Journalistically speaking, one sup-poses they were entitled to this news-splashing and head-lining. In point of fact there was no real news in it at all. Everyone, both literate and illiterate, had long known the truth. So little did Scott value this public admission that he made only a passing reference to it in his *Journal*.

At no time in his life was Scott working more concen-tratedly, more avidly than during this period when he was struggling to recover from his ruin. The *Journal* tells of long days and nights devoted to his task. Sometimes when his hand or health failed him he would have need of an amanuensis. One of these was Robert Hogg, a nephew of the Ettrick Shepherd. Robert recorded an instance when he came to Walter Scott's lodgings to take down dictation. Dictation lasted from six o'clock in the morning till six in the evening—breakfast and luncheon being served to him as he worked. His amanuensis was nearly done with fatigue when this marathon ended; but Scott did not, according to him, show any signs of tiredness.

With one ignoble exception Scott's creditors were aware of his gigantic effort to repay them. The exception was a firm of Jews in London who had got hold of one of his old backed bills. Lockhart records this fact.

He had, while toiling his life out for his creditors, received various threatenings of severe treatment from the London Jews formerly alluded to, Messrs. Abud and Co.; and, on at least one occasion, he made every preparation for taking shelter in the Sanctuary of Holyroodhouse. Although these people were well aware that at Christmas 1827 a very large dividend would be paid on the Ballantyne debt, they could not bring themselves to comprehend that their interest lay in allowing Scott the free use of his time; that by thwarting and harassing him personally, nothing was likely to be achieved but the throwing up of the trust, and the settlement of the insolvent house's affairs on the usual terms of a sequestration. The Jews would understand nothing, but that the very unanimity of the other creditors as to the propriety of being gentle with him, rendered it extremely probable that their own harshness might be rewarded by the immediate payment of their whole demand. They fancied that the trustees would clear off any one debt, rather than disturb the arrangements generally adopted; they fancied that, in case they laid Sir Walter in prison, there would be some extraordinary burst of feeling in Edinburgh—that

201

private friends would interfere—in short, that in one way or another, they should get hold, without further delay, of their 'pound of flesh'.—Two paragraphs from the Diary will be enough as to this unpleasant subject:

October 31.—Just as I was merrily cutting away among my trees, arrives Mr Gibson with a very melancholy look, and indeed the news he brought was shocking enough. It seems that Mr Abud has given positive orders to take out diligence against me for his debt. This breaks all the measures we have resolved on, and prevents the dividend from taking place, by which many poor persons will be great sufferers. For me—the alternative will be more painful to my feelings than prejudicial to my interests. To submit to a sequestration, and allow the creditors to take what they can get, will be the inevitable consequence. This will cut short my labour by several years, which I might spend, and spend in vain, in endeavouring to meet their demands. I suppose that I, the Chronicler of the Canongate, will have to take up my residence in the Sanctuary [a place near Holyrood where debtors could live free of sequestration], unless I prefer the more airy residence of the Calton Jail, or a trip to the Isle of Man.

November 4.—Put my papers on some order, and prepared for the journey. It is in the style of the Emperors of Abyssinia who proclaim, 'Cut down the Kantuffa in the four quarters of the world, for I know not where I am going'. Yet, were it not for poor Anne's doleful looks, I would feel firm as a piece of granite. Even the poor dogs seem to fawn on me with anxious meaning, as if there were something going on which they could not comprehend. Set off at twelve, firmly resolved in mind and body. But when I arrived in Edinburgh at my faithful friend Mr Gibson's—lo! the scene had again changed, and a new hare is started.

The new hare was this. It transpired in the very nick of time, that a suspicion of usury attached to these Israelites in a transaction with Hurst and Robinson, as to one or more of the bills for which the house of Ballantyne had become responsible. This suspicion assumed a shape sufficiently tangible to justify that house's trustees in carrying the point before the Court of Session. Thus, though the Court decided in favour of the Abuds, time was gained; and as soon as the decision was pronounced, Scott heard also that the Jews' debt was settled. In fact, Sir William Forbes, whose banking-house was one of Messrs. Ballantyne's chief creditors, had crowned his generous efforts for Scott's relief by privately paying the whole of Abud's demand (nearly £2,000) out of his own pocket—ranking an ordinary creditor for the amount; and taking care at the same time that his old friend should be allowed to believe that the affair had merged quietly in the general measure of the trustees. It was not until some time after Sir William's death, that Sir Walter learned what had been done on this occasion; and I may as well add here, that he died in utter ignorance of some services of a like sort which he owed to the secret liberality of three of his brethren at the Clerks' table—Hector Macdonald Buchanan, Colin Mackenzie, and Sir Robert Dundas. I ought not to omit, that as soon as Sir Walter's eldest son heard of the Abud business, he left Ireland for Edinburgh, but before he reached his father, the alarm had blown over.

The Abud business roused him from the mechanical stupor in which he was working. He now pulled himself together and aroused his old creative powers.

He embarked upon another novel, *The Fair Maid of Perth*, and *The Tales of a Grandfather*. This eased his private finances and he also liked the comforting thought that he was doing well by his creditors. The Constable trustees proposed to put on the market the copyright of the novels owned by the estate. The Trust thus paid its first dividend— six shillings in the pound. In two years he had won for it £40,000, which meant that he who had made about £10,000 a year when he wrought for himself, had been earning £20,000 in one year for his creditors. He began to see light ahead and recorded the fact in his Christmas entry in his *Journal*: 'If I die in the harness, which is very likely, I shall die with honour; if I achieve my task I shall have the thanks of all concerned . . . and the approbation of my own conscience. . . . I am now perfectly well in constitution, and though I am still in troubled waters, yet I am rowing with the tide, and less than the continuation of my exertions of 1827 may, with God's blessing, carry me successfully through 1828, when we may gain a more open sea, if not exactly a safe port. . . . For all these great blessings it becomes me well to be thankful to God, who in his good time and good pleasure sends me good as well as evil.'

'If I die in harness, which is very likely . . .' Scott was now within six years of his death, and he must have been aware of its approach.

It is distressing to read his private admissions of constant pain at this period in his *Journal*. At the same time one's distress is partially alleviated by the sheer heroism of it. In all our literature there is nothing quite equal to Walter Scott's recovery from his own ruin.

21

Walter Scott's Triumphant Struggles

The more does one contemplate the ruined Walter Scott at the period of his exile in the 'bug-infested lodgings' in St David's Street or in other casual *pieds-à-terre* in Edinburgh, the more is one moved to sympathetic admiration.

His wife, for whom he had a stronger feeling than he had realized during his lifetime, had newly died. His children were not very sympathetic. He who had, through his novels, counted upon an income of £10,000 or more a year, was now uncomplainingly reduced to doing literary jobs for £20 or less. His ruin had been accomplished by the public admission of a not very reputable secret—that was that for some years he had been involved with the Ballantynes in a private printing business.

He was much in pain, and was afflicted by rheumatism which crippled his movements and deprived him of sleep. He noticed blood when he was passing water, yet made a joke of it saying that the 'a' in 'passing' should be an 'i'. It was now that he was deeply distressed by the news that his old friend and colleague, Heber, who had assisted him in *The Minstrelsy of the Scottish Border*, had been caught out in London in 'unnatural practices' and had to flee the country. All around him the friends of his youth were dying and he felt lonely.

He was infuriated by an attempt by one of the most notable Scottish eccentrics, Sir John Sinclair, to relieve his finances by arranging a marriage for him (only a few months after Charlotte's death) with the wealthy Dowager Duchess of Roxburghe. His pride was genuinely wounded by this clumsy attempt.

Other eccentrics, finding out where his lodgings were,

bothered him with boring attentions yet he seems to have treated them with his old courtesy.

His nervous system, once unassailable, showed signs of distress. He wrote in his *Journal*: 'A thousand fearful images and dire suggestions glance along the mind. Command them to show themselves, and you presently assert the power of reason over imagination.'

He had once relished his food, wine and whisky toddy of an evening; now he was reduced to the humblest fare which he bought for himself as he crippled home from the courts to his lodgings; he was forbidden the comfort of wine and whisky.

He had once delighted in full exercise either on horseback or walking; now it was as much as he could do to drag himself across Princes Street to his lodgings. How he ached, ached and ached with his rheumatism! It fills his *Journal*, yet without a sign of complaint. He notes with distress a muddiness in his head, and says he would willingly compound for more pain to be rid of it.

In youth he had been enormously active physically; in middle-age he had had to pull in a bit physically but made up for it by his vehement powers in writing. Now he was verging on sixty, and (though he does not mention it) must have been aware that the end was in sight.

And yet . . . and yet he never let his pen fall idle. In the evenings (sometimes when pain kept him awake all the night) he wrote one more successful novel at high speed, and when this was achieved he tackled his enchanting *Tales of a Grandfather*, a history of Scotland designed for Lockhart's little boy, Hugh Littlejohn. He very much believed in not writing down for children; in consequence his *Tales of a Grandfather* is a history book in which many adults have taken delight and found information. Buchan, who was well versed in his country's history, has this to say about it:

> Here Scott is writing about what he knew and liked best, the long pageant of Scottish history. Since he is writing for his darling grandson he curbs his prejudices, and he admits a little, a very little instruction to balance the heroics. 'When you find anything a little too hard for you to understand at this moment,' he tells Hugh Littlejohn in the preface, 'you must consider that you will be better able to make out the sense a year or two afterwards; or perhaps you may make a great exertion and get at its meaning, just

as you might contrive to reach something placed upon a high shelf by standing on your tiptoes.' The book is never written down to children, but it is all within the comprehension of a child's mind, for the narrative is easy and natural with the sound of a living voice behind it, and every paragraph has something to catch the youthful fancy. When Scott wrote, the history of Scotland had not been attempted on scientific lines, and he often accepts traditions which later research has exposed. Nevertheless he gives us truth, the truth of spirit, and a noble impartiality. Hugh littlejohn, like many a child since, was properly excited by it all, and set out to dirk his young brother with a pair of scissors. But he could not away with the instructive matter. His views were communicated through Mrs Hughes of Uffington: 'He very much dislikes the chapter on Civilization, and it is his desire that you will never say anything more about it, for he dislikes it extremely.'

In 1827 he launched on into a new manner and new style in *Chronicles of the Canongate*, a collection of three short stories. Once again it is worth quoting Buchan, who loved these late-flowerings of Scott's genius.

'The Highland Widow' is a picture of the disruption of the old Highland life after the 'Forty-five and, if Elspeth MacTavish is perhaps too reminiscent of Helen MacGregor, there is tragedy in her stubborn savagery and the son Hamish is drawn with sober faithfulness. In 'The Two Drovers' we have a glimpse into the perverse but logical Highland ethics and an unforgettable picture of the old world of the drove-roads. There is no trace of falsetto in Robin Oig, and his tragic fate is made as inevitable as the return of the seasons. In these stories Scott brought to the study of the Highland character a new psychological insight. 'The Surgeon's Daughter' contains an admirable portrait of a country doctor, based on his old friend Dr Ebenezer Clarkson of Selkirk. The charm of the piece lies in the contrast between the homely world of Middlemas and the mysterious East, and, though Scott's knowledge of India was wholly at second hand, he succeeds in creating a sense of the exotic, and in the scene where Hyder Ali reveals himself he achieves a stirring *coup de théatre*. But we have the feeling throughout that he does not take his puppets quite seriously, they are Croftangry's creations, and with Croftangry he is mainly concerned.

It is the narrator of the tale, and the narrator's friends that give the book its virtue. Scott is writing from his own shadowed retrospect. Croftangry is himself, and Mrs Bethune Baliol has much of his own mother and of his childhood's friend, Mrs Anne Murray Keith. Here there is none of the trait-portraiture, the rejoicing of comedy 'humours' of the earlier novels. The figures of Croftangry's world are seen in a cold autumnal light which has lost the riotous colours of summer. All of them—Croftangry, Mrs Bethune Baliol, Christie Steele, Fairscribe, Janet McEvoy—are done with a sure touch and with a delicate and humorous wistfulness. Croftangry himself is a convincing figure of regret and disillusioned philosophy, and Scott never wrote anything more moving than the scenes where the returning exile finds his old friend the lawyer a helpless paralytic, and where his mother's housekeeper shivers his palace of dreams. Here there is a new philosophy, a 'Winter's Tale' philosophy, and a new technique. He paints in finer strokes and in quieter tints, but with an economy and a certainty which recalls some of the best works of Tourgoniev. The ebbing of the currents of life seems to have left him with clearer eyes.

He occasionally managed to get down to Abbotsford in which the bank trustees allowed him to live, when he willed, rent free. Lord Cockburn visited him there and found the talk as good as ever. 'His simplicity and naturalness after all his fame are absolutely incredible.' In his evening dress he was 'like any other comfortably ill-dressed gentleman', but in the morning 'with his large coarse jacket, great stick and leather cap, he was Dandy Dinmont or Dick Hattrick—a smuggler or a poacher'.

He managed what was to be his last visit to London as a comparatively hale man, and was introduced to the little Princess Victoria, the Queen to be. He found her 'plain but pleasing' and hoped that she would change her name before she came to the throne.

For the rest, it was a sad visit. He had been devoted to his grandson, Hugh Littlejohn Lockhart, the child of Sophia and Lockhart. He saw the little boy again, but noticed what poor health he was, and how near to the end; indeed he was shortly to die. His genial friend Terry of the London theatre, who had presented so many of the novels in stage form, had gone bankrupt.

Scott confided in his *Journal*: 'It is written that nothing shall flourish under my shadow—the Ballantynes, Terry, Nelson, Heber, all come to distress. Nature has written on my brow; "Your shade shall be broad, but there shall be no protection derived from it to aught you favour".' This doleful entry in his brave *Journal* is unusual.

On his return to Edinburgh he mixed as far as he could in

the social life of the capital. He attended the ceremony when 'the auld murderess' Mons Meg came back to the Castle battery. After this there was a form of Celtic Saturnalia under the chairmanship of Cluny Macpherson. Scott cannot have joined in the deep drinking and heavy eating, but his mere presence illuminated the occasion.

One habit he continued to keep up—that was his charity to lame dogs who were trying to struggle on. A characteristic entry in his *Journal* notices one of these. 'A poor young woman came this morning, well dressed and well behaved, with a strong northern accent. She talked incoherently a long story of a brother and lover both dead. I would have kept her here till I wrote to her friends, particularly to Mr Sutherland (an Aberdeen bookseller), to inform them where she is, but my daughter and her maidens were frightened, as indeed there might be room for it, and so I sent her in one of Mr Davidson's chaises to the Castle at Jedburgh, and wrote to Mr Shortreed to see she is humanely treated. I have written also to her brother.'

This is true Christian charity of the kind indulged in by Dr Johnson. But this practiser of Christianity was not happy amongst its official exponents.

He records a meeting with the celebrated religious enthusiast, Edward Irving. Scott was impressed with the dark beauty of the face, marred by the 'terrible squint' of the eyes; but he was repelled by the unction in Irving's talk. Walter Scott was not at ease with those who professed ease with Zion as did the extraordinary and spiritually intemperate Irving.

Yet how well, how brilliantly he could portray these Zionists in his novels, notably *Old Mortality*. But then in his Waverley novels he was in a world of his own private imagination. In the Edinburgh of his increasing age, and as the nineteenth century progressed, he had to meet and face real people, real oddities unsupported by the secret dreams of imagination.

Yes, his life at this period of ruin in Edinburgh fills one with pity and admiration.

But the end was not yet—far from it.

———◆◆◆◆———

22

The Last Two Waverley Novels:
the Character of Lockhart

Health of a kind returned in 1828 to Scott who was encouraged by Cadell (Constable's successor) in the scheme for 'an Opus Magnum'—that was a complete reprint of all the Waverley novels with added notes and introductions. These notes and introductions gave him fresh and invigorating work. He also helped a candidate for the Ministry by composing sermons for him—an unusual task which actually saw print.

In this year he composed and published a Waverley novel well up to the level of many of the ones that had gone before—*The Fair Maid of Perth*. Perth is the gateway to the Highlands and Scott was conscious all the time of its environs in writing this near mediaeval romance. He wisely refrains from dialect, either Highland or Lowland, but the Northern flavour is here in the speech of all the characters. The novel shows very vividly the contrast between the two worlds of Scotland—the Celtic and the South.

'The Fair Maid' abounds in memorable scenes including the clan battle on the North Inch, a wide parkland by the edge of Perth, and there is a vivid murder—that of Rothesay. There is also one episode which is proof of the new technique which Scott was acquiring in this period near the end of his novel writing. That is the scene where Dwinning the Apothecary is compelled to cure the child of a man whose death he had earlier brought about.

Finally, there is a personal element in the book which shows that, with increasing age Walter Scott had learned (while looking back on his life) an increased tolerance.

As a young man Walter Scott had allowed himself one piece of ungenerous behaviour about a member of his own family—the only fault of its kind that all his most assiduous biographers can discover.

In Scott's early days when he had much to do with looking after other members of his father's family, the case of his younger brother Daniel was a deep vexation. 'Daniel Scott, having taken to evil courses, was shipped off to the West Indies. But Jamaica proved no cure, he went downhill in mind and body, and during a negro rebellion on the planta tion where he was employed he did not show the family courage. He returned home with this stigma on his name, was taken to his mother's house and soon died. Scott would not see him; he declined to go to his funeral or wear mourning for him. In those high-flying days he could forgive most faults, but not cowardice, and he felt that by the unhappy Dan the family scutcheon had been indelibly stained. It was almost the only case where Scott's abundant charity failed him. The years were to bring him to a humaner mind, and in *The Fair Maid of Perth* he attempted in his account of Conacher the justification of a temporary coward, an expiation, he told Lockhart, to the *manes* of poor Dan. 'I have now learned to have more tolerance and compassion than I had in those days.'

He added that this put him in mind of Samuel Johnson who had stood bareheaded in the rain in the market place of Uttoxeter as penance for having in youth been ashamed of his father who kept a bookstall there.

Yet one more worthwhile novel succeeded *The Fair Maid of Perth*. Lockhart has this to say about it, and in doing so permits himself some reflections on Scott's frame of mind and character at this period.

Anne of Geierstein came out about the middle of May; and this, which may almost be called the last work of his imaginative genius, was received at least as well—(out of Scotland, that is)—as The Fair Maid of Perth had been, or indeed as any novel of his after the Crusaders. I partake very strongly, I am aware, in the feeling which most of my own countrymen have little shame in avowing, that no novel of his, where neither scenary nor character is Scottish, belongs to the same preeminent class with those in which he peoples and paints his native landscape. I have confessed that I cannot rank even his best English romances with such creations as Waverley and Old Mortality; far less can I believe that posterity will attach similar value to this Maid of the Mist. Its pages, however, display in undiminished perfection all the skill and grace of the mere artist, with occasional outbreaks of the old poetic spirit, more than sufficient to remove the work to an immeasureable distance from any of its order produced in this country in our own age. Indeed, the various play of fancy in the combination of persons and events, and the airy liveliness of both imagery and diction, may well justify me in applying to the author what he beautifully says of his King Rene:

A mirthful man he was; the snows of age
Fell, but they did not chill him. Gaiety,
Even in life's closing, touch'd his teeming brain
With such wild visions as the setting sun
Raises in front of some hoar glacier,
Painting the bleak ice with a thousand hues.

It is common saying there is nothing so distinctive of *genius* as the retention in advanced years, of the capacity to depict the feelings of youth with all their original glow and purity. But I apprehend this blessed distinction belongs to, and is the just reward, of virtuous genius only. In the case of extraordinary force of imagination, combined with the habitual indulgence of a selfish mood—not combined, that is to say, with the genial temper of mind and thought which God and Nature design to be kept alive in man by those domestic charities out of which the other social virtues so easily spring, and with which they find such endless links of interdependence;—in this unhappy case, which none who has studied the biography of genius can pronounce to be a rare one, the very power which heaven bestowed seems to become, as old age darkens, the sternest avenger of its own misapplication. The retrospect of life is converted by its energy into one wide blackness of desolate regret; and whether this breaks out in the shape of rueful contemptuousness, or a sarcastic mockery of tone, the least drop of the poison is enough to paralyse all attempts at awakening sympathy by fanciful delineations of love and friendship. Perhaps Scott has nowhere painted such feelings more deliciously than in those very scenes of Anne of Geierstein, which offer every now and then, in some incidental circumstance or reflection, the best evidence that they are drawn by a grey-headed man. The whole of his own life was too present to his wonderful memory to permit of his brooding with exclusive partiality, whether painfully or pleasurably, on any one portion or phase of it; and besides, he was always living over again in his children, young at heart whenever he looked on them, and the world that was opening on them and their friends. But above all, he had a firm belief in the future reunion of those whom death had parted.

He lost two more of his old intimates about this time;—Mr

211

Terry in June, and Mr Shortreed in the beginning of July. The Diary says:—'July 9. Heard of the death of poor Bob Shortreed, the companion of many a long ride among the hills in quest of old ballads. He was a merry companion, a good singer and mimic, and full of Scottish drollery. In his company, and under his guidance, I was able to see much of rural society in the mountains, which I would not otherwise have attained, and which I have made my use of. He was, in addition, a man of worth and character. I always burdened his hospitality while at Jedburgh on the circuit, and have been useful to some of his family. Poor fellow! So glide our friends from us. Many recollections die with him and with poor Terry.'

In this last visit to London he was surrounded by his children and grandchildren; then Fate played a spiteful prank.

'I have had hard cards since I came here,' he wrote to a friend on May 5th. 'I had just had my family here round me, when poor little Johnny Lockhart was affected with a cough and fever which threatened and still threatens to destroy an existence that has always been a frail one. Lockhart and Sophia instantly removed the little sufferer to Brighton, where the sea air, which has always been of service, has something relieved him. Still the prospect of his attaining health and strength is greatly diminished, and I fear almost equal pain to the parents in watching this frail and flickering light perhaps for a few years longer, or in seeing it now brought to a sudden and violent conclusion.

'Anne has thrown up her invitations, tickets to Almack's and all the amusements which her friends were providing for her to attend to Sophia in her distress. So here I am, melancholy enough, and some law matters are like to keep me till the 20th of the month, when I hope we may meet in Edinburgh.'

On return to Edinburgh he found the town filled with the exploits of the 'body snatchers', Burke and Hare who rifled the cemeteries to provide corpses for the medical faculty at the University. He booked a window to see Burke's execution, but at the last moment found himself too busy for so edifying a spectacle. The *Journal* was now temporarily neglected, but after six months he braced himself to resume it. He wrote quite truthfully:

During this period nothing has happened, worth particular notice. The same occupations, the same amusements, the same occasional alternations of spirits, gay or depressed, the same absence of all sensible or rational cause for the one or the other. I half grieve to take up my pen and doubt if it is worth while to record such an infinite quantity of nothing . . . I cannot say I have been happy, for the feeling of increasing weakness in my lame leg is a great afflication. I walk now with pain and difficulty at all times, and it sinks my soul to think how soon I may be altogether a disabled cripple. I am tedious to my friends, and I doubt the sense of it makes me fearful. Everything else goes well though. My cash affairs are clearing, and though last year was an expensive one, I have been paying debts. Yet I have a dull contest before me which will probably outlast my life.

Scott had, in fact, turned himself into a writing machine concerning which the only question was how long it would last and how much could be got out of it before it broke down. For nearly a year it functioned magnificently.

The late Mr Donald Carswell wrote penetratingly and well about this period of decline in Scott's health and activities:

'But one day in the early summer of 1829 Scott had to go to bed and send in haste for his doctor. He was bleeding profusely from the bowels. Dr Ross, an excellent practitioner of the Sangrade school, treated him *secundum artem*—that is, cupped, bled and starved him and reduced his daily allowance of strong drink to a thing *pour rire*. The best advice would have been to stop work, but if given, it was not taken. The patient recovered and renewed the whole of his labours and some of his liberality in eating and drinking. But he was increasingly sensible of fatigue now, was apt to fall asleep at his desk, and could not take a walk at Abbotsford without the supporting arm of Tom Purdie, the surly ex-poacher who had been his personal attendant and factotum for thirty years. It was Tom's humour to die suddenly towards the end of that year. He was an ill-conditioned dog, but faithful, and his master lamented him if no one else did. A successor of sorts was found, whose duties were to prove more exacting than ever old Tom's had been, for within three months he had to take charge of a difficult paralytic. On the afternoon of 15th February 1830, shortly after getting home from Court, Sir Walter fell down in an apoplectic fit.

'Life, with its abundance of tragic materials, is careless of tragic forms. The four years' magnificent conflict with adversity deserved at the least a clean and decent end, and death could never have come to Scott more fittingly than in the Spring of 1830, when he knew his task was virtually accomplished and that, whether he lived or died, his creditors would in time be paid to the uttermost farthing. But no such appropriate grace was given him. The stroke was not mortal. Drs Ross and Abercrombie were at hand with their bleedings and cuppings and starvings to preserve for two and a half years a mere existence that was yet interwoven with lively and various sufferings—a salvage unsightly and most pitiable. At first it seemed not very bad. There was a specious recovery. In a week or two the patient reappeared in Parliament House, genial as ever and not appreciably altered, save for a new twist in the smiling mouth and an unaccustomed stammer when in reply to enquiries about his illness he explained that his stomach was giving him trouble—a foolish placebo of the doctors that he did his best to believe. But presently headquarters began to hint that his retirement on pension would facilitate a re-organization of the clerical staff of the Court of Session. Subject to some heart-searchings—mainly as to the proportion of his salary the Treasury would agree for pension —he accepted his dismissal calmly enough. It meant so much more time for writing—more notes for the *Magnum*, more romances, more histories, more curious and voluminous odds and ends for the reviews. Hitherto his writing had been a means to an end; now it was a sick man's obsession.'

The copy was produced as punctually as ever and even more abundantly; but publisher and printer took to glancing at each other in alarm, and soon dreaded the arrival of each succeeding parcel from Abbotsford with its unconscious instalment of the new tale of physical and mental decay. To appeal to Scott to stop work for his health's sake was useless. Already his doctors had warned him and received churlish answers. To a remonstrance from the favoured Lockhart he was more amiable but not less obstinate. 'I understand you, and thank you from my heart,' he said, 'but I must tell you at once how it is with me. I am not sure that I am quite myself in all things; but I am sure that in one point there is no change. I mean that I foresee distinctly that if I were to be idle I should go mad. In comparison with this, death is no risk to shrink from.' And so it went on. It vexed him, as he covered sheet after sheet, that the mere mechanism of writing should have become so difficult. His fingers played unaccountable pranks with the pen and suffered cruelly from chilblains when the weather turned cold, but, anyhow, he felt his mind was as clear as ever. So much so that he was very insistent upon its clearness.

One day towards the end of the year Cadell and Ballantyne met in agitated conference. The opening chapters of a new novel, *Count Robert of Paris*, had come to hand, and they were shocking. James, who since the death of Will Erskine was the only man who possessed the licence to criticize the master's work, was deputed to explain in writing that the subject of the novel was unsuitable and that not even the genius of the author of *Waverley* could make the Byzantine Court interesting to the British public. A tart reply came back from Abbotsford:

> If I were like other authors, which I flatter myself I am not, I should send you an order on my treasurer for a hundred ducats, wishing you all prosperity and a little more taste; but having never supposed that any abilities I ever had were of a perpetual texture, I am glad when friends tell me what I might be long in finding out myself. Mr Cadell will show you what I have written to him. My present idea is to go abroad for a few months, if I hold together so long. So ended the Fathers of the Novel—Fielding and Smollett—and it would be no unprofessional finish for yours,—Walter Scott.

The letter to Cadell was a jumble of obstinacy, vacillation and wounded pride. No doubt his day was done, and he ought to retire—not because he was failing, but because there was so much competition nowadays. 'The fact is, I have not only written a great deal myself, but, as Bobadil teaches his companions to fence, I have taught a hundred gentlemen to write nearly as well, if not altogether so, as myself.' He could not admit that *Count Robert* was a bad book, so for the present let the printing proceed.

Cadell and Ballantyne were dismayed. This quavering arrogance raised a question that would hardly bear thinking about—would they be driven to tell Scott that he must either stop or be stopped? While they paused the post brought Cadell another letter. The stricken man's mood had changed. Here were no more reproaches, only a piteous appeal for friendly consideration and counsel, for he had to confess something that he had kept from them, viz. that lately he had had a second stroke.

> Now in the midst of all this, I began my work with as much attention as I could; and having taken pains with my story, I find

215

it is not relished, nor indeed tolerated by those who have no interest in condemning it, but a strong interest in putting even a face upon their consciences. Was not this, in the circumstances, a damper to an invalid, already afraid that the sharp edge might be taken off his intellect, though he was not himself sensible of that? and did it not seem, of course, that nature was rather calling for repose than for further efforts in a very excitable and feverish style of composition? It would have been the height of injustice and cruelty to impute want of friendship or sympathy to J.B.'s discharge of a doubtful and, I am sensible, a perilous task. . . . It is the consciousness of his sincerity which makes me doubt whether I should proceed with the County Paris. I am most anxious to do justice to all concerned, and yet for the soul of me, I cannot see what is likely to turn out for the best. I might attempt the Perilous Castle of Douglas, but I fear the subject is too much used, and that I might again fail in it. Then being idle will never do, for a thousand reasons. All this I am thinking of until I am half sick. I wish James, who gives such stout advice when he thinks we are wrong, would tell me how to put things right. One is tempted to cry 'Wo worth thee! is there no help in thee?' Perhaps it may be better to take no resolution till we all meet together.

The very pain and reason of this letter, witnessing as it did that whatever had happened to the novelist the correspondent was able to collect himself, made the problem worse. Before it could be answered came this intimation; having been obliged to lay *Count Robert* aside, yet being incapable of idleness, Sir Walter had composed a very serious pamphlet on the great political question of the moment, wherein was shown by many clear and abundant proofs— that is, to anyone who was not a Whig or a blackguard—the absurdity as well as the infamy of Lord Grey's proposals for Parliamentary reform. It was intended for immediate publication. Sir Walter was sure it would make a profound impression on the public.

Cadell and Ballantyne shared his certainty—so much so that they hastened down to Abbotsford, quaking in concert but resolved that at all costs this madness must be stopped. They were given pause by their reception. Sir Walter, looking fairly well, greeted them with perfect composure and affability. He was eager to discuss the good news he had just had from Edinburgh—now his creditors had received a second large dividend, and how generously they had shown their appreciation of his efforts by releasing from the trust assets his plate, library and collection of curios and armour.

His mind was easy now, he said, and he could make his will in the knowledge that, thanks to the *Magnum Opus*, the rest of the debt would be wiped out in a few years, even if he never wrote another line. So seriously and sensibly did he talk that evening that Cadell and Ballantyne went to bed greatly relieved.

The morning brought a different story. Immediately after breakfast the great pamphlet was produced, and until noon the two men had to sit in patient misery while their host droned and stammered and drivelled, through interminable periods of stale argument, labouring rhetoric and unhappy invective. Cadell, trying to combine tact with emphasis, asked if Sir Walter had realized the consequences of such a publication. Sir Walter, calling his bushy eyebrows into play, replied that the consequences might be damned. Cadell rejoined that they certainly would, and the *Magnum Opus* would be damned into the bargain if the author appeared in the character of an anti-Reform pamphleteer. Sir Walter, never having thought of that, looked blank and appealed to James. Poor James tremulously ventured to homologate *in toto*. A painful half-hour ensued. It ended in an awkward compromise. James had for many years issued from his press a little Tory newspaper, which called itself by the name of the *Weekly Journal*, and it was agreed that, subject to some modification and the very strictest anonymity, Sir Walter's diatribe might appear in its columns without doing harm to anybody. It never did appear. When James sent the proofs he had so many alterations to suggest that Scott in a pet flung the whole wretched thing upon his study fire.

But if he might not use his pen he could still raise his voice against the abomination of desolation. As Sheriff of Selkirk he was returning officer for the county, a situation which, according to the public morality of the day, was regarded as an opportunity rather than a disqualification for party activity, and it was certainly no part of Scott's political creed to be in advance of his time. Crippled, palsied, dying, he could see himself as the Tyrtaus of the Border Tories. The Border Tories saw otherwise, and snubbed Tyrtaus so cruelly that he was in half a mind to quit the field. Yet no— his neighbours might be poor rats, but at least he would do his duty. 'I will make my opinion public at every place where I shall be called upon or expected to appear,' he wrote in his *Journal*, 'but I will not thrust myself forward again. May the Lord have mercy upon us and incline our hearts to keep this vow!' His prayer was not answered, for within ten days of writing these words he announced his intention of moving an anti-Reform resolution at a meeting of the Roxburgh freeholders at Jedburgh. His daughter, the last child now living at Abbotsford, weeping bitterly, implored him not to go. Her solicitude was rewarded with one of the terrible outbursts of fury that for the past year had made Abbotsford an ill place to live in. Sir Walter went to Jedburgh to face, not a decent meeting of county free-holders, but a mob of Reform townsfolk who were in no mood to endure a long, rambling mumbled discourse, of which they could hear little and that not to their liking. They howled him down. When the meeting ended he bowed gravely to the jeering artisans and pronounced with as much audibility and scorn as his trembling lips could compass, the words 'Moriturus vos saluto'.

The dying gladiator had one more blow to strike. On 23rd April, the Reform Bill having been wrecked in the Commons, Lord Grey appealed with confidence to an infuriated country. When the crisis came Scott was lying speechless at Abbotsford in a third attack of apoplexy so grave that Walter, Scott's eldest son and heir, and the Lockharts hastened to his bedside hardly daring to hope that they would see him alive. Yet once more he rallied, got something like speech back, contrived after a fashion to attend to his duties as returning officer for Selkirk, and even resumed writing a little. A less satisfactory aspect of his sense of recovery was his avowed purpose of going to Jedburgh on election day to cast his last vote and make his last speech. The protests of his family were eagerly seconded by his political friends, including the Tory candidate himself, who assured him that his assistance was not needed, yet dared not say what was the fact, that it was not wanted. With the cunning of a clouded mind Scott pretended to be persuaded, but secretly gave orders for his carriage to be ready early on the morning of the poll. When he reached Jedburgh the town was in an uproar. The local rabble, reinforced by a horde of weavers from Hawick, were parading the streets with drums and banners and demonstrating the virtue of democracy by maltreating anyone who did not sport the Whig colours. They pelted Scott's carriage with stones, howled, cursed and spat at him as he hobbled slowly to the Court-house, supported by two friends. When all was over and the Tory had been ruturned by the handsome majority of forty votes to nineteen, a kindly Whig smuggled him through a back lane to his carriage. The mob, inflamed by defeat and an arduous day's drinking, pursued him out of the burgh with yells of 'Burke Sir Walter!' and sped him homeward over the bridge with a parting shower of brickbats. 'Sad blackguards,' he wrote in his *Journal* that evening; 'Troja fuit'.

The times were out of joint—that was certain. Nobody could be trusted, not even James Ballantyne. Two years before James had had the misfortune to lose his wife, and had never been the same man since. Scott, speaking with the authority of one who was himself a widower, had exhorted him to fortitude in affliction, but James, who had loved his wife, would not be comforted. He became excessively devout, which Scott might have forgiven if the new-found faith in God had not been accompanied by a loss of faith in the Tory party. During the summer the *Weekly Journal* announced James's definite adherence to Reform. Scott passionately vowed that never more would James Ballantyne be his literary adviser—a punishment that the poor printer accepted philosophically, for it relieved him of the painful duty of saying what he thought of *Castle Dangerous*. The appearance of friendship was kept up, however, and one Saturday in July James went down to Abbotsford for the weekend. It was not a fortunate visit. Scott could not keep off politics and broke out in railing accusations against his oldest friend, who could only reply, 'The Lord rebuke thee'. Early next morning, without waiting to see his host, James departed. He left word that his spiritual health demanded more strenuous devotional exercises on the Sabbath Day than Abbotsford afforded, on hearing which Sir Walter swore a little. They never met again.'

We must consider another cause of trouble to Sir Walter for some time. This had been the behaviour of his son-in-law, John Gibson Lockhart, who was to write a great, if flawed, biography of Scott well after his father-in-law's death. Lockhart was a strange individual—and as one so close to Scott, it is well worth considering his character.

We can forgive Lockhart a good deal, for he genuinely

loved Scott; and his huge life of him is a quarry in which all who wish to know about Sir Walter or to write about him must delve. Still, there is much to forgive Lockhart.

Born in Glasgow, the son of a minister there, and subsequently a scholar of Balliol, Oxford, he reacted against the vulgarity of the commercial city of his origin and despised the place. He came to Edinburgh and idled away much of his time there. His only occupation at first in Scotland's capital was the writing of anonymous and ferocious satire and abuse in *Blackwood's Magazine*. The following is a fair specimen of his spleen: 'Our hatred and contempt of Leigh Hunt as a writer is not so much owing to his shameless irreverance to his aged and afflicted king—to his profligate attacks on the character of the king's sons—to his low-born insolence to the aristocracy with whom he would in vain claim the alliance of an illustrious friendship—to his paid pandarism to the vilest passions of the mob of which he is himself a firebrand—to the leprous crust of self-conceit with which his whole moral being is indurated—to the loathsome vulgarity which constantly clings round him like a vermined garment from St Giles—to that irritable temper which keeps the unhappy man, in spite even of his vanity, in a perpetual fret with himself and all the world beside, and that shows itself equally in his deadly emnities and capricious friendships—our hatred and contempt of Leigh Hunt, we say, is not so much owing to these and other causes, as to the odious and unnatural harlotry of his polluted muse. We were the first to brand with a burning iron the false face of this kept mistress of a demoralising incendiary. We tore off her gaudy veil and transparent drapery, and exhibited the painted cheeks and writhing limbs of the prostitute.'

He followed this up with an attack on the young poet Keats which is notorious even to this day. Keats's job when he was not writing immortal verse was that of an assistant in a chemist's shop. Lockhart does not let him forget this.

He attacked his poetry with sneering condescension, adding: 'Back to the shop, Mr John, back to plasters, pills and ointment boxes etc.' It is said that in later years Lockhart was prepared to admit that poor Keats 'had some merit'; but the evidence for this is slender; and, as he treated Tennyson in 1833 in the same way, he cannot be excused on the grounds of youth and inexperience.

His meeting with the figure of Walter Scott was fortuitous, but, as it turned out, happy. He found himself sitting next to the great man at a dinner party, and in order to make conversation told him of a journey to Weimar, the home of Goethe. He had asked, he said, whether Goethe 'the celebrated poet' was in town, and got nothing but blank looks, until his landlady suggested that possibly he meant '*The Herr Geheimrat von Goethe*'.

This humble anecdote at once tickled Scott's humour. He grinned broadly and said: 'I hope you will come and see me at Abbotsford, and when you reach Selkirk or Melrose be sure you ask the landlady for nobody but the Sheriff.' This was the beginning of an acquaintance which led to Lockhart eventually becoming engaged to and marrying Scott's daughter, Sophia. Though Sophia later remarked to a friend that, if she had had time to reflect, she 'might have done better'.

After his marriage Lockhart settled down at Chiefswood near Abbotsford and, on the whole, got on very well with his distinguished father-in-law.

His bent for satire and abuse did distress Scott much who pled with him, and with some effect, to abandon the style of anonymous authorship. He was not in time, however, to prevent a disgraceful duel which arose out of Lockhart's writing and intrigue and which caused Scott much heart-burning and personal anxiety. He had to go to London to settle the aftermath of the duel.

One of Lockhart's more disgraceful outburts had been a long poem called 'The Testimonium' in which he had, in terms offensive even for him, attacked McCulloch, the editor of the newly-founded *Scotsman* newspaper. This evoked a stern rebuke from Sir Walter who wrote to him in these terms:

If McCulloch were to parade you on the score of stanza XIII, I do not see how you could decline his meeting, as you make the man your equal (*ad hoc* I mean), when you condescend to insult him by name. And the honour of such a rencounter would be small comfort to your friends for the danger which must attend it. I have hitherto avoided saying anything on this subject, though some little turn towards personal satire is, I think, the only drawback to your great and powerful talents, and I think I may have hinted as much to you. But I wished to see how this matter of Wilson's would turn before making a clean breast on this subject. . . . Besides all other objections of personal enemies, personal quarrels, constant obloquy, and all uncharitableness, such an occupation will fritter away your talents, hurt your reputation both as a lawyer and a literary man, and waste your time in what at best will be but a monthly wonder. What has been done in this department will be very well as a frolic of young men, but let it suffice 'the gambol has been shown' . . . I am sure Sophia, as much as she can or ought to form any judgment respecting the line of conduct you have to pursue in your new character of a man married and settled, will be of my opinion in this matter, and that you will consider her happiness and your own, together with the respectibility of both, by giving what I have said your anxious consideration.

But say what we will about John Gibson Lockhart, one must admit that he not only admired his father-in-law but loved him as far as his somewhat reserved, shy character permitted. Also one cannot but be grateful to him for his great biography of Walter Scott, and for the care and deep affection he showed him on his deathbed, and when he was taking leave of his beloved Abbotsford for ever.

Lockhart had hoped for brilliant success from his writings. It is ironically sad to reflect that he wrote his greatest work, the biography, without profit, and that when the world eventually saw its merits and praised it, he was past caring whether he received praise or not.

Though Lockhart's bent in his anonymous writing was savagely abusive and satirical, he had his tender side—especially towards his children. He did his best to do what he could for his second son, who was a sad scapegrace. A point came at last when even Lockhart's patience failed and he broke off relations, which he only resumed when the boy lay broken and dying abroad at Versailles.

23

The Last Journey. The End

Apoplexy had killed Scott's father; and as the years of decline gathered round Sir Walter he began to be aware that the same fate was threatening him. Nevertheless he showed courage during the attacks.

At Abbotsford one of his lady guests noticed that he interrupted himself when walking up and down the room. He stood silent while, with difficulty, he took out his watch and examined it. At length he spoke and revealed the fact that he had been calmly measuring the time during which a stroke had made his features slip on one side of his mouth. He then continued to walk and talk as if nothing had happened.

There came a time in 1831 when it became obvious that he should leave Abbotsford to winter abroad in a summer climate; and he yielded to his doctors' entreaties and commands to this end. His last autumn at home was cheerful enough. His debts were nearly all paid off and he had convinced himself, poor hardworking man, that he had done it himself—indeed he had done much, and soon after his death the last penny was paid.

Hearing of his poor health Lord Grey's Government in London magnanimously put a frigate at his disposal to take him abroad in the coming winter. Scott accepted this generous proposal. Thinking of the Mediterranean where he was to go, he could not help reflecting that Smollett and Fielding, on whom he had written in earlier days, had been driven abroad by ill health never to return.

Just before the autumn's ending Wordsworth came to visit Scott at Abbotsford. Together the two men forded Tweed at an easy passage and when the hills were purple in an eerie gloaming. Wordsworth, himself sick and blind, saw in the light a presage of death for his old friend, from whom he had much differed, yet had loved. Before Scott's departure to winter abroad, he wrote this sonnet:

A trouble, not of clouds, or weeping rain,
　Nor of the setting sun's pathetic light
Engendered, hangs o'er Eildon's triple height;
　Spirits of power assembled there complain
For kindred power departing from their night;
　While Tweed, best pleased in chanting a blithe strain,
Saddens his voice again, and yet again.
　Lift up your hearts, ye mourners! for the might
Of the whole world's good wishes with him goes;
　Blessings and prayers in nobler retinue
Than sceptred King or laurelled Conqueror knows
　Follow this wondrous potentate. Be true,
Ye winds of ocean, and the Midland sea
　Wafting your charge to soft Parthenope!

I have referred to Wordsworth as an old friend of Scott's. This is perhaps too strong, too intimate a word. The two men had much in common—a love of wild, natural scenery at a time when it was not usual to see any merit or attraction in such—particularly in what the late-eighteenth-century writers called 'horrid mountains'. The great poet Wordsworth felt deeply on the beauty of the Lake scenery of Northern England and expressed his feeling in great English poetry. Scott, too, saw the beauty of wild scenery, especially in his native Scotland, but his feelings were a trifle more facile than Wordsworth's. Nevertheless, he made a very great deal more money out of his epic poems and novels on these themes. It would be too much to say that Wordsworth ever suffered from jealousy on this score, but he was aware of it; and this prevented complete intimacy.

In his *Journal* for September, before his departure Scott wrote: 'I am perhaps setting . . . Like a day that has been admired as a fine one, the light of it sets down amid mists and storms . . . I have no fear on pecuniary matters. The ruin which I fear involves that of my King and country.'

The spirit of reform which was in the air everywhere brought his old conservatism to the surface and compelled him to look on all he saw. London slightly revived his appetite. He could not but reflect that a Whig Government which had generously sponsored his voyage in search of health must 'have gentlemen in it'.

The doctors in London examined him and found traces of incipient disease of the brain, but hoped that if he would give up working the malady would be checked. This, of course, was a hopeless condition to put before Walter Scott. While he breathed he *must* go on working.

After some contrary winds the *Barham*, the vessel the Government had put at Scott's service, sailed from Portsmouth. The Bay of Biscay proved its usual uncomfortable self, but Scott managed to get about on deck, with his lame leg supported by some creaking device.

On the 20th November an extraordinary phenomenon occurred which brought out all Scott's old curiosity. Out of the sea there emerged a floating island caused by a submarine explosion. Nothing could stop Sir Walter from getting off the ship and exploring it on foot. He described this adventure in a letter to his friend Skene.

> Not being able to borrow your fingers, those of the Captain's clerk have been put in requisition for the enclosed sketch, and the notes adjoined are as accurate as can be expected from a hurried visit. You have a view of the island, very much as it shews at present; but nothing is more certain than that it is on the eve of a very important change, though in what respect is doubtful. I saw a portion of about five or six feet in height give way under the feet of one of our companions on the very ridge of the southern corner, and become completely annihilated, giving us some anxiety for the fate of our friend, till the dust and confusion of the dispersed pinnacle had subsided. You know my old talents for horsemanship. Finding the earth, or what seemed to substitute for it, sink at every step up to the knee, so as to make walking for an infirm and heavy man nearly impossible, I mounted the shoulders of an able and willing seaman, and by dint of his exertions, rode nearly to the top of the island. I would have given a great deal for you, my friend, the frequent and willing supplier of my defects; but on this journey, though undertaken late in life, I have found, from the benevolence of my companions, that when one man's strength is insufficient to supply my deficiencies, I had the willing aid of twenty if it could be useful. I have sent you one of the largest blocks of lava which I could find on the islet.

When he reached Malta harbour he felt some vigour returning to him and he stayed three weeks there. The place gave him the idea for a novel to be called *The Siege of Malta*, and a short story called *Il Bizarro*, at which he worked. The manuscripts still exist, but (in the words of one of his biographers) 'it is to be hoped that no literary resurrectionist will ever be guilty of the crime of giving them to the world'.

Lockhart, despite his somewhat stilted phraseology, describes these Mediterranean last days in detail.

He continued, however, to be haunted with a mere delusion—on the origin of which I can offer no guess.—'In our morning drives' (writes Gell) 'Sir Walter always noticed a favourite dog of mine, which was usually in the carriage, and generally patted the animal's head for some time, saying—"poor boy—poor boy". "I have got at home," said he, "two very fine favourite dogs,—so large, that I am almost afraid they look too handsome and too feudal for my diminished income. I am very fond of them, but they are so large it was impossible to take them with me." He came one morning early to my house, to tell me he was sure I should be pleased at some good luck which had befallen him, and of which he had just received notice. This was, as he said, an account from his friends in England, that his last works, *Robert of Paris* and *Castle Dangerous*, had gone on to a second edition. He told me in the carriage that he felt quite relieved by his letter; "for," said he, "I could have never slept straight in my coffin till I had satisfied every claim against me. And now," added he to the dog, "my poor boy, I shall have my house, and my estate round it, free, and I may keep my dogs as big and as many as I choose, without fear of reproach."—He told me, that, being relieved from debt, and no longer forced to write for money, he longed to turn to poetry again. I encouraged him, and asked him why he had ever relinquished poetry?—"Because Byron *bet* me," said he, pronouncing the word, *beat*, short. I rejoined, that I thought I could remember as many passages of his poetry by heart as of Byron's. He replied—"That may be, but he *bet* me out of the field in the description of strong passions, and in deep-seated knowledge of the human heart; so I gave up poetry for the time." He became extremely curious about Rhodes, and having chosen for his poetical subject the chivalrous story of the slaying of the dragon by De Gozon, and the stratagems and valour with which he conceived and executed his purpose, he was quite delighted to hear that I had seen the skeleton of this real or reported dragon, which yet remains secured by large iron staples to the vaulted roof of one of the gates of the city.'

'It had been his intention not to leave the Mediterranean without seeing Rhodes himself—but he suddenly dropt this scheme, on learning that his friend Sir Frederick Adam, Governor of the Ionian Islands, who had invited him to Corfu, was ordered to

India. From that hour his whole thoughts were fixed on home—and his companions soon ceased from opposing his inclinations. Miss Scott was no doubt the more willing to yield, as having received intelligence of the death of her nephew, the "Hugh Littlejohn" of the Grandfather's Tales—which made her anxious about her sister. But indeed, since her father would again work, what good end could it serve to keep him from working at his own desk? And since all her entreaties, and the warnings of foreign doctors, proved alike unavailing as to the regulations of his diet, what remaining chance could there be on that score, unless from replacing him under the eye of the friendly physicians whose authority had formerly seemed to have due influence on his mind? He had wished to return by the route of the Tyrol and Germany, partly for the sake of the remarkable chapel and monuments of the old Austrian princes at Innspruck, and the feudal ruins upon the Rhine, but chiefly that he might have an interview with Goethe at Weimar. That poet died on the 22nd of March, and the news seemed to act upon Scott exactly as the illness of Borthwickbrae had done in the August before. His impatience redoubled; all his fine dreams of recovery seemed to vanish at once—'Alas for Goethe!" he exclaimed: "but at least he died at home—Let us to Abbotsford." And he quotes once more in his letters the first hemistic of the lines from Politian with which he had closed his early memoir of Leyden—"*Grata quies patriae*".

'At Rome, Sir Walter partook of the hospitalities of the native nobility, many of whom had travelled into Scotland under the influence of his writings, and on one or two occasions was well enough to sustain their best impressions of him by his conversation. But, on the whole, his feebleness, and incapacity to be roused by objects which, in other days, would have appealed most powerfully to his imagination, were too painfully obvious: and, indeed, the only, or almost the only lively curiosity he appeared to feel regarded the family pictures and other Stuart relics preserved at the Villa Muti—but especially the monument of Charles Edward and his father at St Peter's, the work of Canova, executed at the cost of George IV. Excepting his visits at Frascati, the only excursion he made into the neighbouring country was one to the grand old castle of Bracciano; where he spent a night in the feudal halls of the Orsini, now included among the numberless possessions of the Banker Prince Torlonia.'

And so, with interruptions due to his failing health, the *Via Dolorosa* continued by sea and land until he reached home. And at length his carriage descended the glen of Gala Water and he awoke to consciousness, and murmured familiar names, and when it rounded the hill at Ladhope, and the Eildons came in view, he exclaimed with delight.

At Abbotsford, Laidlaw and his dogs were waiting for him to greet him. 'Ha Willie Laidlaw!' he cried, 'O Man, how often have I thought of you.' For a few days there was a break in the clouds of his mind. 'I have seen much,' he said over and over again, 'but nothing like my ain house.'

Though he tried to write even at this last hour, his hand would not hold his pen. He cried out, 'No repose for Sir Walter, but in the grave'.

That was all but the last gleam of light. He sank into a melancholy half-consciousness. Talking to John Purdie he repeated the Jedburgh crowd's savage cry, 'Burke Sir Walter!' In happier moods he recited the great Latin hymn, the *Dies Irae*, and some verses from the *Stabat Mater*.

Lockhart's well-known statement that he said, 'Lockhart, I may have but a minute to speak to you. My dear, be a good man—be virtuous—be religious . . . nothing else will give you any comfort when you come to lie here', is probably untrue. This was a pious ejaculation introduced by Lockhart at the request of a female correspondent. She may have *hoped* that some such remark had been made, but we have no certainty that it ever was. 'Walter and Charles were summoned, and in the presence of all his family Scott died in the early afternoon of 21st September. His eldest son kissed his eyes and closed them, while through the open window in the bright autumn weather came the gentle murmur of Tweed.'

He was buried by right of his Haliburton blood in the ruined Abbey of Dryburgh. The day was dark with cloud and high wind. The whole countryside in the same dark apparel followed the coffin to the grave.

The news of his death reached Edinburgh late that night. During the following weeks and months it penetrated to all corners of the world. Men felt that an era had closed.

◄►►►

24

Scott Today
and a Hundred Years Ago

Walter Scott, from his childhood to his death offers the noblest example in our literature of the conquest of imagination and mind over matter. A large statement, but one difficult to deny.

As a small child he rose above infantile paralysis and, at his grandfather's farm at Sandy Knowe he played with the shepherds on the hills whilst greedily absorbing the Border lore. As a youth, despite his lame leg he was the equal of his contemporaries in physical exercise, on horseback and on foot—sometimes outstripping them in the miles he could cover. In his forties he suffered an agonizing illness combined with the savage, useless attentions of the doctors. But it was in agony that he forced himself to write some of his finest novels—only, and it was at rare intervals, howling in pain before taking up his pen to resume. In his fifties he faced financial ruin and some disgrace unflinchingly, and wrote on and on. Only when hereditary apoplexy struck him did he weaken. Even then he did not abandon writing. All this is still remembered in his own country and by all who study his life, wherever they may be.

For decades after his death he was almost universally read throughout the world, and today his poetry still has living echoes, if only for the number of well-known lines that have stuck in the public memory. His novels are far less read than they used to be, but everyone knows about them, and most people have heard of the characters he created.

I refer the reader back to M. Georges Simenon, the well-known French novelist of whom I spoke in Chapter 1, who asked me in Edinburgh what 'that huge spiky building in Princes Street' was, and upon being informed that it was the monument to Walter Scott, the novelist, said, 'How right! He invented us all'—that is, all later novelists.

Scott was the first author, certainly the first novelist to choose his heroes and characters (and some of the most memorable of them) not from great folk, but from the humbler people—peasants, obscure countrymen, lawyers' clerks, the bourgeoisie of cities and so on. Admirers of Walter Scott have said that there was a Shakespearean quality about him. True, but Shakespeare only chose his heroes and heroines from noble blood or from the great ones of the world.

Then there is the matter of romance. Cervantes (whom Scott had admired) in his universally read *Don Quixote* almost killed romantic tale-telling stone dead. Walter Scott triumphantly revived it to such an extent that there are innumerable romantic fiction authors going on writing and publishing today who have never read a word of Scott's novels.

But there was a time, continuing to well after his death, indeed until well into the nineteenth century, when his novels were very widely read here and abroad, and when his influence on other writers was not only potent, but acknowledged. That influence was once as great as Byron's, and more long-lasting.

In France Alfred de Vigny, Mérimée, Dumas, Balzac and Victor Hugo, to mention only some, were inspired by him. He was the leader of a new romantic manner of writing in Germany and Italy; Manzoni was his follower; and it was *Quentin Durward* that caused Ranke to become a historian. In Russia Dostoevsky admitted Scott as his earliest master. Spain was full of his imitators, and Scott had much to do with the rise of Catalan nationalism. Scandinavia, as one might have expected, re-echoed Scott, and even Strindberg said that he never tackled an historical subject before putting himself through a course of reading Scott. No writer in English except Shakespeare had been so much translated and reprinted abroad.

All this despite his obvious faults. Owing to the astonishing speed at which he wrote, his style was slapdash and sometimes ungrammatical. Not for him the *mot juste* or the agonized literary parturition of Flaubert, or, to come nearer our time, of Henry James. He bashed ahead, and achieved or missed his effects by a kind of happy accident.

That other Edinburgh author, R. L. Stevenson, who much admired him and was influenced by him, made a charge against him. 'His characters will be wading forward with an ungrammatical and undramatic rigmarole of words. He could often fob us off with languid, inarticulate twaddle. . . . He conjured up the romantic with delight, but he had hardly patience to describe it. He was a great day-dreamer, but hardly a great artist.'

Maybe, but what a day-dreamer! What an example of potent day-dreaming to such an effect that he caused the world of his time, and long after, to be bedazzled by his dreams! And not all his day-dreams were mere fantasy. He had been more widely read than he admitted in his *Journal*, and his memory, verbal and factual, was one of the most remarkable in the history of our literature. When he chose he could evoke the past without re-reading books about it and never put a foot wrong in fact or in character drawing. An example is to be found in *Quentin Durward*.

In the foreword I said that I did not intend to indulge in literary criticism of his novels, and I think and hope that I have largely avoided this. But these reflections on how Walter Scott wrote and why he wrote are so much involved with the character and personality of the man, that they are relevant in a life and study of one of the greatest (certainly one of the most famous) Scotsmen our country has ever produced.

The world-wide interest in Walter Scott and his works continued, as has been said above, well into the nineteenth century. It reached, however, what may properly almost be described as an explosion at the centenary of his birth held in Edinburgh in August 1871. The final burst of the explosion took place in the Corn Exchange, a building which once stood in the vast space of the Grassmarket under the towering and precipitous south face of the Castle Rock. The old Corn Exchange was capable of holding a huge audience. Even its capacity, however, must have been strained to the utmost, for everyone of consequence in Scotland, and many who were not, as well as a large number of representatives from abroad were there. But much had happened elsewhere and before.

Apart from the proceedings in the Grassmarket, the whole of Edinburgh was *en fête* for days; indeed the city of 1871 seems to have been all but smothered for many days in

231

flags, tartans, thistles and coloured decorations representing Scott, his family, his dogs and the characters from his Waverley novels. Episodes from the novels and poems were the subjects of large processions on horseback and on foot. When night fell the junketings were continued under blazing artificial illuminations.

Junketings! One is compelled to admit that the central point of the organization was opposite the Scott Monument and in a large temperance hotel still standing there. Scott would hardly have approved of this. But Edinburgh being Edinburgh, her citizens were not put off by this geographical accident of the 'temperance hotel'. They drank toasts in profusion and without heeltaps to the memory of their great man in howffs, homes and in the open streets.

The centenary proceedings are described and set forth in full in *The Scotsman* and the *Edinburgh Evening Courant* in eleven long and closely printed columns containing over ten thousand words in each journal.

I have told in Chapter 1 how I put forward to M. Simenon the strong probability that the Scott Monument in Princes Street is the largest stone building of its kind in the world put up in memory of a man of letters. Reading the accounts of the Scott centenary junketings in the Edinburgh of 1871, one doubts whether any civic celebrations in honour of an author have surpassed those which Edinburgh organized for Walter Scott. Not even the admirers of Shakespeare have been able to mount and organize so massive, so populous an affair at Stratford. It is true there isn't room there in the restricted Warwickshire town; and even Garrick's famous eighteenth-century jamboree, at which Boswell made such a characteristic, if endearing ass of himself had not the sheer weight and volume of the capital of Scotland celebrating the memory of Sir Walter Scott a hundred years after his birth. And London has never had a Shakespearean festival of the size and glamour of Edinburgh's on Scott in 1871.

From the lengthy, numerous, yet minutely printed pulullating columns of *The Scotsman* and the *Edinburgh Evening Courant* it would appear that the nobility and gentry of Scotland were largely represented in the Corn Exchange. The lawyers, too, were present and the learned and literary professions were there in force. Every burgh and town in Scotland sent their Provosts or most prominent citizens. England showed up well as did many nations overseas, from the Americas to the Russias. Ambassadors were thick upon the ground and vociferous.

As was customary in mid-Victorian Edinburgh the speeches (certainly those of Edinburgh and Scottish natives) were enormously long! Having begun at six o'clock, the proceedings lasted till well after eleven. At intervals in these marathon outpourings, Mr Kennedy, 'the Scottish vocalist', entertained the company with song. The quality of these lyrics may be judged by the following one, the words of which were written by Mr James Ballantyne, a son or grandson of Scott's Ballantyne.

> Come, let us raise a grateful song
>   On this our Minstrel's natal day;
> And all the world shall round us throng,
>   Heart-homage to his name to pay.
> One hundred years have passed away,
>   Since first awoke that watchful eye;
> Whose sparkling glance and genial ray
>   Have kindled light that ne'er can die.
>
> *Refrain:*
>
> See his glory brightly shining
>   Over palace, hill and cot;
> See the myriad nations twining
>   Laurel wreaths round Walter Scott.

The words deteriorated as the song went on, but eventually all the mighty audience caught the refrain and bellowed it.

At this point one should add that many toasts were proposed and loudly welcomed. It is clear from internal references in the report of the proceedings that 'refreshments' were provided for this large gathering, not only on the platform but on the floor of the house, to drink these toasts.

The Chairman, the Earl of Dalkeith, spoke of the tributes from without Scotland, including one from the Emperor of Brazil. He also read a letter from the British Prime Minister, Mr W. E. Gladstone, who expressed his sorrow at not being able to be present:

'I wish I could convey to you adequately the regret with which I find myself cut off from any possibility of joining in the tribute to be paid to the memory of the first among the sons of Scotland. He was the idol of my boyhood. . . . In his case the feeling is towards the man as much as towards his

233

works. Did we not possess a single line from his pen, his life would stand as a true epic. . . . He is above fluctuations of time for his place is in the Band of the Immortals.'

The strong yet agreeable twang of Mr Cyrus W. Field (the inventor of the Atlantic telegraph) leading for the United States then stimulated the two thousand members of the audience. They received with cheers his eloquent account of Scott's influence in North America.

There were plenty of other spokesmen from European countries, including a touching one from Dr Beets speaking for Holland.

But the most distinguished speaker from abroad was the great Russian novelist, Turgenev (hats off to the Edinburgh organizer who had procured from somewhere in Western Europe this great exile from the Empire of the Tsars!).

Mr Turgenev could read and understand English and could speak it after a fashion, but he had mugged up his address and learnt it by heart in advance. His few slips and errors in our tongue were sympathetically cheered. This is what he had to say:

I will not dwell upon the feelings of personal gratification has given rise to my being here—honoured and flattered as I am by it—but hasten to say what pleasure I experience at representing on so memorable an occasion at so distinguished a meeting, and, I may add, in the midst of a city so illustrious as Edinburgh—to speak of Russia and its literature. Russia, my country, is so little known in Western Europe that it may be that I shall astonish you when I say how great has been the influence of English literature there—and when I tell you that never has that influence been greater than it now is. (Applause.) Of this great influence—one at which I, for my own part, cordially rejoice; for we Russians cannot but gain by our contact with this classic land of liberty and free thought. (Applause.) Of this influence I say the chief founders were Byron and Scott. (Applause.) The study of Shakespeare dates from a more recent period. All our best writers have been admirers, some of them happy imitators of your great master of Romance. Our poet Pourhaine, above all, paid a tribute to Walter Scott. He used to say of him, amongst other things, that, if Scott had treated with so much calmness and simplicity the kings and heroes and other historical personages of the past, it was because he felt himself their equal before posterity (cheers) and they formed what was for him his natural and everyday society. And not only our writers, but our men of science and our statesmen have felt the power of Scott; and through them our whole nation also has felt the effect of his healthy and bracing influence on their views of the worth of genuine historical sentiment and true national feelings. Of all that sacred legion of great men who, though foreign to its soil, have taken part in the intellectual development of Russia, no one, perhaps, has earned more gratitude, has gained more affection than Walter Scott. And proud and happy as I am to be this day the interpreter to Scott's compatriots of that affection and that gratitude. (Loud cheers.)

After more speeches and well after eleven o'clock and to the strains of Auld Lang Syne the two thousand members of the audience in the Corn Exchange streamed out into the Grassmarket under the shadow of the Castle Rock. As they wound their way round into the Lothian Road they could hear the sounds from the open-air celebrants in Princes Street who, late into the night, were still carrying on the week-long festivities in honour of Walter Scott's hundredth birthday.

It has been a strange experience for me to explore these columns of close, minute print recording these events of 1871—events so full of vigour and occasional absurdity. I can scarcely believe that they happened in the Edinburgh in which I was born and which I know so well. My father and my grandfather, a well-known Victorian citizen and politician, were in Edinburgh for these junketings. What did they think of them? Did they take notable parts in them? I have never heard mention of it from any of my family.

It has indeed been a strange experience soaking myself in the Walter Scott junketings in Edinburgh of a hundred years ago. It was humorously invigorating, yet had a slight touch of melancholy about it.

Nothing of this kind on this scale will ever take place in Edinburgh again in memory of a great author, or, indeed, in any city in Europe or America.

Have we lost some faculty of public enjoyment of public celebration of the great past in our streets? I think we have.

There is talk nowadays of our 'battery-hen' human society. The words battery-hen are derived from those cruel contraptions in which laying fowls are cut off from their kind in order to get on in privacy with the job of laying eggs. People are pointing out that human beings are now voluntarily undergoing the fate of these fowls. They stay at home content with television, the radio and other domestic inducements to stay indoors. They don't even lay eggs.

The talk about our battery-hen human society may be exaggerated, but the tendency is certainly there. It is sufficiently in us to make it impossible today that, in the foreseeable future there will be in Edinburgh, or anywhere else, ceremonial public explosions like that of the Scott centenary of 1871. People would just not be interested enough to go out of doors to jollify in the streets in memory of a great man—still less of a great author.

But I do not intend these words written about Edinburgh to be gloomy. Much remains from the past—even from the past of Sir Walter Scott's day.

His Edinburgh is now filled with motor traffic and the air of it poisoned with fumes he never dreamed of. Architectural horrors intrude here and there; and the gracious eighteenth-century New Town is subject to the attack of the motor-car. *But* the New Town is still there, still what it once was—the noblest piece of neo-Georgian town-planning in the world.

Much else, however, is still with us from Walter Scott's day. The splendidly theatrical drop curtain piece of scenery above Princes Street to the south—the Castle and the Old Town streaming down that Castle Rock. Arthur's Seat—the only example of a mountain to be found within a city's official border. The Pentland Hills rising to over two thousand feet, and the glimpses of far-off Fife, and even the first Highland hills beyond that are clear also to their summits from within the city border.

But what remains even more unchanged than these architectural and natural circumstances is something more living—more encouraging—the people.

The people of Edinburgh and the people you will find down in the Borders near Abbotsford and elsewhere are refreshingly unchanged. Their faces, their manners evoke the past. Even their speech, their choice of words have resisted apparently without conscious effort nearly fifty years of the all-out attack of the radio and some fifteen years of television.

The bourgeoisie of Edinburgh often speak much as Walter Scott spoke, and in the poorer quarters of the town there remains, though somewhat debased, a living version of the old broad Scottish tongue. All over the Borders and not only by Abbotsford, you will find and hear plenty of men and women still speaking as James Hogg, the Ettrick Shepherd, spoke and as did the characters of the Waverley

236

novels. In Glasgow Baillie Nichol Jarvie from *Rob Roy* still lives to delight everyone who goes across from Edinburgh to make his acquaintance.

So long as the people of Scotland in Edinburgh, Glasgow and the countryside from Berwick westwards to the Solway Firth (that Solway where were enacted the scenes from *Redgauntlet*) remain, the people of Walter Scott's Scotland and of his Waverley novels shall remain alive. Walter Scott is still with us in the people of Scotland.

Bibliography

The Life of Sir Walter Scott by J. G. Lockhart. Adam & Charles Black. 1898.

Sir Walter Scott by John Buchan. Cassell Ltd. 1932.

Walter Scott, His Life and Personality by Hesketh Pearson. Methuen. 1954.

Sir Walter, A Four-Part Study in Biography by Donald Carswell. John Murray. 1930.

Critical and Miscellaneous Essays by Thomas Carlyle. Chapman & Hall. 1899.

Memorials of his Time by Henry Cockburn. T. N. Foulis. 1856.

Robert Louis Stevenson. Collected Poems. Edited by Janet Adam Smith. Rupert Hart-Davis. 1950.

Life on the Mississippi by Mark Twain.

The Files of:

> The *Scotsman*
> The *Times*
> The *Glasgow Herald*
> The *Edinburgh Evening Courant*
> The *Richmond Examiner*

Index

241